CAMBRIDGE

City of Dreams

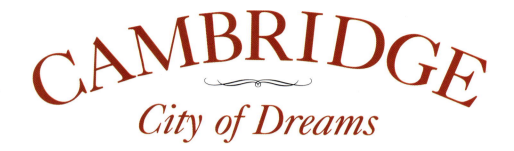

CAMBRIDGE
City of Dreams

LOUIS T. STANLEY

PLANET BOOKS
Published by
W.H. Allen & Co Plc
London

Copyright © Louis T. Stanley, 1987

First published in 1987 by Planet Books,
a division of W.H. Allen & Co Plc

Typeset by Phoenix Photosetting, Chatham, Kent
Printed and bound in Barcelona, Spain by Cronion, S.A.
for the publishers W.H. Allen & Co Plc,
44 Hill Street, London W1X 8LB

ISBN 1–85227–030–6

Designed by Christine Simmonds

British Library Cataloguing in Publication Data

Stanley, Louis T.
   Cambridge: city of dreams.
   1. Cambridge (Cambridgeshire)—Description
   —Guide-books
   I. Title
   914.26′5904858   DA690.C2

   ISBN 1–85227–030–6

CONTENTS

PREFACE

Cambridge, City of Dreams, provides a colourful series of impressionist insights. It is full of fascinating cameos of Colleges, University Institutions, Churches, the Town, its river and surroundings. An international variety of characters, learned and not so learned cross the pages. There are nuggets of offbeat history, together with glimpses of mainline history seen through the windows of Cambridge life.

The early history of University Education emerges: nothing happened in a hurry at this level of British life. It took from 1834 to 1871 for the firm proposal to abolish the Religious Test Act to be accepted. That cautious creeping forward is paralleled by the time it took for women to be allowed to receive degrees and full membership, only granted in 1947. I sat on the most cautious and conservative body I have ever met, while I was in Cambridge. This was the "Blues Committee", in which the captains of the different University sports would meet under the Chairmanship of the President of the Boat Club, to whom the "Blue" theoretically belongs. Applications for full-blue or half-blue status would come to the Committee, often prefaced with the words, "The Blues Committee at Oxford has agreed . . ." The inevitable retort followed, "We do not automatically do what Oxford does."

The book is lovingly evocative, both to the visitor who has caught the charm of Cambridge and to those of us who have long been in love with it. For me it is the place where my Christian faith came alive and turned my life around, and where I met Grace, my wife, who was training to be a teacher at Homerton. So for me personal memories are stirred – by the Union Society where Grace and I admired each other from afar, each thinking we never stood a chance with the other, or by Great St Mary's Church where I was first shaken out of my lukewarm half-believing at a Christian Union Mission. I had gone to Trinity Hall with the eventual intention of becoming a barrister; that dream slowly faded, until the one thing I most wanted to do was to offer for the ordained ministry of the Church.

I had a room in Trinity Hall during my third year from which I looked across Henry James' "prettiest corner of the world" to Clare Bridge and to the roof of King's College Chapel. Then cricket at Fenner's immediately evokes the smell of spring blossom together with the damp and cold days waiting in the pavilion. My cameo is of walking back to that pavilion, having been bowled out for a duck by the fourth ball of a match, when the clock struck 11.30, and I felt like going back and protesting that we shouldn't have started the game yet. Louis Stanley reminds me of some of the very successful cricketing days when the University side could hold its own with the best professional teams. Today students are two years younger and are under greater pressure to put their studies first.

I am glad of the opportunity to commend a beautiful book about a beautiful place.

David Sheppard
Bishop of Liverpool

INTRODUCTION

Coaches pour into Cambridge every day during the summer months. They come from all parts of Europe. You read locations like Amsterdam, Frankfurt, Geneva, Copenhagen, Milan, Stockholm and Vienna, yet in one sense they all look alike. Inside are tired rows of tourists isolated from the landscape in mobile glasshouses of chrome. Everything is regimented and superbly organised. Never before have so many people seen Cambridge from behind plate-glass. Official estimates put the figure in the region of four million, an invasion that horrifies many residents who resent having their placid lives interrupted, but tourism is big business for operators and tradespeople. A world-famous city of rare architectural beauty and historic associations cannot be kept under wraps for a select few.

The big moment comes when the pilgrims emerge into the un-airconditioned atmosphere. Reactions vary according to nationality. Italians are perhaps the most explicit with gesticulations that cover the gamut of emotions – *pianissimo, andante, robusto, fortissimo* and *furioso*, the last expressing ultimate exasperation. Gestures are inevitable, for sightseeing can be tough. Crocodile-formations wend their way through quadrangles, College grounds, galleries, churches and chapels to the accompaniment of verbal bombardment from guides. Even the most resilient wilt under the barrage. When that happens the mask of intelligent appreciation is dropped. Signs are unmistakable. With downcast, glazed eyes, they plod along behind the others. It is, of course, unfair to generalise or exaggerate. Given physical stamina, concentrated tours can be enjoyable, an appetiser for a more leisured approach when the time factor is of secondary importance.

Unquestionably the best way to get to know Cambridge is to walk everywhere, beginning before the place is awake, when the air is still fresh from the night. There is no traffic, no stream of cycles or crowded pavements. The sun is low, touching the spires of King's and the erratic roof-lines of houses in the Parade. Half the street is sunlit, the other half still in the shadow. Walk down the narrow Mill Lane, opposite the church of St Botolph, appropriately patron saint of wayfarers and beggars, and site of Trumpington Gate, the southern entrance to the medieval town. The Gate has disappeared, but the church stands as a reminder of those early days. At the end of the lane is a low wall by the Millpool, within sound of the mill race and the water coming through the floodgates, an ideal vantage point for several Cambridge vignettes.

The river is ever-changing. It glides towards the shadow of willows with the green of wavering weeds, the soft grey of a wood-pigeon. Occasionally a kingfisher speeds by like a flash of sapphire. A frequent early visitor is the heron that watches as the last traces of morning mist recede. In winter months the scene is striking in a different way. Everything is dead-white. Trees are transfigured and powdered with snow-dust, a treatment more beautiful than hoar-frost witchery. Not a bird sings. A squirrel leaps up a tree-branch only to fall backwards, half-blinded by a snowfall. When the sun eventually rises above the snow cloud, it momentarily fills the landscape with dazzling splendour. Or maybe the visit coincides with the beginning of the academic year in October. The most we can hope for is an Indian Summer that recalls sunnier days, the warmth of St Luke's Summer adding to the illusion with autumn crocus, wood-sage, wild mint and ivy. The probability is that the trip will be in high summer. In that case one feature by the mill pool is certain: there will be rows of empty punts by Scudamore's Boatyard. No other craft, not even the Venetian gondola, has contributed so much to what the French call the *doux plaisirs* of love. The punt is only a small boat in which one, or better still two, can lounge in comfort without fear of suddenly being upturned into the water. In May Week or on Madrigal Nights, it becomes an elegant setting for a special occasion. But now they lie unwanted, line upon line, sleeping as the water gurgles, reminders of what life once was like.

Given sensitivity, the past is never far away in Cambridge, but it needs a sprinkling of knowledge of what has gone before. The scene by the Mill has immediate appeal, but aesthetic pleasures alone are impersonal. Look across Lammas Land and the Little Island and you see an attractive house with adjoining granaries, a site that has been in continual use for some 500 years. This is now Darwin College, founded in 1964 by the Colleges of Caius, St John's and Trinity. It was so named because of the association with Cambridge of Dr Erasmus Darwin and his grandson, Charles Darwin, and the fact that Newnham Grange was the home of Sir Charles Darwin's son, Sir George Darwin, and his family. It has interesting associations, many captured by Gwen Raverat, daughter of Sir George, in a charming book called *Period Piece*, compulsory reading for anyone seeking the charisma of the place. This talented writer and artist was sadly stricken by a stroke, but though severely handicapped she could still sketch and write. For several years she was a familiar figure on the river-path, slumped in a wheelchair, wrapped in an old rug and dark cloak with a black, wide-brimmed clergyman's hat rammed on her head, sketching in all kinds of weather until a Swiss nurse took her back

Punts come into their own during May Week

9

Opposite: *A familiar scene in summer by Mill Lane*

Left: *The Bohemian backwater of Portugal Place*

to Newnham Grange for lunch. If ever a place is haunted by friendly shades those of Gwen Raverat must surely return to the Granta. Her home was equally evocative and was loved by such figures as Bertrand Russell, Arthur Clough, Rupert Brooke and Augustus John, whose horse-drawn gaudy caravan with Dorelia in gypsy-looking clothes would cross Silver Street bridge on the way to Grantchester, invariably pausing for a while at Newnham Grange.

The mathematical bridge of Queens' in the distance is a reminder that whilst we are among the latest visitors, what we see in the Colleges would be familiar to famous figures of many centuries. In that sense Cambridge is a constant reminder of the past. The undergraduates we see walking in the Great Court of Trinity are the counterparts of those young men whom Hugh Balsham, Bishop of Ely, insisted in 1284 should "in everything live together as students of Oxford who are called of Merton". The span covers seven centuries and actively involves kings and queens of England from the Plantagenets of the thirteenth century to Elizabeth II. It is interesting to recall some of the names. Erasmus taught French at Queens' between 1510 and 1513. Samuel Pepys was at Magdalene, Wordsworth at St John's, Cromwell at Sidney Sussex, Horace Walpole at King's, and Harvard at Emmanuel. Also at Cambridge were the historians Macaulay, Acton and Trevelyan, the jurist Coke, and the economists Marshall and Keynes. There have been numerous scientists such as Newton, Thomson, Rutherford and Chadwick, and philosophers like Bacon, Whitehead and Russell. Classical scholars include Bentley and Porson, and poets Milton, Dryden, Byron, Tennyson and Brooke. *The Golden Bough* was written by Fraser in Trinity. The catalogue of fame is endless. It is a strange thought that their likenesses looking down on us from the walls of the Halls are in settings that would be familiar to their eyes. It is impossible not to be influenced by the atmosphere of such traditions always providing that we know what to look for and the meaning of what we see.

Sir Arthur Quiller-Couch used to say that "Oxford and Cambridge are so amazingly alike while they play at differences and so amazingly unlike anything else in the world." The latter is still true, but I am not sure that "Q" would have emphasised the similarity between the two places had he lived today. Industrial development and traffic problems have done so much damage to Oxford that Cambridge, in spite of architectural additions in appalling bad taste, is now more beautiful. Its harmony has not been blighted by commercialism. That gem known as Petty Cury has been replaced by a monstrosity known as Lion Yard, but there is no need to visit it. Such changes as have been made serve to highlight the good taste of previous centuries. Unchanged are inherited glories. Nothing can detract from the beauty of the weeping willows, the balustraded bridges of stone, the romantic Gothic of St John's or the narrow alleys by the Church of the Holy Sepulchre and Portugal Place which hint at how these places must have been. It is a scene waiting to be explored, but before doing so it is useful to know something of the origins of Cambridge and the University, a search that can be elusive.

Tradition would have us believe that Cambridge was founded by a Spanish prince, yclept Cantaber, in the 4321st year from the Creation and restored in A.D. 637 by Sigbert. Unfortunately, proof relating to these theories put forward by Doctor Caius of Gonville and Caius College was destroyed some centuries ago when the Charters granted to Cantaber's foundation by King Arthur and Cadwallader, together with the Rules of Sergius and Honorius, were lost by fire or riot. If the origin of the city is problematical, the evolution of the name Cambridge is equally confusing. The range of choice is wide. Some scholars have tried to identify it with the Roman *Camboritum*, but the evidence is unconvincing. Other variations include *Grantanbrycge* in A.D. 875, *Grantebrigge* in the Domesday Book, and *Cantebrugescir* in about 1142. *Cantebrigge* was used by Chaucer, the Latinised form of *Cantabrigia* appeared in the thirteenth century, and over the next two hundred years there are such versions as *Cauntbrigge*, *Cantbrigge*, *Cawnbrigge*, *Caumbregge* and *Cambrigge*.

Even as regards the beginnings of the University there is speculation rather than certainty. We find a legendary founder in the guise of that mythical king named Cantaber. Much more likely is the theory that the inauguration of the University was preceded by instruction in religious houses or monasteries, with the University of Paris as the model when the point of formal organisation was reached (Bologna and Paris were the archetypes of all later foundations). Here it is pertinent to point out that a *universitas* meant a body of persons, a corporation. In time it came to mean a guild of students or teachers, i.e., a *universitas scholarium* or a *universitas magistrorum*. A *universitas* was thus a body of students, not a building where studies were followed. A *studium generale* was a place where students were absorbed. An Oxford historian has claimed that a disturbance in that town in 1209 caused many students to leave and form the prototype of the University in Cambridge, but it is more likely that a school of learning was by then already in existence in Cambridge.

The distinguishing mark of a university is the right to confer degrees. In that sense Bologna and Paris were recognised in the thirteenth century, but in the following century it became customary for schools to revive the ranking of a *studium generale* by means of a Papal or Imperial Bull. Cambridge received such rights and privileges from Pope John XXII in 1318 and was formally declared a *studium generale*. Being modelled on Paris, Cambridge had a Chancellor as head of the University, and two Proctors, whose duties related to university finance and the arrangement of disputations. There were also the two legislative bodies of Regents or active teachers, and non-Regents or Masters of Arts not engaged in teaching.

The development of the College system followed a clear-cut pattern. In Paris students lived together in hostels of their own choice under the surveillance of a master nominated by his fellows. Gradually they came under the direction of the University. Early in the thirteenth century benefactors endowed certain of these Paris hostels for use by needy scholars and gave them the title of *collegium*, one of the most famous being the Sorbonne, inaugurated in 1257 for the study of theology. Cambridge had similar hostels. In fact, a Royal Edict of 1231 nominated two Masters of Arts and two good and loyal men of the town to assess their rents. The first founder of a College in the recognised sense of the word was Walter de Merton, who in 1264 outlined a set of statutes for the control of the everyday life of his scholars. The House of the Scholars of Merton formed the pattern on which the collegiate life of Cambridge was based. When Hugh de Balsham, Bishop of Ely, founded Peterhouse in 1284, he stipulated that the men should live together as students on the Merton principle.

It is interesting to note the fluctuating level of scholarship in those early days. A school of theology was founded by the Franciscans, but not until the middle of the fifteenth century did its fame as a centre of learning exceed that of Oxford. The Renaissance brought renewed interest in classical literature and academic attention was focused on the new learning. The first holder of the Chair of Divinity was John Fisher. It was largely through his influence that his patroness, Lady Margaret Beaufort, the mother of Henry VII, founded the Colleges of St John's and Christ's. He was also instrumental in bringing Erasmus to the turret room in Queens' where he worked upon the New Testament and the volume on Jerome. Erasmus was the first to teach Greek in the University.

The relationship between the University and the Crown has not always been harmonious. The first disagreement came when Henry VIII expressed his wish that marriage with Catherine of Aragon should be declared illegal. The universities eventually concurred with his wishes in 1530. The Reformation period saw Cambridge vitally alive from the doctrinal viewpoint. It became a bastion of Protestantism in the sixteenth century. The religious houses came to an end with the dissolution of the monasteries. The Benedictine hostel known as Buckingham College was closed and reopened as Magdalene College. Any threat to the existence of the Colleges was averted by the favourable attitude shown towards the University by Henry VIII, whose direct intervention resulted in professorships of Divinity, Civil Law, Physic, Hebrew and Greek being introduced. He was also responsible for the founding of Trinity College, into which was incorporated King's Hall, Michaelhouse, and another medieval hostel. On the other hand, the Dissolution of Monasteries affected the University adversely in as much as the needy students who normally lived in the monastic houses had to fend for themselves with the result that their numbers decreased. New University statutes were introduced in 1549 revising the curricula, at the same time attempting to stamp out popery, a policy that had an adverse effect on education. The accession of Mary I to the throne added to the existing upheaval. The aim was to eliminate Protestantism and bring back the study of scholastic philosophy. The period marked the refounding of Gonville Hall by Doctor Caius, whilst Trinity became the recipient of additional benefactions.

During the reign of Elizabeth, Cambridge developed and matured. Much credit for this goes to William Cecil, Lord Burleigh, Secretary and chief Minister to the Queen and later Lord High Treasurer, who was Chancellor of the University for some forty years. The new statutes approved by the Queen in 1570 resulted in College Heads taking a more definite role in University government, a constitutional innovation whereby instructional powers were transferred from the University to the Colleges. Under the new system the Vice-Chancellor was taken from their nominees, proctorial authority was modified, and the office was filled by nomination in College rotation. The Chancellor took over financial control from the proctors. In 1573 Cambridge received its charter of incorporation. As a result all undergraduates over sixteen years of age had to acknowledge the Thirty-nine Articles and the Royal Supremacy. Two Colleges were founded in the Elizabethan era: Emmanuel in 1584, and Sidney Sussex in 1594.

The reign of James saw the University granted the privilege of selecting two "grave and learned" men to act as burgesses in the House of Commons. Their responsibility was to inform Parliament of what was happening in the University and in each College. Francis Bacon was one of the first Cambridge representatives. The reign also saw the clash in the University between the Anglicans and the Puritans, the latter being particularly strong in Cambridge (the Synod of Dort in 1618 had four Cambridge men among the five English delegates). Trinity College was rebuilt by the Master, Thomas Nevile, the alterations adding greatly to its beauty.

Charles I found Cambridge more than sympathetic. In 1641 Trinity and St John's welcomed him with loyal addresses, and when the need for exceptional assistance arose the following year, many Colleges came to his aid. Several attempts to contribute College plate to the cause resulted in Cromwell making Cambridge a garrison town and sentencing the Heads of St John's, Jesus and Queens' to prison. They were released in the Restoration, every Fellow of a College having to declare his intention of observing the liturgy of the Church of England, a form of discipline that would not go amiss in the Church of England Synods of today.

I must mention the intellectual movement linked with Cambridge in the seventeenth century and associated with a company of scholars known as the Cambridge Platonists that included Benjamin Whichcote, a Provost of King's; Henry Moore, author of the *Enchiridion Ethicum*; John Smith, the celebrated preacher; and Ralph Cudworth, author of *The True Intellectual System of the Universe*. Their aim was to exchange sectarianism and scholasticism for more thoughtful philosophy. As regards particular individuals, this was the era of Sir Isaac Newton, who gave Cambridge its mathematical renown. He became the second occupant of the Lucasian Chair of Mathematics upon the resignation of Isaac Barrow. Twenty years later Newton published his famous *Principia*.

A word is not out of place about the system of examinations. In medieval times the age of entry into a university was about fourteen. The desired qualification was ability to talk in Latin. The threefold course, or *trivium*, comprised Logic, Latin Grammar and

Rhetoric. If the student satisfied the test of disputation in Logic and Rhetoric, he went on to the fourfold course of *quadrivum*, of Arithmetic, Geometry, Music and Astronomy as a "commencing" or "incepting" bachelor. Upon completion of the four years, he could take the degree of Master of Arts with teaching qualifications. If the student wished to proceed to a doctorate in Canon or Civil Law, Medicine or Theology, eight additional years had to be completed. In the reign of Henry VIII, Grammar was taken from the *trivium* and Mathematics substituted. The first tripos list appeared in 1747–8. The name was medieval in origin. The "ould bachelor" who disputed with the students used to squat on a three-legged stool and was identified as "Mr Tripos". He indulged in writing tripos verses, light-hearted Latin lines on the topic of disputation. In 1747 the names of the candidates were printed in order of merit on the back of the verse-sheets. In due course, the name Tripos was taken to refer to the examination alone. Roughly twenty years later, the system of written answers was introduced.

The controversial religious tests roused considerable opposition. A group of graduates petitioned the House of Commons in 1834 to have the system abolished, but the request was not granted until 1871. The nineteenth century saw many changes in the field of university education. The Royal Commission of 1850 recommended that university supervision over studies be restored and advised the recognition of fresh branches of knowledge by which academic honours could be gained. It recommended sweeping away restricted elections to scholarships and fellowships. The Caput at Cambridge was succeeded by elective councils comprising Heads of Houses, Professors, and resident Masters of Arts. The range of possible fields of study was extended and Natural Science, Law and History were included in the Honours Schools. The Royal Commission of 1872 was responsible for the Universities of Oxford and Cambridge Act of 1882, which permitted a married Fellow to retain his Fellowship, an innovation that affected the lighter side of University life. Other changes touched on educational departments: Life-fellowships were abolished with the exception of those earned by long College service; entrance scholarships were given a uniform value; University funds were increased by a scale of College contributions; inter-collegiate lectures were proposed. The 1926 Royal Commission on the universities resulted in new statutes. Only Masters of Arts engaged in administration or teaching had legislative powers; all lectures were classified as University lectures; Colleges were obliged to give a set number of their fellowships to University lecturers and professors; State aid was to supplement the existing endowments which were insufficient to cope with scientific expansion. Complaints still persist on the same line in the eighties.

Royal visits to Cambridge form a centuries-old chapter rich in pageantry and tradition. Today they have become so frequent that reaction has become almost blasé, but not so in the past. Two instances suffice. The visit of Elizabeth I is recorded in detail. In 1564 the University was gathered at King's College. The Chapel was decorated with fine tapestries and strewed with rushes. Near Newnham, the royal party was met by the Mayor on horseback. The Chancellor received the Queen at the west door of the Chapel and in a speech lasting half-an-hour the Orator proclaimed the Queen's virtues. The Provost made his obeisance inside the Chapel, after which the Te Deum and Evensong were sung. Upon completion of the service six boxes of fine comfits and four pairs of Cambridge double gloves were presented. At the close of the ceremony, the gathering broke up, the Chancellor "riding upon a little black nagg". On the following day the *Aulularia* of Plautus was played in King's Chapel, and on the Monday a large stage was erected in Great St Mary's for disputations, the Queen enquiring "why some masters went in white silk and others in mynever".

The act of physick had two questions: 1 *Simplex cibus praeferendus multiplici*; 2 *Coenandum liberalius, quam prandendum*. Doctor Caius and two other professors disputed. They spoke so low that the Queen asked them in Latin to raise their voices, apparently without much effect for "Her Grace made not much of that disputation". The Queen visited individual Colleges over a period of days. An address was given in Greek at Christ's, the Queen replying in the same language. Apparently her visit inspired a surfeit of plays, and the tour was not completed by Her Majesty being "over-watched with former plays".

The visit in 1843 of Queen Victoria and Prince Albert had an equally full programme. The Queen stayed at the Master's Lodge of Trinity College, following the example set by James I in 1614. Elaborate preparations were made. The Queen and Prince Albert travelled from Windsor to Slough by road, from there by the G.W.R. to Paddington in a train driven by the famous engineer, Brunel. From Paddington to Cambridge the Royal party proceeded by road, a triumphal procession through towns and villages decorated with flags and floral arches. The Queen, escorted by Lord Hardwicke, Lord Lieutenant of the County, and by a body of the Whittlesea Yeomanry Cavalry, came into Cambridge from Royston, passing under an archway of flowers and evergreens at the end of Trumpington Street. With the Mayor walking alongside the royal carriage, she arrived at the Great Gate of Trinity College. The Queen was met by Dr Whewell, who offered first, as Vice-Chancellor, the staves of the Esquire Bedell, then, as Master, the keys of the College, all of which tokens were returned.

After refreshments at the Lodge, the Queen held a court in the Hall. The tables had been removed and Her Majesty sat upon a temporary throne erected on a dais beneath the portrait of Newton, which, flanked by Barrow and Bacon, occupied the space now filled by the huge picture of the royal founder. University, College and county dignitaries occupied the floor of the Hall and the Minstrels' Gallery was filled by ladies. Lengthy addresses of welcome, loyalty and devotion were read in English. After short replies, the royal party went to King's Chapel, later returning to Trinity Lodge. In the evening the Queen expressed a desire to see Trinity Chapel, and a torchlight procession across Great Court was improvised. Of an incident on the return journey, a contemporary wrote: "On leaving the Chapel, it was perceived that there was a short deficit in the carpeting that led to the Lodge, and, quick as a thought, a hundred gowns were off, and strewed three deep beneath the royal path. This incident gave Her Majesty more gratification than all she had as yet witnessed since her arrival within the precincts of the University. The following day, after the Prince had been admitted as a member of Trinity and had matriculated, the Queen and Prince went to the Senate where, the Queen being seated upon a throne, the scarlet robe of a doctor's degree was conferred upon Prince Albert. After this ceremony, the royal party went on a rapid tour of all the Colleges, lunched at Trinity, then later in the afternoon left for Wimpole to spend a few days with the Earl and Countess of Hardwicke before returning to Windsor."

Royal visits were a ponderous affair unlike the informality of today when members of the Royal Family walk freely in the streets with the minimum of fuss. An exception is when Prince Philip carries out his duties as Chancellor of the University, particularly during the ceremony of conferring honorary degrees in May Week.

Times change, but the essentials remain. During our tour of Cambridge there will be reminders of the days when the supreme issue was whether England should be Roman Catholic or Protestant; of Tennyson and Arthur Hallam; Byron and his wine parties of pugilists and poets; and Newton walking abstracted in his garden. These are but incidents in Cambridge's past. They can be multiplied many times and all are interesting.

KING'S COLLEGE AND CHAPEL

Walk under the octagonal dome of the Gatehouse with its cluster of independent pinnacles and enter one of the best known colleges in the world. Familiarity dulls the senses. Those of us who live in Cambridge take many things for granted and the sight of King's is one of these. Not so the first-time visitor. Initial impact is dramatic. In the centre of an immaculate lawn is the bronze figure on a pedestal of King Henry VI, who had the imagination to found his Royal College of Cambridge to the glory of God and of the Blessed Virgin and of St Nicholas. That was in 1440.

His plan was far-seeing, but too modest in size, the site being only forty yards by twenty-five. A petition pointed out this weakness: an amended charter went to the other extreme. Instead of a community of a rector and twelve scholars, it became a college with a provost, ten priests, six clerks, sixteen choristers, and seventy scholars – an ambitious undertaking over 500 years ago. To build such a complex meant disrupting the life of the town. Clearing the site required demolition of existing property. Contemporary documents list what had to be knocked down. Three buildings stood on the site of the Chapel. God's House, a grammar school, occupied the ground needed for the antechapel. St Thomas's Hostel had to make way for the choir. The vicarage of St Edward's became the Porter's Lodge. The White Canons of Sempringham were on the land earmarked for Gibbs, being partly owned by the nuns of St Radegond with a tenement belonging to Bartholomew Morris of Trinity Hall. Kitchens would replace the hostel of St Austin. A garden of the Carmelites became Bodleys Court. Others affected included the church of St John Zachary, the White Horse Inn and Le Boreshede tavern by King's Lane. An important road, Milne Street, would be resited by Gibbs' Buildings.

Gutting the centre of the town inevitably led to strong opposition. The six Colleges of Peterhouse, Trinity Hall, Pembroke, Corpus Christi, Clare, and Gonville and Caius seemed adequate. Dominican Friars occupied the site of what later became Emmanuel College and Trinity had not yet amalgamated with Michael House and King's Hall. The Senate House had not been built. King's Parade was the High Street. The critics had no immediate anxieties for the project was dogged with ill-fortune. Lack of finance was a problem, whilst disruption through civil war cost Henry VI his crown in the Wars of the Roses. Gradually the fabric took shape, helped financially by Edward IV, Richard III and Henry VII. The eventual structure was a modified version of Henry VI's plan. What it might have looked like is detailed in *The Will of King Henry VI*, in which the two Royal Colleges of Eton and Cambridge are described in detail.

From the porter's lodge we would have seen a square court – 230 feet by 238 feet – with the chapel on the north side. On the east side, instead of the seemingly transparent stonework of the screen with its seven light Perpendicular windows, there would have been dwellings as far as the Provost's lodge on the south side. The hall with buttery adjoining and the library were to be on the west, and behind the hall a bakehouse, kitchen, court and offices. Behind the library would be a cloister cemetery, and between the kitchen courts and the cemetery a path led to the river and the bridge.

It would have been a fine example of medieval asymmetry, not unlike the plan of New College, Oxford. Seventy years earlier Winchester College and New College had been founded by William of Wykeham. Henry VI had similar plans for Eton and Cambridge. He records, no doubt with satisfaction, that his college chapel would be twenty feet higher, seventeen feet longer, and eight feet wider than New College.

The link between King's and Eton has always been close. This is reflected on their coat of arms. Both College seals were engraved in 1443. King's had a shield emblazoned as follows: sable mitre pierced by a crozier, between two lily flowers proper; a chief per pale azure, with a fleur-de-lys of France and gules a lion of England. The mitre and crozier were for St Nicholas, the lilies for Our Lady – the patron saints of King's. Eton was similar, except for a third lily flower substituted for the crozier and mitre. The founder in both instances is represented by the chief, derived from the Royal Arms. In 1448 both Colleges were authorised to bear arms by royal patents. The seal of the Eton arms was confirmed, but with King's, three silver roses were substituted for the mitre and crozier. The intention of Henry VI was clear: he wanted to co-ordinate as far as possible the educational programme of these twin foundations. The scholars of Eton were to proceed to Cambridge once the rudiments of grammar had been mastered. That wish was to be gratified, but the College itself was very different in size and style.

Henry had wanted the buildings to be majestic but plain and unadorned with architectural frivolities. This wish was observed by Hawksmoor when he was asked by the Provost in 1713 to design new buildings. Wren's brilliant pupil adopted Henry VI's ground plan as the basis for a new court. Gothic style gave way to Palladian in contrast to the flamboyant tastes of the Tudors. Again there were delays. When building eventually began in 1724, the architect was James Gibbs, who constructed one side, the Fellows Building. In 1784 Robert Adam submitted plans to complete the court. Had they been accepted King's would have had a circular hall, but nothing happened for forty years when William Wilkins took over as designer, and added the screen facing King's Parade, the Porter's Lodge, entrance gate and the range of buildings that included the Hall, Combination Room, Library and Provost's Lodge.

King's has always been a law unto itself, but in 1851 it accepted change by forgoing

Below: *Silhouette of the Gatehouse of King's College with its cluster of pinnacles and immaculate lawn*

the privilege of claiming degrees for its students without them having to take any University examinations. Then, in 1873, non-Etonians became acceptable for scholarships and the first non-Etonian Fellow was elected. It seemed that democracy had arrived.

KING'S COLLEGE CHAPEL

King's College Chapel is itself worth the visit to Cambridge. Conceived on the lines of a cathedral though serving as a chapel, it is one of the finest examples of medieval architecture in England. It was an inspiration to writers, artists and composers. Canaletto painted the interior, Turner the exterior, Wordsworth added three sonnets, and Saint-Saens praised the choir that once included the composer, Orlando Gibbons. Dimensions indicate something of its overwhelming size: 310 feet overall in length; 289 feet inside; 40 feet wide; 94 feet high; interior height 80 feet; 146 feet high to the top of the turrets. The figures are almost the same as those listed in Henry VI's *Will* of 1448. Documentation records the identities of the Master Masons: John Wolrich; Reginald Ely; John Langton, Master of Pembroke and Chancellor; and Nicholas Close, Fellow of King's. The first stone was laid on the 25th July, 1446 by Henry VI, but ninety-nine years had to pass before the High Altar was in place. The stonework was finished by 1515, the windows completed about 1530. We are told that financial assistance came from Edward IV (£1,100), Thomas Rotheram (£100), Richard III (£750), and Henry VII (£5,000 plus a further £5,000 in his *Will*).

As many visitors have limited time to sightsee, it is helpful to list some of the features to note. First and foremost, the *fan-vaulting*, the most glorious in England. There are smaller versions at St George's Chapel, Windsor and Henry VII's Chapel at Westminster Abbey, but neither are on such a scale. The delicate filaments of stonework are

Below: King's College Fellows Building by James Gibbs

exquisite. There are thirteen fans, each with twelve sections, these divided into four groups by cross-pieces. The tapering cross-pieces have rows of fleurs-de-lys. Each section has innumerable arches, each fan having sixty-two. There are some two miles of slender ribbons of stone with more than 5,000 trefoiled arches, plus tiny fleurs-de-lys in the fan-sections. The overall effect is misleading, for the fan-vault serves no practical purpose, the roof being supported on a timber frame.

The *screen and choir stalls* are examples of the finest craftsmanship in Early Renaissance style in this country. Dating is helped by the cyphers H.R., the King's monogram, and A.B., the initials of Henry VIII's second wife, Anne Boleyn. They were probably completed between 1531 and 1536, the years spanning the marriage and Anne's execution. The rich stalls were contemporary, though the canopies were added in the seventeenth century. The cost of the stalls and screen is recorded as £1,333.6s.8d., which today sounds reasonable! Built by Thomas Dallam in 1606, the *organ* is a composite of several alterations, with parts of the organ-case dating from the Henry VIII period. The angels with trumpets were a later addition in 1859. The lectern should be studied. It was designed by the craftsmen responsible for the screen round Henry VII's tomb in Westminster Abbey. Exquisitely wrought in latten, it has a statuette of Henry VI, and was the gift of Provost Hacumblen in the early sixteenth century.

The *stained glass* is very important for it represents the most complete set of church windows existing of the Henry VIII period. The documentation is interesting, reflecting the work of two crafts, that of glaziers and enamellers. At the time of Henry VI, no instructions for glazing the windows appear to exist – in fact, possibly due to the civil war and the slow rate of building, windows are not mentioned in the records until 1515. That entry records an advance payment of £100 to Barnard Flower, the King's glazier. He died ten years later, and a fresh contract was made with four London glass workers. The terms were specific. They were to glaze the east and west windows, and sixteen others, "with good, clene, sure, and perfyte glasse . . . and oryent colours and imagery of the story of the old lawe and of the newe lawe . . . after the fourme, maner, goodenes, curyousytie, and clenelynes, in every poynt of the kynge's newe chapell at Westmynster . . . and also accordingly and after suche maner as oon Barnard Flower, glasyer, late deceessed, by indenture strode bounde to doo." The contract was executed on the 30th April, 1526. The four men concerned were Galyon Hone, of St Mary Magdalene's parish in Southwark, who had been made master in the gild at Antwerp in 1492, probably originated in Holland, and was in Eton Chapel in 1492; James Nycholson, of St Thomas's in Southwark, a German craftsman who worked in Great St Mary's 1518–19 and in Christ Church, Oxford, in 1528–9; Thomas Reve of St Sepulchre, Newgate; and Richard Bownde of St Clement Danes.

Three days after this contract was signed, an agreement was made with two Flemish men, Fraunces Wyllyamson, of St Olave's, Southwark, and Symond Symondes, of St Margaret's, Westminster. Their task was four windows, two on either side of the Chapel, the glass to cost 1s.4d. per foot, working from designs by Hones.

Studying the windows it is remarkable how glass so in sympathy with Mariolatry survived the iconoclastic attentions of Dowsing. His diary has notes that 1000 superstitious pictures in King's were to be destroyed. His statutable fee of 6s.8d. is recorded, but no action was taken. Various theories have been put forward, the most plausible being that Cromwell granted immunity in order to keep his relationship with the University on a friendly footing.

Intelligent appreciation of the windows is made difficult because the designs are interrupted by lead bars, a feature of medieval glass. Identification of the figures is not always easy. There are twenty-five main windows, twelve on each side of the Chapel and one at the east end. With the exception of No. 12 on the north side, the rest pursue the type and antitype theme with incidents from the Old Testament or Apocrypha being paired with corresponding scenes from the New Testament. The last two windows on the south side are exceptions. They depict legendary scenes of the Death of the Virgin. The key that follows emphasises the iconographical unity of the lay-out, the sequence of parallels between the Old and New Testaments:

East Window
| Christ nailed to the Cross | The Crucifixion | The Deposition |
| *Ecce Homo* | Pilate washing his hands | Christ bearing the Cross |

North Window: 1 from East
| Job tormented by Satan | Solomon crowned |
| Christ scourged | Christ crowned with thorns |

North 2
| Jeremiah imprisoned | Noah shamed by Ham |
| Christ before the High Priest | Christ before Herod |

North 3
| Cain killing Abel | Shimei cursing David |
| Betrayal of Christ | Christ mocked |

North 4
| Manna in the wilderness | Fall of the Angels |
| Last Supper | Agony in the Garden |

North 5
| Elisha raises the Shunamite's son | Triumph of David |
| Raising of Lazarus | Entry into Jerusalem |

North 6
| Naaman washing in Jordan | Esau sells birthright |
| Baptism of Christ | Temptation of Christ |

North 7
| The Golden Calf | Massacre of Seed Royal by Athalia |
| Fall of Idols in Egypt | Massacre of Innocents |

North 8
| Purification of Women under the Law | Flight of Jacob from Esau |
| Purification of the Virgin | Flight into Egypt |

North 9
| Circumcision of Isaac | Queen of Sheba visits Solomon |
| Circumcision of Christ | Adoration of the Magi |

North 10
| Eve tempted by the Serpent | Moses and Burning Bush |
| Annunciation | Nativity |

North 11
| Golden Tables presented in the Temple of the Sun | Marriage of Tobias and Sara |
| Presentation of the Virgin in the Temple | Marriage of Mary and Joseph |

North 12
| Rejection of Joachim's Offering | Angel appears to Joachim |
| Joachim and Anne at the Golden Gate | Birth of the Virgin |

South Window: 1 from East
Moses and the Brazen Serpent, by
   Hedgeland, 1845
Naomi mourns her husband   Lament over Christ

South 2
Joseph cast into Pit   The Exodus
Entombment of Christ   Descent into Hell

South 3
Jonah cast up by Whale   Tobias returning to his mother
Resurrection   Christ appears to Virgin

South 4
Reuben finds Pit empty   Darius finds Daniel alive in Lion's
                                Den
Women at the Sepulchre   Christ appears to Mary Magdalene

South 5
Raphael appears to Tobias   Habakkuk feeds Daniel
Christ appears on the way to   The supper at Emmaus
   Emmaus

South 6
Return of the Prodigal Son   Joseph welcomes Jacob
Incredulity of Thomas   Christ appears to Apostles

South 7
Elijah carried up to Heaven   Moses given Tables of the Law
Ascension   Pentecost

South 8
Peter and John heal the Lame Man Arrest of Peter and John
Peter preaching   Death of Ananias

South 9
Conversion of Paul   Paul disputing at Damascus
Paul and Barnabas at Lystra   Paul stoned at Lystra

South 10
Paul casting out a spirit of   Paul before Lysias
   divination at Philippi
Paul saying farewell at Miletus Paul before Nero

South 11
Death of Tobit   Burial of Jacob
Death of the Virgin   Burial of the Virgin

South 12
Translation of Enoch   Solomon receives Bathsheba
Assumption of the Virgin   Coronation of the Virgin

West Window
19th century glass, work of Clayton and Bell, depicting the Last Judgment

---

Opposite: The exquisite sixteenth century lectern wrought in latten with a statuette of Henry VI

This key will help to identify figures and hopefully encourage closer study of significant details. For instance, the glass depicting the *Bearing of the Cross* shows Veronica offering Christ the linen cloth to wipe His face. That same cloth was said to retain His likeness miraculously. In *The Last Supper*, Judas Iscariot is shown as red-headed in line with the legend that red-heads were treacherous. There are many other details to be discovered.

The final note about King's Chapel is more personal. It concerns a service that takes place every Christmas Eve. Through radio and television, the Festival of Nine Lessons and Carols has become global. The order of service remains constant. The Provost leads the Bidding Prayer. Carols, some familiar, others new, are sung by the world-famous choir. Lessons are read by a chorister choral scholar, Fellow of King's, Vice-Provost, Free Church Minister, Mayor's Chaplain and a representative of the Sister College at Eton. For many people this service is the prelude to the Festival Season with the emphasis on its true significance. For centuries King's Chapel has roused the wonder of visitors, even those who are familiar with the world's largest churches. This Chapel offers an immediate transition from the noise of the outside world to the calm and quiet of the eternal values. On a dull and sunless day one gropes one's way like a dwarf lost in a wood, twilight translated into stone, but at this Festival of Carols on the eve of Christmas, the mass of delicate filaments of stonework in the fan-vault and the sheer size of the Chapel's mighty medieval architecture become friendly and companionable, even lovable. It is in every way a unique structure. Before returning to King's Parade, the *Adoration of the Magi* by Rubens should be studied. Presented to the College by Alfred Alnatt in 1961, it was sited with immense care. The floor was lowered and the High Altar removed. In its place is the simplest of altars with a cloth designed by Joyce Conway Evans with pearls and gold thread from Japan. The paving was renewed with a thousand black marble slabs from Belgium and 850 white Italian slabs.

In dealing with the Colleges, it is interesting to comment on members who were distinguished in many fields of endeavour. Among such Kingsmen is the seventeenth century poet, Edmund Waller, who entered the College in 1621. Horace Walpole was admitted as a Fellow-Commoner in 1734–5. His letters provide interesting side lights on the social and political scene as well as autobiographical touches. Christopher Anstey, a Fellow in 1745, is recalled if only for his eccentricities. He wrote the *New Bath Guide*, a light-hearted series of letters in anapaestic verse describing the affairs of the Blunderhead Family at Bath and the droll humour of that time. At King's he rebelled at being called upon to declaim in Latin in the Schools before preceeding to the degree of Master of Arts. Claiming that the Kingsman's privilege was threatened, he phrased his declamation in lampooning vein. He was suspended from the degree. Several years later, he wrote:

> Granta, Sweet Granta, where studious of ease
> Seven years did I sleep, and then lost my degrees.

The former Provost, M. R. James, is perhaps better remembered as a weaver of ghost stories rather than a medievalist. His remarkable knowledge of Christian iconography helped him to reconstruct some of the stained glass in the Chapel that had been disarranged by earlier restorers. Lord Keynes, the economist, left his mark on King's in many ways. As Bursar, shrewd investment of capital made the College considerably wealthier. He married the Russian ballerina, Lydia Lopokova, who had danced solo parts with the Imperial Ballet in St Petersburg. He also built and financed the Arts Theatre in Cambridge. Rupert Brooke was a Kingsman who never aged. His poems belie the fact that he was born in 1887. At Cambridge he helped to found the Marlowe Society and was elected a Fellow of King's in 1912 with a dissertation, *John Webster*. His stay at the Old Vicarage, Grantchester, is described with nostalgia in his poem of that name. His tragic death by blood poisoning at Skyros in the First World War was poignantly recalled in *1914 and Other Poems* and *Collected Poems* that were published posthumously. They reflect something of the romantic patriotism of that time. The church clock and honey for tea lines have become such clichés that a Grantchester vicar used to halt the clock permanently at ten-to-three. A more appropriate epitaph of this brilliant young Kingsman is in his poem *Clouds*:

> They say that the Dead die not, but remain
> Near to the rich heirs of their grief and mirth.

To single out one Kingsman of eminence, my choice would be E. M. Forster, the novelist and man of letters, whose rooms in College were a time warp of a nineteenth century way of life. They reflected Edwardian taste in a Victorian setting. High-ceilinged, spacious, armchairs draped with Indian shawls, books galore, period portrait frames, and a piano which he used to say was not ornamental – no one could disagree – it was there if wanted and the mood was right. He performed indifferently from a strictly limited repertoire, but enjoyed particularly Beethoven and Verdi and was a thwarted musician. It gave him immense pleasure to assist Eric Crozier in writing the libretto for Benjamin Britten's opera, *Billy Budd*.

After *A Passage to India* Forster wrote no more novels. Not that it affected his standing for he used to say that his reputation as a novelist grew with every book he didn't write. *A Passage to India* was probably Forster's most satisfying novel. It was translated into twenty-one languages and won the Femina Vie-Heureuse and James Tait prizes. Begun in 1913, it was not completed until 1924 and at times he admitted there were doubts whether it would ever be finished. In the narrative he captured accurately the speech and mannerisms of the Indian characters – it is a true reflection of the oriental mind. He handled the thorny question of Anglo-Indian relations with sympathy and gained approval from both Hindu and Muslims.

Forster was conscious of the break in the flow of his writing. He would have liked to have done more, but never succeeded. It was not due to pressure of other commitments, for he had all the time in the world to develop a theme. For some reason inspiration died. But he was not forgotten. When his mother died, he was invited to return to King's as an Honorary Fellow. He refused a knighthood offered by Clement Attlee. In 1953 he became CH. His eightieth birthday was celebrated by a lunch party in the Hall attended by aging literary friends of the former Bloomsbury days, figures like Leonard Woolf, Clive and Vanessa Bell, Duncan Grant, David Garnett, and the Greek poet, George Seferis. The following year was marked by the conferring of an honorary degree by Cambridge University. His ninetieth birthday was celebrated by a concert in the Chapel for which he selected the music, and the ultimate honour of being admitted to the Order of Merit.

E. M. Forster is remembered as a brilliant writer, shy and retiring in manner but, like many Kingsmen, with the spirit of a rebel and a touch of conceit.

ALFRED, LORD TENNYSON (Trinity College)
1809–1892

> *Therefore your Halls, your ancient Colleges*
> *Your portals statued with old kings and queens*
> *Your gardens, myriad-volumed libraries,*
> *Wax-lighted chapels, and rich carven screens,*
> *Your doctors, and your proctors, and your deans.*

AN INTERNATIONAL
THOROUGHFARE

Before leaving King's, notice the Victorian letter-box on the cobbled forecort, then take stock of a thoroughfare as well-known as Fifth Avenue in New York, Bond Street in London, Rue de la Paix in Paris and Via Condotti in Rome. Like Princes Street in Edinburgh, it is only half a street. In Scotland the focal point is the Castle: in Cambridge it is the fabric of King's College and Chapel, yet the opposite side of King's Parade has its own claim to distinction. Initial impressions are influenced by the irregular roof-lines and gables, but the houses they protect have interesting histories. No. 19, for instance, was where Edward Fitzgerald lodged as an undergraduate. This English translator and poet published anonymously an English poetic version from the Persian of the *Rubaiyat* and made Omar Khayyam a household word in this country. The combination of melancholy and sensuality, with the rhythm of an original four-line stanza, gave the poem widespread publicity. King's Parade was a favourite base of this reserved scholar with eccentric tastes in clothes. He was a familiar figure in flowered-satin waistcoat, handkerchief tied over his hat, and an Inverness cape. His first published work *Euphranor* describes his idyllic vision of Cambridge. No. 19 knew many literary figures, for example Tennyson, described by Fitzgerald as "something like the Hyperius shorn of his beaus in Keats' poem, with a pipe in his mouth". Others include W. B. Donne, Carlyle and Thackeray, the last a close friend of Fitzgerald. They shared a common sense of humour.

No. 11 also cast a spell. Here it was that Mary and Charles Lamb lived in the shadow of insanity, an illness that caused Mary to kill her mother in a spasm of madness, whilst Charles was similarly deranged for a long period. No. 57 was the lodging of Alfred Tennyson. This time only the memory has survived. In place of a door is now an iron railing. The entrance has become a window, the bell-push a token, and the number 57 is just discernible. During the war, rooms over No. 15 housed the restless spirit of Harold Laski, the guru of the Socialist Party who was always ready to act as Devil's Advocate for the joy of arguing.

These are but a few of the well-known figures who have frequented King's Parade. I must not forget some of the more recent tradesmen who served both Town and Gown. Peck's Chemists opposite King's used to have the traditional jars in the windows with the sign of the owl and pestle with mortar above the door, and the manager, "Pip" Orange, was a boon to several generations of students. Dorothy Crisp at No. 16 was the fourth generation to sell prints, whilst her father carved the wooden spoons given unkindly to undergraduates who had failed the Tripos. John Leach at No. 18 was a rare craftsman and an authority on local history. He was a keen golfer and after his death in 1986 his ashes were scattered on his beloved Gog Magog links. Ryder and Amies, robe-makers at No. 22, have another distinction. Their windows are used to display University teams. Many future cricket, rugby and golf stars have rushed to see if they had been selected. Of current interest, Clive Sinclair, the computer genius, has a base at No. 6a.

Several generations of undergraduates and countless visitors will recall the KP restaurant at No. 17 run by Grace Marsh, daughter of the Beckhampton racehorse trainer, Sam Darling. I have left it to the last because the establishment was unlike any other in Cambridge. The number of famous people who walked down that narrow passageway would make a celebrity *Who's Who*. The restaurant's success was due to the personality of the proprietor who on racing lore was almost a legend.

"Mops", as she was affectionately known, presided over the KP in regal style. In appearance, she never varied. Stylishly dressed to the last detail with an Edwardian touch, she sat in a small, elegantly furnished room on the left as you entered from the passageway. Only the chosen few were invited to have a glass of sherry in the sanctum. When she reminisced it was total recall of the days when her husband, Richard Marsh, trained Persimmon to win the Derby and St Leger for the Prince of Wales. Those familiar with the deeds of this spirited bay should visit the National Horseracing Museum in Newmarket where his stuffed head is on loan from the Queen's racing collection. "Mops" would describe how Persimmon almost missed the Derby. His high-mettled temperament rebelled at the thought of the box on the horse-train. Attempts failed with the first two special trains at Dullingham Station. The last train was about to leave. Marsh took drastic action. Twelve men literally carried Persimmon aboard. Once installed, he settled down with no further trouble.

Other recollections were how Richard achieved the Triple Crown with Diamond Jubilee, who arrived at Egerton House, the family home, in 1898 as an unbroken year-ling and something of a handful. A devilish temper made training a nightmare. After victory in the Grand National with Ambush II, the Prince of Wales became the only owner to have won the Derby and this famous steeplechase in the same year. In 1909 Marsh won another Derby and the rare distinction of recording a win for a reigning sovereign in the Classics. In Grace Marsh's world memories never aged. In her mind Richard's influence was still felt, a belief doubtless helped by her interest in spirit-

Below: King's Parade with an international reputation as a street of memories

ualism. Her son, Marcus, added his quota of success when he came to Cambridge. He inherited much of his father's flair, winning the 1934 Derby and St Leger with Windsor Lad for the Maharajah of Rajpla and the same Classics in 1952 for the Aga Khan, whilst two years earlier he took the Derby with Palestine.

The KP Visitors' Book contained the signatures of royalty, statesmen, politicians and the successful from all walks of life. Of Americans Grace Marsh would recall Clark Gable and Humphrey Bogart, but she had an eye for future talent. Several Cabinet Ministers can look back to those early days. One habitué I recall was Norman St John Stevas, in those days somewhat foppish with impeccable manners. On one occasion I was present when the Gaekwar of Baroda was enjoying her hospitality, before the Indian Government had deposed him as ruler of Baroda, a decision that killed any chance of rivalling the Aga Khan's position in the Turf. That evening he was pleased with himself, having created a record at the Newmarket Sales by paying 28,000 guineas for a yearling. Conversation was interrupted when an undergraduate from his country was about to leave. Seeing the Gaekwar, he prostrated himself on the ground, a diversion that did not upset the head waiter who stepped over the body to announce that dinner was ready.

Only once in my experience did I see Mrs Marsh embarrassed. Among my guests one Saturday evening was a somewhat rotund man wearing plain-rimmed glasses who looked a good trencherman. He had a rare ability to enjoy himself, occasionally unleashing a body-shaking laugh that was infectious. The echo reached downstairs. The head waiter whispered to me that perhaps the robust laugh might be modified if only for the other diners. After the meal I introduced my guests to "Mops". He was William Temple, Archbishop of Canterbury, who the following day would preach the University Sermon. The good lady looked in need of a confessional.

The closing of the KP was a loss. It confirms that the houses on King's Parade hold the secrets that only a few know.

THE UNIVERSITY CHURCH

Great St Mary's, once called St Mary-by-the-Market, has been the site of a church since 1205, but what we see today dates from the fifteenth and sixteenth centuries. Its past history has been chequered. Fire damaged the structure in 1290: de Lisle, Bishop of Ely, consecrated the High Altar in 1351, but the clunch used in the rebuilding deteriorated and the foundation had to be rebuilt. Fuller compiled notes of the operation: "Begun May 16th, 1478, when the first stone thereof was laid in the 17th of Edward the Fourth. The Church ended (but without a tower or a belfry) 1519 in the 11th of Henry the Eighth. The tower finished 1608 in the 6th of King James; so that from the beginning to the ending thereof were no fewer than an hundred and thirty years."

This church was dogged by alterations. Drastic changes involved the screen, rood-loft, west door and south porch. A third gallery was added in the eighteenth century to accommodate the Vice-Chancellor, Professor and Doctors when they assembled to listen to the University Sermon preached from an outsized pulpit set in the centre of the congregation, then in 1863 the lot was swept away. More enduring was the roof made from hundreds of oak trees from Chesterford Park and the gift of Henry VII in 1505.

From the outset it has been known as the University Church and served in that capacity. Before the Senate House was built, degrees were conferred there and charters stored in it. The cost of many of the alterations came from University funds, supplemented by contributions from Richard III and Henry VII. One tradition remains and can be watched every Sunday in Full Term. On the strike of half-past two, a procession walks from the Senate House to Great St Mary's led by the Esquire Bedells carrying their silver maces. The Vice-Chancellor accompanies the Select Preacher, followed by the Heads of Houses, Doctors and Professors, re-enacting a time-old ceremony. At one time attendance was virtually compulsory as laid down by University regulations in 1750. A more liberal attitude was sounded in the *Ten Minutes' Advice* to Freshmen of 1785: "It is not reckoned fashionable to go to St Mary's on a Sunday – But I know no harm in going, nor that it is any reproach to a man's understanding to be seen publickly in the same place with the most dignified and respectable persons of the University." Today such advice might be needed by senior members of the University who often are thinly represented.

Another feature about the University Church should be mentioned. Not many people know that the quarter-hour chimes of the church clock, composed in 1793 by Joseph Jowett, professor of Civil Law, and aided by Dr Critch, organist of Christ Church, Oxford, were copied over sixty years later for the chimes of Big Ben at the new Houses of Parliament. The Cambridge Quarter Chimes are sometimes called the Westminster Chimes and have been copied at the Royal Exchange. "Congregations" in the Senate House are summoned by the great bell that lives up to its name.

An unusual tradition has grown round the University Church for some years. It would seem that the vicars anticipate being elevated to vacant bishoprics. Among those who have swopped their trousers for gaiters are Joseph Fison, Hugh Montefiore, Stanley-Booth Clibborn and Mervyn Stockwood. The pattern was broken in 1986 when Michael Mayne was appointed Dean of Westminster. He came to Cambridge after being head of the BBC religious programmes, and made the pulpit of Great St Mary's a forum for debating the ethical issues of the day. With an eye to popular appeal, he invited such figures as Billy Graham, Lord Ramsey, Princess Anne, Edward Heath, Cliff Richard, David Owen, Hans King, Alec Guinness, Shirley Williams and Lord Scarman. His duties at the Abbey began with the marriage of Prince Andrew and Sarah Ferguson after being in office for only a few days. After serving as a bishop's chaplain, he had no ambitions to change places. His reaction to episcopal duties was echoed by Mervyn Stockwood. Over lunch he described his attempts to discipline an erring priest. The cleric had fallen out with his parishioners. The choir left, wardens resigned, finally no one turned up for Sunday services. Routine thereafter on a Sunday morning was fixed. Candles were lit, a few prayers said, a week's work over on full pay. Stockwood remarked that a priest could only be defrocked if he committed two major offences. One is unlikely, the other often physically impossible. He ended with a comment I have never forgotten – "As long as there's death, there's hope."

In case the visitor imagines that all University Church vicars are destined for high office, glance at a brass set in the floor by the sanctuary. It records that the reformer, Martin Bucer, was buried in the chancel, but that in 1557 his bones were disinterred and with those of Fagius from St Michael's Church, burnt in the Market Place.

Overleaf: The University Church of St Mary's, a recruiting ground for gaiters

THE CORE OF THE UNIVERSITY

O pposite the University Church stands the dignified Senate House, designed by James Gibbs and completed in 1730. Many experts rate it as the finest work of the architect who also designed the church of St Martin-in-the-Fields in London. The Senate House was intended to form part of a three-sided court, but happily the scheme was shelved. The building blends into its surroundings: an eastern block could have upset the balance. The interior is pleasing with woodwork and plaster-work by Artari and Bagutti, Italians frequently employed by Gibbs. An outside wall every year knows moments of suspense. On it are posted Tripos examination results. Students approach the lists warily and often from a distance hopefully try to spot their name in the short number of First Class Honours, then switch to the crowded columns of lesser degrees. It can be a humbling experience to have public assessment of your work.

Many visitors to Cambridge imagine the University as one building with a visual identity. The nearest approach to this conception is a small court near the Senate House that is rarely discovered. It is older than any of the Colleges, literally a fragment

Below: *The Senate House designed by James Gibbs and completed in 1730*

of medieval Cambridge left behind. It is the core of the University. Records show that this plot of land was given to the University by Nigel de Thornton in 1278. By the end of that century the first teaching building or Divinity School was built and can still be seen in the Cobble Court of the Old Schools. The first floor was the *Domus Congregationis* or Regent House, eventually to become the University Combination Room. At the outset it served as the Chapel and Senate House. The religious side ceased after the Reformation. The centre of University legislation was later transferred to the present building.

It is not easy to understand the framework of the University. Although in many ways flexible, its organisation is complex. The Colleges, whilst self-autonomous, are subject to the University. They contribute financially and reserve a number of fellowships for professors. The University examines and confers degrees. Statutes are separate and can only be changed through the Privy Council. In practice many of the divisions between University and College are theoretical. Most of the dons hold teaching posts as lecturers or professors, which in turn are tied to faculties or university teaching departments, each being responsible for the faculty curriculum and setting of examinations.

Protocol is all-important. This is emphasised during the ceremony involved in the conferring of honorary degrees. Many watch the procession through the handsome cast-iron railings that were among the earliest to be erected in England. In the centre of an immaculate turfed square is the copy of the Warwick Vase presented by the Duke of Northumberland in 1842. The procession of dignitaries highlights the ritual, dress and office of all the principal University officials. Everything about it observes tradition. The order is: Esquire Bedells; Chancellor; University Marshal; recipients of honorary degrees; Vice-Chancellor, accompanied by the Registrary and the Orator; Heads of Colleges; Regius Professors of Divinity, Hebrew, and Greek; Professors, if Doctors, in the order of their complete degrees; Doctors of Divinity, Law, Medicine, Science, Letters, and of Music; the Librarian; remaining Professors; Members of the Council of the Senate; Bachelors of Divinity; Doctors of Philosophy . . . altogether sufficient shades of protocol to satisfy any purist, but for the ordinary onlooker more than confusing. For that reason I am adding a few details about the main University officers, their functions, dress and origin.

The *Esquire Bedells* are not only picturesque in appearance, but have been practical officers of the University for over 700 years. Originally they were not graduates or members of the University, but enjoyed certain privileges and were exempt from the jurisdiction of the town because of their official academic standing. In due course they were recruited from graduates of eminence and are today the link between the oldest traditions and more recent ceremonies.

The first reference to the title of Bedell is in a deed that refers to John Canterbury. With his brother-in-law, Provost Woodlarke, they were the first University members to hold the post. We know that Canterbury was a Fellow of King's and married the Provost's sister, Elizabeth. The official title was *Bedellus* with occasional variations. The style was *Serviens Universitatis Cantabrigiae*, whilst his Oxford counterpart was the *Serjeant* of the University. Just to confuse matters, Fuller in his *History of the University* refers to *Illuminatores, Scriptores, Stationarii*, and other officers, whilst in statutes and deeds, Bedells are referred to as: *Apparitor*, or *Stator; Praeco; Viator; Serviens Universitatis; Caduceator; Accisus; Lictor*. Clearly the Esquire Bedell was a man of many duties.

The uniform of the Esquire Bedell has always been distinctive. The Tailors' Statute of Oxford (1358) stipulates that the vestes of Masters and Bedells were to be wide and long to distinguish them from the laity. In 1790 John Cobbould painted the well-known picture detailing University customs and costumes. Half-a-dozen Bedells are shown in distinctive gowns and caps. The virges were wands of office, not staves. The dress was a long gown with a girdle, but no hood. Later it became compulsory and may have been the *Caputium* or *Epomis* worn by Bedells who had no degree.

Matthew Stokes recorded the scene during a visit by Queen Elizabeth I: ". . . in the

Opposite: University procession of dignitaries preceded by mace-bearing Esquire Bedells leading the Vice-Chancellor

time of this disputation (that took place in Great St Mary's Church) the Bedells according to the Custom put on their quifs and Hoods, and so entered and kneeled down. Unto whom after she had for a little while looked upon their habit, she with her hand beckoned to stand up."

The maces of the Bedells have had many names. Fuller refers to virges or wands and staves: others speak of sceptres and maces, with their Latin titles *Virgas, Sceptra, Caducea* and *Baculi*. Maces were presented in the seventeenth century by George Villiers, Duke of Buckingham, who was Chancellor in 1626. There is also the Yeoman's Mace, presented by Henri Rich, Earl of Holland, and Chancellor in 1628. The Royal Arms of the mace-heads were removed under the Commonwealth but restored in 1663. Before the Sovereign or Chancellor, the maces are carried upright. When the Sovereign visits the University, the staves are surrendered, but immediately returned to the Bedells.

The list of these gentlemen is lengthy and includes some who were hardly serious holders of this academical office. The case of Thomas Burrowes (1734–67) suggests that moonlighting is not so modern. Cole tells the story of Burrowes' mode of life . . . "Jovial and sociable, marrying a lady of Cambridge of the name of Yardley; by indolence and carelessness, they eat and drink their fortune almost all up: so that they were always in the utmost distress. The Duke of Newcastle got him a place of about £100 per annum: I think it was Chimney Sweeper to the King, which was of great use to him. His wife was one of the most slatternly, bad-tempered women he could have met: always lolling her head out of the window, if the season allowed it. They had a son of Trinity College (BA 1768) who was very wild and extravagant, and what was left of the estate at the father's death he soon made an end of." Looking at the current Esquire Bedells making their way in solemn progress, it is difficult to imagine such behaviour. It is more rewarding to concentrate on their historic maces.

Nerve-wracking moments known by generations of undergraduates when Tripos results are listed on notice-boards outside the Senate House

FRANZ JOSEF HAYDN

On 30th November 1791 I was three days in the country a hundred miles from London, with Sir Patrick Blake. In going I passed the town of Cambridge, inspected all the Universities, which are built conveniently in a row but separately. Each University has behind it a very spacious and beautiful garden, besides a stone bridge, in order to afford passage over the stream which winds past. The King's Chapel is famous for the carved work of the roof which is all of stone, but so delicate that nothing more beautiful could have been made of wood. It has already endured 400 years and everybody judges its age at about ten years, because of the firmness and peculiar whiteness of the stone.

The students are dressed like those at Oxford, but it is said they have better instructors. There are 800 students in all.

CLOTHES A LA UNIVERSITY

Convention unquestionably influences clothes. A regulation of the University decreed that the person *in statu pupillari* must wait on his tutor in his gown: that once a day at Hall, all present, from master and don to undergraduate, must be robed according to their standing or degree, but, in the liberated eighties, time-honoured customs tend to be ignored. Some students look scruffy by any standard, but history shows there is nothing new. Even in the fourteenth century there were rebels among priest-students. "... They disdained the tonsure, the distinctive mark of their Order, wore their hair either hanging down on their shoulders in an effeminate manner, or curled and pow-dered: they had long beards, and their apparel more resembled that of soldiers than of priests: they were attired in cloaks with furred edges, long hanging sleeves not covering their elbows, shoes chequered with red and green and tippets of an unusual length: their fingers were decorated with rings, and at their wrists they wore large and costly girdles, enamelled with figures and gilt: to the girdles they hung knives like swords." It was hardly surprising that Archbishop Stratford issued an order in 1342 that no student, unless he reformed his "person and apparel", would receive any ecclesiastical degree or honour.

The Proctors are readily recognisable. First mentioned in 1275, there is a complete record of each appointment since 1314. They are dons nominated every year by the University to represent the authority of the Vice-Chancellor and to discipline students. Their duties have varied over the centuries. In earlier times they regulated the hours of disputing and lecturing, of burial services, inceptions and festivals, acting for the Uni-versity in all kinds of business. They destroyed bad herrings exposed for sale, bought vestments, bell-ropes and candlesticks, and had charge of the University Chest. They also patrolled the streets to quell disturbances. Their activities are now on a lesser key. After the last war an undergraduate caught out of doors after sunset without cap and gown was fined 6s.8d. Today a chapel service is one of the few occasions when gowns are compulsory, though most colleges insist on gowns for dinner in Hall. Another restriction is that no undergraduate can keep a car unless permission is granted by a special pro-proctor. This eases traffic congestion in Cambridge streets and explains the flood of bicycles.

The traditional insignia of a Proctor is a linstock and small partisan for the Senior Proctor, and halberd and butter measure for the Junior Proctor. On ceremonial occasions these are carried by the Proctor's bull-dogs or constables, bowler-hatted University policemen chosen from college servants. The books they carry are not chained Bibles but ancient volumes of *Statuta Academiae Cantagrigiensis*, printed by J. Archdeacon in 1785. In the Senate House the proctorial ceremonial dress is the Congregation Habit, a hood set in the usual manner over the ruff which is worn over the gown. In the University Church the *Ad Clerum* habit is worn, a squared hood with three buttons in front and no ruff.

The role they play when degrees are conferred in the Senate House can be confusing to a visitor. An official reads, almost gabbles, a series of formal propositions, pauses, raises his hat, and says *placet* (approved). This ritual represents the completion of University legislation. If there is no opposition to the Grace read, the Proctor declares *placet*, but if it is *non placet* a vote can be demanded by any members of the Regent House. When that happens, the *placets* take their place on one side of the Senate House, the *non placets* on the other. An obvious majority means the Proctor pronounces *placet* or *non placet*. A request by not less than ten members means a scrutiny has to be taken.

There are still four important University officials to be recognised. The Public Orator is the correspondent of the University. He writes addresses and formal letters, and presents to the Chancellor or Vice-Chancellor those who are to receive honorary degrees, reciting a Latin speech in honour of each recipient. The office was founded in 1552. *The Historical Register of the University of Cambridge* has the complete list of Public Orators, headed by Richard Croke, the Greek scholar. He is entitled "to have precedence of all other Masters of Arts; and, as a mark of honour, to walk in processions and sit in public acts separate from the rest." The Registrary is one of the chief administrative University officers. As a permanent secretary to the Council of the Senate, he keeps records of proceedings in the Registry, attends all meetings or congregations of the Senate House and Regent House, deals with Boards and Syndicates, and edits the *Reporter*, the official gazette of the University. The office dates from the beginning of the sixteenth century, the first Registrary being Robert Hobbs, an Esquire Bedell.

The active head of the University is the Vice-Chancellor, elected annually by the Regent House from among the Heads of Colleges. Automatically he becomes chairman of a considerable number of University bodies, though in practice he only retains the chairmanship of the Financial Board, the General Board and the Council of the Senate – the rest are delegated. Finally, comes the Chancellor, who is first among University officials. The privileges of the University were confirmed in 1317 by Pope John XXII at the request of Edward II. The following year a bill was issued decreeing that Cambridge should not only be a *stadium generale* with masters and scholars having the rights of a university, but the University should be independent of the jurisdiction of the Bishop of the diocese, ultimate power resting with the Chancellor as Head of the University. The earliest mention of the office is 1248. From the outset the Chancellor was chosen by annual election, the system being retained for over 300 years, but early in the sixteenth century Bishop John Fisher was elected and remained in office for over thirty years. From that period the holder was an eminent public figure from outside the University, ordinary affairs being the responsibility of the resident Vice-Chancellor. The present Chancellor, Prince Philip, must be thankful that times are more settled than the old days. The first eight Chancellors elected after Bishop Fisher included six who died on the scaffold.

GONVILLE AND CAIUS COLLEGE

So much for academic protocol. Resuming our tour, the frontage of Gonville and Caius College is unmistakable. It is matter of taste. The purist finds difficulty in equating the mishmash of statuary, ungainly chimney-stacks and high tower with the elegant lines of the Senate Houses and University Church. Short-sighted critics accept it as a Victorian montage with vulgar overtones. There are many compensations. Caius Court is a pleasing reminder of its autocratic benefactor who indulged in symbolism. There are three gateways that mark a student's progress through the College. The gate in the Master's garden has engraved on it the word *Humilitatis*, hopefully indicating the student's mind on entering the College. The sequence from the Gate of Humility, with its plain fluted pilasters, was through a more imposing structure, the Gate of Virtue, inscribed with the word *Virtutis* on the east side and *To Caius Posui Sapientiæ 1567* on the west. The progress from Humility to Virtue and Wisdom leads finally to the third Gate that leads into Senate House Passage. This is the Gate of Honour through which the student goes to the Schools to gain a degree. This Gate is a choice example of Renaissance work taken from the designs of Dr Caius, but built after his death and completed in 1575.

It is customary to refer to this College as Caius, which is unfair to its first founder, Edmund Gonville, vicar-general of the diocese of Ely and rector of Terrington and Rushworth in Norfolk. In January 1348 Gonville founded a College of twenty scholars in dialectic and other sciences, naming it the *Hall of the Annunciation of the Blessed Virgin*. Little is known about Gonville, apart from the fact that he came from an established county family and had founded a Dominican House at Thetford. His Cambridge College was a modest establishment in tenements near Luteburgh Lane, now Free School Lane behind Corpus Christi College. When Gonville died three years later, the task of completing the plans became the responsibility of his executor, Bishop Bateman, founder of Trinity Hall. He moved Gonville Hall to a site by his own College, adding a Master's chamber over the Gatehouse, Fellows' chambers and a kitchen.

Even then Gonville Hall was still minute and remained so for some 200 years. Several benefactors added embellishments. Stained glass windows in the library were presented by John of Ufford, son of the Earl of Suffolk; William Lyndwood, the English canonist and Bishop of St David's also contributed. Others were more materialistic, like the bequest from the Lestrange family of "seven score ewes and three score lambs" that were to be given to the Master and Fellows each midsummer. A Cluniac monk, John Household, left in his will, dated 1543, the bequest, "To the College in Cambrydge called Gunvyle Hall, my longer table-clothe, may two awter (altar) pillows, with their bears of black satten bordered with velvet pirled with goulde: also a frontelet with the salutation of Our Lady curely wroughte with goulde; and besides two suts of vestments having eveythinge belonging to the adorning of a preste to say masse: the one is a light greene having white ends, and the other a duned Taphada." As a footnote the monk left his books, "protesting that whatsover be founde in my bookes I intent to dye a veray Catholical Christen man, and the King's letheman and trewe subject".

The Bursar's accounts for the half-year ending Lady Day, 1513. tells the size of the College. It has a Master, seven Fellows, three scholars, four servants and fifteen pensioners or undergraduates, one of whom was a nobleman, the rest were monks – Austin Friars from Westacre, Black Benedictine from Bury, Cistercians from Lewes, and Suffolk Monks of Butley. In accordance with Gonville's religious schemes, all approved candidates took doctorates, whilst Fellows were priests. In 1529 one of the students admitted was John Caius. The *Ordo Senioritatis* for 1532–3, that was similar to today's Tripos List, shows that Caius was brilliant for he ranked first, became a Fellow at twenty-three, and President of Physwick's Hostel, later incorporated into Trinity College. He turned his attention to medicine, went to Padua to work with the brilliant Vesalins, took M.D., and eventually returned to England in 1544 after extensive travels. His skill as a medico was recognised: he became President of the College of Physicians and physician to Edward VI and Queen Mary. His impressions on revisiting Cambridge are interesting, ". . . struck with the marvellous transformation which everything had undergone . . . faces and things, manners and dress were new. I saw books; I heard a new pronunciation; the forms of teaching, learning, disputing all were new. Not to mention all the novelties about me – and they were endless – I found scarcely a soul who either knew me or was known to me." Unfortunately Gonville Hall was in decline. The Reformation and suppression of religious houses had ruled out monk-students. Caius saw the need for the foundation of a new college and chose "that pore house now called Gonville Hall". A royal licence was granted in 1577 to refound and rename the Hall as Gonville and Caius College. Two years later Caius became Master and made an immediate impression, in more ways than one. He argued with the Fellows about "College copes, vestments, albes, crosses, tapers, and all massynge abominations"; approved architectural improvements; began the Admissions Registers; weeded out the archives; refused to take any salary as Master; introduced unusual measures. He declared that no persons "deaf, dumb, deformed, lame, chronic invalids or Welshman" should be admitted to the College. He came to an understanding with the town authorities that every year the bodies of two criminals should be delivered to the College for dissection purposes. Afterwards they would be buried in St Michael's Church before the entire College.

The College owed much to its second founder. Endowments were such that it became financially wealthy. Largely through Caius' influence it became a medical college, its best known physician being William Harvey, who went to the medical school at Padua where he studied under Fabricus, became a doctor of medicine at twenty-four, and returned to England in the first year of the reign of James I. At that time anatomists thought there were two blood systems in the body and that the blood flowed to and from the heart through each. Twenty-six years later Harvey published *The Movement of the Heart*, proving that the blood flows from the heart in the arterial system, through the tissues, and then back towards the heart in the venous system. *Of the Animal Species* in 1651 summed up his important work on embryology. From such a beginning came this medical trend. Fuller listed twenty-seven Doctors of Physic who were Caius' men.

Sadly Dr Caius did not find the happiness and recognition he might have expected from Cambridge. This was partly due to disputes with Fellows who were Puritans. He was denounced as a Papist and protests were made to the Chancellor. Dr Caius' reaction was forthright. Several Fellows were dismissed and one was put in the stocks. In 1572 the Vice-Chancellor wrote to Lord Burghley about the "superstitious rags" and "popish trumpery" hidden by Dr Caius in his Lodge, adding that "it had been thought good by the whole consent of the heads of houses to burn the bookes and suche other thinges as servid most for idolatrous abuses, and to cause the rest to be defaced, which was accomplished . . . with the willing hartes as appeared of ye whole company of that house."

Dr Caius resigned. In poor health, he visited the College, and supervised details of his tomb in the Chapel. Carvings were executed by Theodore Haveus of Cleves, who was described by Caius as "a skilful artificer and an eminent architect", whose bill for alabaster and transport amount to £10.10s.0d. The inscriptions *Fui Caius* and *Vivit post funera Virtus* were chosen by Dr Caius. The heavy brackets on which the monument is raised were fitted in 1637. A stickler for detail, he left instructions in his will for keeping

Opposite: The Gate of Virtue of Caius College, dated 1567

the College clean. A servant was to be paid to clean the pavements and gutters outside and inside the College courts. Two other tombs in the Chapel are noteworthy. One is to the physician, Stephen Perse, who died in 1615, leaving money to found a *Grammar Free School*, that became the Perse School; and the memorial to Thomas Legge, a former Master.

Among other distinguished Caius' men was Thomas Badwell, Poet-Laureate and fierce critic of John Dryden, the English poet and dramatist; Edward Thurlow, a Perse scholar in 1784, who left the College without a degree because of idleness and became the Lord Chancellor who presided over the trial of Warren Hastings; and Sir Thomas Gresham, English merchant and royal financial agent, who established the Royal Exchange in London as a bankers' meeting house. In many ways Gresham came second to Harvey as the most brilliant of Caius' products. He was ahead of his time in proposing a national equalisation fund to stabilise the exchange rate of the pound sterling, which had dropped since Henry VIII debased the coinage. He expounded what later became known as Gresham's law, stating that money of greater intrinsic value is hoarded while that of equal monetary but lesser intrinsic value is circulated. Among the relics of interest in the College is the flag flown at the South Pole in the Scott Expedition of 1912 by Dr Wilson, a Caius' man. On feast nights the silver Sceptre, or Caduceus, is brought out on its original yellow silk cushion. This treasure was presented by Dr Caius to the Royal College of Physicians and then transferred to his own College.

Of all the distinguished figures linked with Gonville and Caius, my choice would be Sir James Chadwick, who was Master in 1945. As a physicist, he began the research on radioactivity in co-operation with Lord Rutherford. In 1921, as Assistant Director of Research at the Cavendish Laboratory, he became responsible for the detailed organisation of research on the artificial disintegration of light elements by alpha particle bombardment. In his Bakerian lecture in 1920 Rutherford had predicted the existence of the neutron. In 1932 Chadwick proved its existence, a major landmark in nucleur physics for which he received the Nobel Prize for Physics. During the Second World War, Chadwick was actively concerned with mastering the problem of nuclear fission, was closely involved with the development of the atomic bomb, and led the team of scientists who co-operated with the Americans on the Manhattan project, finally determining the operational application of the bomb.

Chadwick was introspective. After Nagasaki he became even more aloof and inaccessible. Like Sir Martin Ryle, later Astronomer-Royal, but in another branch of science, he discovered his social conscience. The positive values of the civil application of atomic energy had his approval and as Chairman of the Committee dealing with such matters he was influential in establishing the pattern of the British nuclear power programme, but always nagging was the memory of what atomic power can do in war. That recollection never left him, but, as he often said, there is no way of going back. If he hadn't discovered the neutron, some other physicist would have done so with the same result, but it was a heavy mental burden to carry.

The fact that much of his technical research was difficult for a layman to understand had its lighter moments. I shared a platform with him in Liverpool. Sitting beside me was Lord Leverhulme who had hearing problems. To overcome this disability and maintain contact with what was being said, he had a box-like contraption that acted as a microphone, regulated for loudness by a dial and a listening ear-plug. After a time, the struggle to comprehend was too much. He switched off and enjoyed the peace of silence with a quiet smile of contentment that was not missed by platform or audience. Afterwards I told Chadwick of the incident. He thought that many of the listeners must have been envious.

The Gate of Honour through which the Caius student would pass to the Old Schools to receive his degree

DAVID'S BOOKSTALL

For years David's bookstall on Market Hill was famous. Every Saturday morning a fresh selection of books at ridiculously low prices was laid out on the trestle-tables. Many were the 'finds' made by don and student. It was a recognised meeting-place for the bibliophile, on a par with the Quays of Paris. Today it is not the same. David's has gone, Sidney is dead. Both were 'characters' known to generations of undergraduates. Attempts have been made to provide similar stalls, but the magic and quality are no more. They are memories like the flower-seller who used to sell bunches of violets in the doorway of the Red Lion in Petty Cury after spraying them with cheap scent; the don who strode through King's Parade carrying a pile of old newspapers under his arm; the Professor of Economics who walked in Newnham snipping privet hedges with a pair of scissors; the newspaper-seller, invariably drunk, who refused to sell a newspaper unless he liked your face. The list of eccentrics was long and accepted as part of the scene. Unfortunately, like David's, there is no room for nonconformity unless an earring is worn!

After David's bookstall left Market Hill, bibliophiles now frequent his well-known little bookshop in St Edward's passage

TRINITY HALL

The adjoining Trinity Hall, like Gonville and Caius, owed much to that far-sighted cleric, William Bateman, Bishop of Norwich. He saved Gonville Hall after the death of its founder in 1351 by transferring it to a site opposite Trinity Hall which he had founded the previous year. Bateman was no ordinary man of God. After studying Canon and Civil Law at Cambridge, his astuteness in diplomacy was noted by the Roman Pontiffs and in due course he was consecrated bishop by Pope Clement VI. The appointment coincided with the Black Death, a plague that decimated the ranks of clergy in the eastern counties: gaps had to be filled. Bateman, recognising the need to create trained logicians to strengthen Papal authority against the Statutes of Praemunire and Provisors, sought and obtained a royal licence to found a college with a Master, twenty Fellows and several scholars. The Fellows were required to be candidates for Orders, but only seven Canonist Fellows had to be priests. The intention was to have experts in Canon Law for the service of the Church.

A site was chosen behind the University Schools where John de Crauden, Prior of Ely, housed monks studying at Cambridge. Bateman transferred them to Burden's Hostel that stood between Rose Crescent and Green Street. In 1350 the Hall was founded as the "College of the Scholars of the Holy Trinity of Norwich". The plan was not popular. When Bateman died five years later in Avignon, there were only three scholars, three Fellows and a Master. The Hall survived and for some 600 years produced advocates in Canon law, ostensibly for the service of God. In some ways progress was slow. The Chapel was licenced in 1352 – the earliest Chapel earmarked for a College – but it was not consecrated until 1513. During those years Trinity Hall shared with Clare Hall the church of St John Zachary. Henry VI's enthusiasm for demolishing churches to suit his own ends led to St John Zachary being pulled down to make room for his new foundation, King's College. Both Colleges were forced to transfer their worship to St Edward's Church. At the beginning of Edward VI's reign, a proposal was made, probably by Somerset, that as both Colleges worshipped in one church, they should be amalgamated into one College called St Edward's College, after the eleven-year-old monarch. Nothing came of the scheme. To make it possible for both Colleges to use St Edward's Church, Simon Dalling had approached the royal commissioners for permission. This entailed Henry obtaining the gift of both livings in 1444 and transferring them to the Master and Fellows of Trinity Hall. The grant was made on the 21st March, 1446, the King's grant being confirmed the same year by the Bishop of Ely. As a result, St Edward's became a church outside the jurisdiction of the diocese and is still a Peculiar.

Trinity Hall has several features of interest, particularly the Library which ranks as the finest sixteenth century example in Cambridge. In those days they provided sloping desks above each shelf and seats alongside for anyone who wanted to study a book. Each press ends with an Elizabethan finial. Many of the books are chained, but the chains are not original. The Combination Room anticipates the needs of diners. The large semi-circular table has fitted an ingenious tramway obtained from a London club and installed in 1838. It enables Fellows to move their after-dinner port with the minimum of difficulty.

No visit to Trinity Hall is complete without appreciating the gardens, particularly the terraces down to the river. In 1905 Henry James wrote, "If I were called upon . . . to mention the prettiest corner of the world, I should draw out a thoughtful sigh and point the way to the garden of Trinity Hall.'' Such praise is still justified, even for so small an area.

Trinity Hall has had a long and distinguished legal tradition. The Regius Professorship of Civil Law was a College monopoly for over 300 years. A Master of Trinity Hall was responsible for establishing the Doctor's Commons in London. Among the many legal figures who were Hall men are Jowett, ''an elegant scholar and a man of mild and amiable manners''; Lord Chief Justice Cockburn; Sir James Marriott, a Judge of the Admiralty Court; and Stephen Gardiner, Bishop of Winchester, Chancellor of England, and Master of Trinity Hall from 1525–52. This inspirer of the Six Articles and known as ''the great instrument of Henry VIII'', can be seen in the Combination Room through the eyes of Holbein. Gardiner's likeness has little in common with a contemporary description – ''The doctor had a swart colour and hanging look, frowning brows, eyes an inch within the head, a nose hooked like a buzzard, wide nostrils like a horse, ever snuffing into the wind, a sparrow mouth, great paws like the devil, talons on his feet like a grype, two inches longer than the natural toes.'' This jaundiced pen-portrait was by a critic who would have won the approval of Wilkie Collins.

The rooms of Trinity Hall did not know just men of Law: there were eminent figures of other professions. One of them was Robert Herrick, the English poet and clergyman whose *Hesperides* (1648), an assortment of some 1200 poems, included the lyric ''Gather ye rosebuds while ye may'', plus countless references to the pastoral names of mistresses and the physical presence of women. This hedonistic philosopher of verse studied first at St John's, but found it too expensive and transferred to Trinity Hall where costs were less. He studied law and informed his uncle that he intended ''to live recluse''. Good resolutions did not last. He left Cambridge with an M.A. in 1620 and became one of Ben Jonson's young poets in London. Thomas Tusser, the farmer-poet,

Below: *Trinity Hall, known for its legal traditions*

came to Trinity Hall from Eton and is remembered for his "Hundreth good pointes of husbandrie" in verse of quaint expression that was published in 1557. He enjoyed more practical fame by introducing the culture of barley at his Cattiwade farm in Suffolk.

Lord Chesterfield, who was at Trinity Hall in 1712, left a series of pungent letters to his bastard son. One comments on the Cambridge of his day: "I find the college where I am infinitely the best in the university; for it is the smallest, and it is filled with lawyers, who have lived in the world, and know how to behave. Whatever may be said to the contrary, there is certainly very little debauchery in this university, especially amongst people of fashion, for a man must have the inclinations of a porter to endure it here."

Other former members include Viscount Fitzwilliam, founder of the Fitzwilliam Museum, and Henry James who dwells on the joys of a Sunday morning walk in Cambridge in his essay *English Vignettes*: ". . . the loveliest confusion of Gothic windows and ancient trees, of grassy banks and mossy balustrades, of sun-chequered avenues and groves, of lawns and gardens and terraces, of single-arched bridges spanning the little stream, which is small and shallow, and looks as if it had been turned on for ornamental purposes. The thin-flowing Cam appears to exist simply as an occasion for these brave little bridges – the beautiful covered gallery of John's or the slightly-collapsing arch of Clare."

Sir Leslie Stephen entered Trinity Hall in 1850 and appeared to have enjoyed the stay, later becoming a typical mid-Victorian don who glowed with mental and physical fitness. He enjoyed tobacco sessions at midnight in College rooms, sipped wine in the Fellows' Garden, listened to nightingales along their Backs, periodically walked to London, and even smoked a pipe on the summit of the Eiger. Such activities were not to the taste of Edward Bulwer-Lytton, later Baron Lytton, who preferred to imitate Byron's lifestyle even to the point of taking up pugilism. He had the satisfaction of gaining the Chancellor's English Medal for 1825 on the strength of his poems on Cambridge. Edward Carpenter (1844–1929) was a don at Trinity Hall, but resigned as a Fellow and curate of St Edward's Church through the influence of Walt Whitman's poems and recognition of his own homosexuality. The decision was understandable for Trinity Hall's physical activities like rowing hardly appealed to the aesthete. The same was true of Ronald Firbank (1886–1926) who modelled his life on a decadent dandy. He tried to make his rooms in the Hall the most elegant in the College and gave sumptuous dinners to a circle of friends that included Rupert Brooke, E. J. Dent and Shane Leslie. Dent, who was a Fellow of King's, repaid the hospitality in a bitchy letter to Clive Carey in 1915 . . . "Do you remember an absurd thing at the Hall called Firbank who tried to look rather like Lord Alfred Douglas of the sonnets? A great adorer of Rupert? He has written a novel . . . It is very 1890 – incredibly artificial and absurd."

J. B. Priestley was like a breath of Yorkshire cold air. No messing about, just blunt speaking. He entered Trinity Hall on an ex-officer's grant, and maintained that the wool office in Bradford offered more educative experience than Cambridge. A popular chronicler of English life, his first two books were published by Bowes and Bowes of Trinity Street in 1922. In many ways he was an ideal Trinity Hall product.

Two last snippets. Trinity Hall is the only foundation in Cambridge to retain its ancient title of Hall; it also has the smallest College Chapel in Cambridge.

JOWETT'S LITTLE GARDEN

Trinity Hall Lane has a reminder of Joseph Jowett, Professor of Civil Law from 1782 to 1814. It applies to a small piece of ground in an angle of Trinity Hall wall that produced a satirical epigram:

A little garden little Jowett made
And fenced it with a little palisade;
But when this little garden made a little talk
He changed it to a little gravel walk;
If you would know the mind of little Jowett
This little garden don't a little show it.

The author of these lines is said to be Archdeacon Wrangham. There is also a Latin rendering:

Exiguum hunc hortum, fecit Jowettulus iste
Exiguus, vallo et muniit exiguo;
Exiguo hoc horto forsan Jowettulus iste
Exiguus mentem prodidit exiguam.

CLARE COLLEGE

A few yards from Trinity Hall and almost under the shadow of King's Colleg Chapel and the New Schools is the unobtrusive, classical-styled Clare, secona oldest of the Cambridge Colleges and founded by the University in 1326. The architecture is pleasing. Iron gates are superb examples of English Renaissance craftsmanship. All the buildings blend into the background, although none is original. Civil War interrupted a 1638 rebuilding scheme and the work was not finished until 1715. Prior to that Clare's history was chequered. The original foundation had languished. After ten years the revenue could only afford ten scholars. Then in 1338 a remarkable woman came on the scene. Elizabeth, Domina de Clare, granddaughter of Edward I, and youngest sister of Gilbert de Clare, 4th Earl of Gloucester, who died at the Battle of Bannockburn, inherited with her two sisters an estate of considerable size. Possibly influenced by the action of her friend, the Countess of Pembroke, in founding Pembroke College, she became interested in education in a practical fashion. A deed dated the 6th April, 1338, states that Richard de Baden, "Founder, Patron and Advocate of the House called the Hall of the University surrendered all the rights and titles of University Hall to Lady de Clare", who refounded it, settled endowments, and changed the name to Clare House. A few years later it became Clare Hall, the title remaining until 1856 when the Master and Fellows approved a resolution altering the title to Clare College. Elizabeth de Clare was no stranger to change. She had three husbands: John de Burgh, Earl of Ulster; Theobald, Lord Verdun; and Roger, Baron Damory, who died in 1332. The College arms are those of Clare impaling de Burgh, her first husband.

The early years were not without drama. The Colleges seemed prone to fire: in 1362 "a casual fire reduced their house to ashes"; then in 1521 the Master's Chambers, the treasury and the archives were destroyed. Fuller adds a footnote: "Here, by way, whosoever shall consider in both Universities the ill contrivance of many chimnies, hollowness of hearths, shallowness of tunnels, carelessness of coals and candles, catchingness of papers, narrowness of studies, late reading and late watching of scholars, cannot but conclude that a special Providence preserveth those places. How small a matter hath sometimes made a partition betwixt the fire and the fuel? Thus an hairsbreadth fixed by a Divine finger shall prove as effectual a separation from danger as a mile's distance. And although both Universities have had sad accidents in this kind, yet neither in number or nature (since the Reformation) so destructive as in other places: so that, blessed be God, they have been rather scare-fires than hurt-fires unto them."

That year it was proposed to amalgamate Clare with Trinity Hall, the new college to be called St Edward's, specialising in the study of Civil Law with the eleven-year-old Edward VI as Patron. Vigorous opposition came from Nicholas Ridley. He argued that a College founded to the glory of God and His Word should not become a mere legal institution. Hugh Latimer, a Fellow of Clare, acted as his mouthpiece, only to be rebuked by Nicholas West, Bishop of Ely, for the tone of his sermons. Latimer ignored the ban imposed and preached his famous Card Sermon. He took as his theme a game of cards. "And whereas," he said, "you are wont to celebrate Christmas in playing at cards, I intend, by God's grace, to deal unto you Christ's cards, wherein you shall perceive Christ's rule. Then further we must say to ourselves, 'What requireth Christ of a Christian man?' Now turn up your trump, your heart (hearts is trump, as I said before), and cast your trump, your heart, on this card; and upon this card you shall learn what Christ requireth of a Christian man – not to be angry, be moved to ire against his neighbour, in mind, countenance, nor other ways, by word or deed."

Below: *Classical-styled Clare, second oldest of the Colleges*

The mood of the incoming tide of Reformation was bitter. It was not only the Protestant reformer, Hugh Latimer, but others like Nicholas Ridley, later Master of Pembroke, Thomas Cranmer, compiler of the English Prayer book and Archbishop of Canterbury, with Miles Coverdale and William Tyndale, translators of the Bible, who perished at the stake because of their beliefs. As Macaulay summarised, "Cambridge had the honour of educating those celebrated protestant Bishops whom Oxford had the honour of burning."

Another remarkable young man who came to Clare at the age of thirteen in 1626 was Nicholas Ferrar. He must have been somewhat precocious for, after a year in residence, the Fellows invited him to become a Fellow-Commoner so that "he might be their companion". In 1624 he was elected to Parliament, but when the Plague erupted the following year he retired to Little Gidding, became a cleric, and formed an Anglican community consisting of his brother's and brother-in-law's families, who consecrated their lives to devotion and prayer. On three occasions this small group was visited by Charles I, also by George Herbert, the English churchman and metaphysical poet. T. S. Eliot refers to it in *Four Quartets*.

A window in Clare Chapel shows Nicholas Ferrar, in red court dress, and Hugh Latimer, in the black-and-white garb of a priest, kneeling by a cross. In another window Richard Badew, the original founder, kneels on a sphere and offers University Hall and its band of scholars to the Virgin. Most noticeable is the altarpiece of Cipriani's *Annunciation*, a beautiful painting by one of the founder members of the Royal Academy.

Distinguished members of Clare include William Whitehead, who became Poet-Laureate after Gray had declined the office in 1757. The son of a baker, he is the only Laureate born in Cambridge and went to Clare on a scholarship designated for orphaned sons of bakers. Peter Gunning, a Royalist cleric, was imprisoned during the Civil War after delivering an inflammatory sermon from Little St Mary's pulpit, but became Master of Clare at the Restoration. John Tillitson became Archbishop of Canterbury. William Whiston, Newton's successor to the Lucasian professorship of Mathematics, was accused of Arian heresy, deprived of his Chair and excluded from the Royal Society. George Ruggle, whose satirical onslaught on the legal profession in his Latin play, *Ignoramus*, so appealed to James I's humour, that in spite of it lasting some five hours he asked for a repeat performance.

Nathaniel Vincent attracted royal attention in a different way when he preached before Charles II at Newmarket in a long periwig and Holland sleeves. The King was not amused and ordered the Chancellor of the University to discipline the priest. As a result all clerics were warned about "wearing their hair and perukes of an unusual and unbecoming length", whilst sermons, either English or Latin, had to be delivered "by memory or without book, as being a way of preaching which his Majesty judgeth most agreeable to the use of all foreign churches, to the custom of the University heretofore, and the nature and intendment of that holy exercise."

Clare can also claim the eccentric Mansfield Forbes and the American poet, John Berryman, who entered the College in 1936 on a two-year scholarship to study English and left impressions in *The Other Cambridge*. It includes these lines:

Opposite: Impressive window in Clare Chapel showing Nicholas Ferrar and Hugh Latimer kneeling before a cross

Spires, gateways; bells. I like this town:
its bookshops, Heffer's above all and Bowes & Bowes
but Galloway & Porter too, & Deighton Bell
& sparkling Gordon Fraser's in Portugal Place
for days outranked for me the supernatural glass in King's Chapel,
the Entrance Gateway of John's, the Great Court of Trinity.
Slowly, as rapidly my books assembled every afternoon,
I strolled to look & see, & browsed, and began to feel.

No visit to Clare is complete without walking over one of the most attractive bridges in Cambridge. It was built by Thomas Grumbold from an original drawing for a fee of three shillings and is popularly known as the bridge of uncountable balls – the answer being thirteen and four-fifths as one has a segment missing. The garden has been laid out with imagination: from the pool it looks like a natural theatre with entrances and exits through gaps in the yew hedges. In May Week it is the ideal setting for Shakespearean and Elizabethan plays. The garden itself has endless surprises, credit for which is shared by Professor Nevill Willmer, a College Fellow, whose interest in the physiology of colour perception is evident, and two College botanists, Professor Godwin and Gilmour, a former Director of the Botanic Garden.

Across Queen's Road is the Memorial Building designed by Sir Giles Gilbert Scott, a pale-grey brick building in Neo-Georgian style with Adam details. Across a spacious court is the University Library, also designed by Scott. The front lawn has a sculpture by Barbara Hepworth, whilst Henry Moore's *Falling Warrior* is in Thirkell Court. A final word about the College collection of plate. It includes the Poison Tankard, made in Germany about 1580 of silver with filigree work. Its name is due to the crystal in its cover. Should poison be added to the wine, this conical crystal will either change colour immediately, or else shatter. It has yet to be tested.

FRANCES CORNFORD

I ran out in the morning when the air was clean and new
And all the grass was glittering, and grey with autumn dew
I ran out to the apple tree and pulled an apple down,
And all the bells were ringing in the grey old town.

Down in the town off the bridges and the grass
They are sweeping up the leaves to let the people pass,
Sweeping up the old leaves, golden-reds and browns
Whilst the men go to lecture with the wind in their gowns.

TRINITY STREET

It is impossible to confine Trinity Street to the limits of a normal thoroughfare. A better description would be a meeting-place for Town and Gown with a strong cosmopolitan flavour, foreigners galore walking against the human tide instead of observing tradition. Mid-morning is the best time when everything and everybody seem unhurried. A focal point used to be the establishment run by the Misses Walliker, preferably by the fireplace in the Big Room of the Whim, famous for its coffee and known by generations of students scattered across the world. It attracted a cross-section of the community, not all of whom were young. Middle-aged women openly flaunted their maturity. Between eleven and noon they came into their own, then melted into the obscurity of domesticity in Newnham, Huntingdon Road and Trumpington. Old Blues, like the importunate widow, were common. An occasional female don would appear with hair in a stringy bun. There were plenty of slim young women with pretty faces and shapeless clothes that somehow held together, chatting to inarticulate young men and long-haired curiosities who might have been either sex. The air was full of idle gossip, gentle slander and casual looks. Extremes rubbed shoulder with shoulder. Confined space emphasised the height of Boat Race crewmen and the brawn of Rugby Blues. Graduates with ordinary degrees tried to forget the fact. Clever students never listened but delighted in debunking the pseudo-culture of Union debating irrelevances: stupid ones seldom talked but eyed the Bright Young Things who turned up with eyelashes in bundles of three.

The Whim had a fascination peculiar to itself. It had the intimacy of a community the farthest from the work-a-day and all for the price of an excellent cup of coffee, sometimes served by genteel young women who gave the impression that the very act meant social degradation, but only a few were Andromedas chained to a cash-till. The majority were more than pleasing to the eye. Cambridge was unquestionably poorer when the Miss Wallikers retired. Cambridge life has always benefited from individuality and individual enterprise. In the same premises and in the name of progress we now have Libertys

Another household name disappeared when Bernard Matthew sold his grocery business and restaurant. The family had plied their trade for three generations. Many famous University figures made their domestic purchases in his well-stocked grocery establishment and will recall the tempting aroma of freshly-roasted coffee that wafted down the street, whilst those with a sweet tooth patronised the cake shop with its Victorian ferns and wicker-chairs. Happily Jack Hobbs Sports Shop still remains. This greatest cricketer of his generation was born in Cambridge, the eldest of twelve children. He played for Cambridgeshire, then tried to join Essex only to be turned down. He made his debut with Surrey and in his second match he made 155 off the bowling of Essex – the satisfaction lingered for he often recalled that innings. He always encouraged young talent in Cambridge. I once joined him in a match on Parker's Piece against the Young Working Men's Club organised by Alex Wood, a Fellow of Emmanuel. Although by then Sir John Berry Hobbs, his enthusiasm was tireless. Those who today buy their cricket gear from his Trinity Street shop would do well to remember that in terms of cricketing feats his record was on a par with any of the contemporary greats. Between 1905 and 1934 he scored 61,237 runs (average 50.65). He was forty when he scored his hundredth century and went on to ninety-seven more at an age when many cricketers have been turned out to grass. His opening partnerships with several fine batsmen, including Tom Hayward and Andy Sandham for Surrey, and Wilfred Rhodes and Herbert Sutcliffe for England, helped him to achieve no fewer than 166 century first-wicket stands during his 1,315 innings in first-class cricket. It seems appropriate that a few yards away in Trinity Street "Gubby" Allen had lodgings as a student above the Alma Mater Toilet Saloon. Still a grand character and similarly knighted for his services to cricket, "Gubby" is remembered for clinching victory in the 1936 Test at Brisbane when he bowled unchanged throughout the Australian innings – that lasted three balls more than twelve overs – and claimed five wickets for thirty-five runs, including McCabe's and Bradman's.

Trinity Street has a world-wide reputation for its bookshops. For seniority Bowes and Bowes takes pride of place for in 1981 they celebrated 400 years of bookselling and can claim to be the oldest bookshop in Britain. Previously it was Macmillan's, who took an important step when deciding to publish their own books. From No. 1 Trinity Street came such bestsellers as Hughes' *Tom Brown's Schooldays* and Charles Kingsley's *Westward Ho* and *The Water Babies*. In 1857 Macmillan transferred the publishing side to London. His nephew, Robert Bowes, took charge of the Trinity Street shop and the name was changed to Macmillan and Bowes. In 1953 the business was bought by W. H. Smith, an astute move by a progressive Group but somehow on a par with Libertys taking the place of the Whim.

As a bookshop I prefer Heffer's which in new premises is carrying on a family tradition that was begun in Petty Cury in 1876 by its founder, William Heffer. After William's death in 1928, Ernest assumed charge and many will recall how he would slowly descend the stairs and survey the scene before deciding which unsuspecting browser would have the benefit of his wisdom for about ten minutes. This was never a hardship; at times a positive delight. His son, Reuben, who tragically died whilst swimming in 1985, adopted a gentler, more donnish approach. His place as Chairman has now been taken by his son, Nicholas, who is equally conscious of the establishment's reputation. Quite by chance I was able to extend that standing in an unexpected way. The principal was Ben-Gurion, the Joshua who established his people in their Promised Land. He never relinquished his role as a visionary or allowed himself to forget the horror of Hitler's rule in Europe. Nothing blurred the memory of the *Einstzkommandos*, the gas-wagons or the slaughter-houses. But his campaign exacted a toll on his health: thrombosis symptoms led to frequent private visits to England and the necessary calm of a Cotswold Inn. This gave him an opportunity to indulge, with his wife Paula, his absorbing interest as a bibliophile. It was books, books, and more books, plus the joy of browsing, unbeknown to the Press, in bookshops, sometimes in Charing Cross Road, but mainly in Blackwell's of Oxford. Subject-matter was wide: Greek, Rome, Hebrew and the ancient philosophers. I suggested that Heffer's of Cambridge could match any Blackwell shelves. He put it to the test, found Reuben more than helpful, but unfortunately the "finds" that day were a trifle disappointing. Twice after that I accompanied him on his private foraging. On the last occasion he bought two 'treasures". I was not so fortunate. I enquired of an elderly, continental assistant on the ground floor about a book that had been published on General Booth and the Salvation Army. He directed me to the military section!

Finally, a word about the somewhat unprepossessing Trinity Street post-office. During the Second World War, the Cambridge University Pitt Club had its premises commandeered for the duration. Members looked for alternatives and settled for rooms above this post-office. The removal was marked by changing the name to the Interim Club. In some respects the new site was an improvement on Jesus Lane: windows overlooking the Great Gateway of Trinity College were a constant reminder of the proximity of history and the centuries-old traditions of the University. A frequent visitor to the Club in the afternoons was an elderly man, heavily-built, stooping, with old-fashioned high, stiff, white collar, starched cuffs and rimless glasses attached to a cord. Invariably he sat at the head of the long table. Routine was predictable. He declined the offer by a club servant to pour out the tea, preferring instead to mix the brew himself. So far, so good, but unfortunately the teapot handle was too hot to hold for more than a few seconds and the operation was painful and hazardous. This stubborn masochist was Sir Arthur Quiller-Couch, King Edward VII Professor of English Literature, better known by the pseudonym "Q".

Today his name is almost forgotten, yet before the war "Q" was widely read, with some sixty books, mostly romantic novels, to his credit. He was also Editor of the *Oxford Book of English Verse* and author of several outstanding books of criticism with an enormous following from undergraduates who formed capacity audiences at his lectures. His abrupt fall from fashion was remarkable and there are possibly several reasons for this. As an incurable romantic he was anathema to post-war critics and open to attack from pedants like F. R. Leavis. "Q" was not slow to react. He belittled T. S. Eliot's poetry as unpalatable and muddled, whilst Bloomsbury cliques got short shrift. Inevitably with such polarised views, he attracted both partisan admiration and abuse. Evaluated dispassionately, there was much about "Q"'s work that constituted solid achievement. Knighted in 1910, he had the satisfaction of establishing an independent Honours School in English and was largely responsible for founding an English Tripos at Cambridge. By his enthusiasm he succeeded in making the theme of literature not only uplifting but adventurous.

As to "Q" himself, he was something of an enigma, reluctant to reveal what he was like and how his mind ticked. In that sense time spent with him in the Interim Club and occasionally in the privacy of his room in Jesus College on C Staircase was rewarding. It invoked the thought that sadly what might have been his most absorbing book was never written. The tragic accident that cost his life in 1944 meant that his autobiograply was left unfinished, chapters that would have given insights into the lives of many famous literary and artistic figures. A glimpse of these was given from time to time in his reminiscences.

In an age when "characters" are rare, "Q" was outstanding. A man of panache, he was often flamboyant in dress. During the May Races he wore yachting trousers and reefer jacket, but in the lecture room he was a stickler for academic correctness and always wore morning dress. University rules had to be meticulously observed, so much so that women students in the audience were ignored as he addressed them as "Gentlemen". Even in the war when masculine representation was almost nil, the form of address remained the same. Women as such in the academic sense did not exist, though in no way was he a misogynist. On the contrary he never discouraged feminine attention.

Interim Club musings were varied. He harked back to the days when he was Assistant Editor of the *Speaker* with a staff that included W. B. Yeats, L. F. Austin, Augustine Birrell and J. M. Barrie and recalled how the lay-out used to be finalised in a room at the Craven Hotel. The paper itself was printed at *La Belle Sauvage* in Ludgate Hill, where Oscar Wilde, then editing *Woman's World*, often joined them for lunch. Barrie was a close friend of "Q"'s and often stayed in Cambridge, their joint pleasure being long walks on the bank of the Cam. "Q" described visits to Boxhill with Barrie and Conan Doyle to lunch with Meredith, whose style he regarded as dandiacal, particularly in *Modern Love*, a bleak commentary of human relations based on his first marriage. On other visits to Boxhill he met Swinburne and Rossetti. He also described watching John Sargent paint in his studio the famous picture of Ellen Terry as Lady Macbeth. There were innumerable word-vignettes, like Ruskin replete in velvet cap, Jowett's early morning jog round Trinity Garden and Matthew Arnold at Balliol. The reminiscing was endless and always in good humour.

As to personal matters, "Q" admitted that the Cambridge Professorship was accepted with a degree of hesitation, because having failed to win a Fellowship at Oxford, where he read Classics, he turned to journalism, popular novels, essays and short stories, in fact everything that dons frowned upon. A redeeming feature was editing the *Oxford Book of English Verse*. Even so, alongside many colleagues, he felt unqualified. Such fears were groundless. Rarely has a professor commanded the respect of so many generations of students. He became an integral part of Jesus College. Oxford was his first love, later supplanted by Cambridge, but, first and foremost, he was a Cornishman. He confessed that only in the crooked streets of Fowey and the creepered house called *The Haven*, his home for so many years, did he really know happiness. When he wrote *Troy Town*, he enshrined Fowey and it was fitting that this little town should show its appreciation by making him Mayor and then adding the Freedom of the town.

As an academic, "Q" was one of the best-loved figures in Cambridge. In many ways he epitomised what his novels expressed: their pages contain more about him than he realised.

TRINITY COLLEGE

In terms of age *Trinity College* stands fourteenth in the list of collegiate foundations, senior only to Emmanuel, Sidney Sussex and Downing. The ranking is misleading for technically Trinity in part is next in age to Peterhouse. In 1323 Hervey de Stanton, Chancellor of the Exchequer to Edward II, founded Michaelhouse; then in 1336 Edward III created King's Hall. The difference between these two foundations was distinct. King's Hall was a royal foundation supported by public funds, and consisted at the outset of a Warden and thirty scholars – choirboys sent to complete their education from the Chapel Royal. College affairs came under the direct supervision of the King for over a century, the students being "the King's childer".

Michaelhouse was different, being the private foundation of Hervey de Stanton and independent of outside control apart from nominal supervision by the Bishop of Ely, as visitor, and the Chancellor of the University. Numbers were small, at first consisting of a Master and half-a-dozen students who were in Holy Orders and came from humble parentage. The statutes drawn up by the founder for the maintenance of his College are interesting. They are the earliest College statutes connected with the University, not based on any other similar foundation, but are Stanton's original draftsmanship.

He states that royal and the bishop's consent empowered the founding of a college for the study of divinity. The original members were named: Master Robert De Mildenhale, Master Walter de Buxton, Master Thomas de Kyningham, and Henry de Langham, priests and bachelors in the University engaged in the study of theology or philosophy. Roger de Honyng, sub-deacon, was added to the list. Walter de Buxton appointed the first Master. Details are explicit. The scholars had a common table and a uniform habit – the first reference to a College having its own design of gown. Priests received five marks and deacons or sub-deacons four marks. Meals were to cost not more than 12*d.* a week per head. Two College servants each received 10*d.* a week for their food. The barber and washerwoman each received 40*s.* a year for their wages. No one could be admitted through favour of blood-relationship, but only the best. Any member becoming too ill to live with healthy people should lose his place. A common chest held the title deeds with three locks and the keys kept respectively by the Master and two chaplains. The founder reserved the right to alter the statutes during his lifetime. This was exercised on the 25th July, 1329. The ruling on sickness was modified. Sick fellows were allowed leave of absence and given 12*d.* a week during sickness, the change being in line with King's Hall practice.

On the 2nd November, 1327, Hervey de Stanton died and was buried in St Michael's Church. Bequests to Michaelhouse included these relics: a piece of stone from the column where Christ was scourged; two ribs of St Bartholomew; a crystal box with bones and a tooth of one of the 11,000 virgins; bones of St Anthony in a piece of silver in a purse. None of these relics is in Trinity College.

King's Hall expanded. A College Chapel was built towards the end of the Wars of the Roses. At the accession of Henry VIII in 1509, it was decided to build an impressive entrance gateway. Work commenced in 1518 and was completed in 1535. The Great Gate stood alone. There was no Great Court, neither was there a link with King's Hall or Michaelhouse. An Act of Parliament in 1544 gave the King power to dissolve any hospital, chantry or college, and appropriate its possessions. As the monasteries had already disappeared, the King was urged by certain courtiers to apply the same treatment to Oxford and Cambridge. To avoid that happening, Thomas Smith, the clerk to the Queen's council, and John Cheke, tutor to the Prince of Wales, were asked by the University to assist. The King granted an enquiry, and a commission, dated the 16th January, 1546, appointed Matthew Parker (the Vice-Chancellor), John Redman (Warden of King's Hall), and William Mey (President of Queen's), to submit a report on College revenues and the number of students in residence.

The report favoured the Colleges, so much so that the King declared that "he had not in his realm so many persons so honestly maintained in living by so little land and rent." Pressure on the King continued, aided by the influence of Catharine Parr, his sixth wife, to use monastic spoils to found a royal College of exceptional magnificence. Eventually King's Hall and Michaelhouse were merged into one College with the right to fly the royal standards. A Master was appointed by the Crown and the College endowed with monastic lands and advowsons, and dedicated to "the Holy and Undivided Trinity". It was to occupy "the soil, ground, sites and precincts" of Michaelhouse, Physwick's Hostel, King's Hall, and other hostels; and to become a college of "literature, the sciences, philosophy, good arts, and sacred theology". In size, it was to have one Master and sixty Fellows and scholars and was to be called "Trinity College, within the town and University of Cambridge, of King Henry the Eight's foundation".

If 1546 was a significant date in the history of Trinity, February 1593 proved even more important. It marked the appointment by Queen Elizabeth of Thomas Nevile to succeed John Still as Master of Trinity. Nevile, a favourite of the Queen, had been Master of Magdalene from 1582 to 1588, Vice-Chancellor, and Dean of Peterborough. He came to Trinity with ambitious plans and exceptional imagination. The results are there for us to enjoy today. The Great Gate should be studied in detail. Above the Royal Arms is a niche over the outer entrance containing a statue of Henry VIII by William Cure the Younger and placed there by Nevile, then seven panels showing: (1) the arms of Edmund, Duke of York; (2) the arms of Lionel, Duke of Clarence; (3) the arms of Edward, Prince of Wales, with the three ostrich feathers and the motto *Ich dien*; (4) the arms, France (ancient) and England, quarterly-Edward III, Founder. Beneath is a small shield, that of Geoffrey Blythe, who was Master when the Gate was begun, and below the inscription, *Edvardus Tertius Fundator Aulae Regis*, that often puzzles the visitor for the anonymous statue of the founder of Trinity, Henry VIII, is set above the name of Edward III; (5) the empty shield of William of Hatfield, who died in infancy; (6) the arms of John of Gaunt, Duke of Lancaster; (7) the arms of Thomas, Duke of Gloucester. Above the Gate, the storey used to be a Treasury. In 1615, the statues of James I, his wife Anne of Denmark, and their only surviving son, Prince Charles, were installed on the inner side of the Gate. They commemorate royal visits to Trinity in that year. After watching Latin and English plays in the Hall, they slept in the Master's Lodge, beginning the tradition that royalty visiting Cambridge stay at Trinity.

THE GREAT COURT

When Henry VIII died, the Great Court did not exist. It was Nevile who built the grandest court in either Oxford or Cambridge, measuring 340 by 288 feet on the west and south sides, 325 by 257 feet on the east and north sides. In the centre he erected the spectacular fountain by Italian craftsmen in Elizabethan design, so ambitious it could house the Gate of Honour of Caius College under its strap-ornamental dome.

THE CHAPEL

On the right through the gate is the Chapel, a traditional Marian structure, its Gothic

Overleaf: The Great Gate of Trinity College, begun in 1519 and completed in 1535, was built before the Great Court existed. This west side has the statues of James I, his Queen and his son

PVGNA PRO PATRIA
1577

TERTIVS EDWARDVS FAMA SVPER ÆTHERA NOTVS

style not particularly impressive, but blending adequately into the Great Court design. The turret, leading to the loft of the original rood-screen, has a stone cupola similar to those of King's College Chapel. The stone used for building came from Ramsey Abbey in Huntingdonshire and the dissolved Grey Friars at Cambridge. The antechapel is divided from the Chapel by a screen of excellent Wren style. The antechapel, white, with white statuary and clear glass in contrast to the gloom of the Chapel, is dominated by the over-life-sized figures that stand or sit: Roubiliac's masterpiece of the standing Newton *qui genus humanum ingenio superavit* completed in 1755; the Victorian and Edwardian-styled sculptures of Bacon in elaborate Elizabethan costume; Barrow who had the Library built; Macaulay by Woolner; Whewell, responsible for Whewell's Court, also by Woolner; and Tennyson by Thornycroft. Most of the wall monuments have protrait busts, and include Daniel Lock, Francis Hooper, Thomas Jones, Porson P. P. Dobree and Sheepshank. On the floor is a Neo-Gothic brass to William J. Breamont. The extravagant screen that holds the organ was installed in Bentley's time by this great classical scholar who was over-fond of grandiose works.

KING EDWARD'S TOWER

To the west of the Chapel is King Edward's Tower, or the Clock Tower, that was originally the gateway to King's Hall and built 1427–33. It was the first of the Cambridge gatehouses and is of stone, not brick like the Great Gate. The niche and statue of Edward III date from 1601 and are by Paris Andrew. Wordsworth refers to the clock in his *Prelude*. Undergraduates try to race the chiming at midnight by running round the Great Court.

THE TRINITY STEPS OR JUMP

Correspondence in *The Times* varies in content. It was lightened some years ago by the publication of a letter from the Master of Trinity College inspired by an incident described to him by Field-Marshal Lord Montgomery who said that his father, when an undergraduate, cleared the steps to the Hall with a single leap. Those who do not know the steps cannot appreciate the feat. There are eight steps, each five-and-a-half inches high and a foot wide. The Master referred to a predecessor, William Whewell, having performed the feat in full academic costume which, apart from his distinguished position and the fact that he must have reached the half-century mark in years, made the performance more striking than that of the youthful Montgomery.

Later letters showed that the feat had been rivalled. Canon Hugh Le Fleming had performed it in 1892, whilst Fred Brittain of Jesus told how in 1934 J. B. Luddington, an undergraduate, set out to walk from Cambridge to Mill and back – a distance of 101 miles – in less than twenty-four hours, the following day to be spent in the hunting field, for a wager of £30. He completed the walk in twenty-one hours, reached Cambridge at 3 am, and spent most of that day "whipping-in efficiently" to win the wager. Sir John Pollock recorded a remarkable kick by C. M. Wells (double Blue, First Class Classical Tripos, and later Eton master). Walking along the Backs one day, Wells was dared to punt the rugby ball he was carrying over the far tower of New Court. He cleared the tower which was some forty feet high and the width of a large set of College rooms. Another incident in the late 'nineties was when a Clare student teed a golf ball in front of the Lodge windows and drove it over the Chapel, apparently without injury to mid-day walkers. Endurance feats were not confined to undergraduates. G. M. Trevelyan used to say that every Cantab and Oxonian ought to walk to Marble Arch from their respective Colleges, adding as an afterthought that the wisdom of our ancestors, surely

Previous page: King Edward's Tower in the Great Court was built in 1427–33 and was the first of the Cambridge gatehouses. The niche and statue of Edward III date from 1601 and are by Paris Andrew

not by accident, had fixed these two sites of learning the same distance from London. He worked out that the Cambridge student should start at five o'clock, encouraged by the prospect of a second breakfast waiting to be eaten at Banyer's in Royston at eight o'clock. Another suggestion was an even stiffer test, namely that a man should walk the eighty miles from St Mary, Oxon to St Mary, Cantab in twenty-four hours, but as Trevelyan added, there is no orthodoxy in walking. It is a land of many paths and by-paths, where everyone goes his own way and is right.

QUEEN ELIZABETH GATE AND MERTON'S OR MUTTONHOLE CORNER

The gate in the middle of the south range is Queen Elizabeth Gate, a simplified version of the usual motif. Like all Nevile's work, it is stone-faced. The statue of Queen Elizabeth was set up in 1597. The south-east corner of the Great Court is Merton's or Muttonhole Corner, and was where Byron used to keep his bear.

THE HALL

The Hall was built by Nevile at his own expense. He detailed the architect, Ralph Symons, to examine the design of similar buildings in London, for which, according to College records, he received the sum of ten shillings, "to Carpenters and Keepers of dyvers Halles to viewe and measure them". The final choice was the Hall of the Middle Temple. It was copied faithfully and dimensions are identical: 100 feet long, forty feet wide, fifty feet high. It has an impressive hammerbeam roof, but the Hall is dominated by the famous portrait of Henry VIII by Holbein. On his right is the morose Mary Tudor by Antonio Moro who looks capable of carrying out her brutal purge of Protestants, the Duke of Gloucester by Sir Joshua Reynolds, a contemporary study on wood of Francis Bacon, Lord Tennyson by Watts, and an interesting portrait of Nevile, who created the Hall.

On the other side of the screens is the old hall of Michaelhouse, now the kitchen and buttery on an impressive scale. Hanging on the walls are turtle shells on which are engraved the dates of special occasions when the soup was made. The doorways in the passage are older than Nevile's time. He added the studded oak doors and the strap-decorated Porch.

NEVILE'S COURT

Leaving the screens we step into Nevile's Court, an ambitious scheme on a par with the Great Court, which he built, also at his own expense. The Cloisters have a Mediterranean touch with stone columns and stylistical elegance. The Court was completed in 1614 with the west side open, the boundary from the water meadows being marked by a low wall. Sixty years later it was closed by the Library, designed by Sir Christopher Wren under Isaac Barrow's Mastership. He drew on his friendship to persuade Wren to design the Library for nothing. It was based on Sansovio's library of St Mark's at Venice and is built of attractive stone from Ketton in Rutland and raised above the cloister. Building began in 1675 and was virtually completed in 1690. The panelled ceiling was finished in 1755.

After seeing it, Sir Christopher Wren's own comments on his scheme become interesting: "I have given the appearance of arches as the order required, fair and lofty; but I have layd the floor of the Library upon the impostes, which answer to the pillars in the

cloister and levells of the old floores, and have filled the arches with relieus stone, of which I have seen the effect abroad in good buildings, and I assure you where porches are low with flat ceilings is infinitely more graceful than lowe arches would be, and is much more open and pleasant, nor need the mason feare the performance because the arch discharges the weight, and I shall direct him in a firme manner of executing the designs. By this contrivance the windowes of the Library rise high and give place for the deskes against the walls . . . The disposition of the shelves both along the walls and breaking out from the walls must needes prove very convenient and graceful, and the best way for the students will be to have a little square table in each celle with 2 chaires." It is interesting to note that the original plan put forward by Wren was a free-standing circular building. This was turned down, eventually appearing in Oxford where Gibb adapted the Wren plan for the Radcliffe Camera.

The result at Trinity is classical simplicity. The insides of the bookcases, shelves, tables and chairs were designed by Wren. He wrote, "We are scrupulous in small matters and you must pardon us; the architects are as great pedants as Criticks as Heralds." The Library has thirty cubicles, the majority open, with two at either end closed by grills superbly carved by Grinling Gibbons. A stone statue of the sixth Duke of Sussex high up in a niche is also by him. Roubiliac busts are outstanding, particularly of Coke, the Lord Chief Justice; others include Cotton, Barrow, Bentley, Newton and Bacon. The naturalists Ray and Willoughby are each side of the entrance. There is also a bust of a beardless Tennyson, and the Byron statue by Thorwaldsen, offered to Westminster Abbey but twice declined because of the poet's unfortunate way of life.

Opposite: *The Hall range of Nevile's Court with the balustrade by Essex*

Below: *The cloisters completed in 1614 have elegant stone columns interrupted every four bays by a broader pier*

The Library holds some 90,000 volumes and roughly 1,900 manuscripts including the following: the manuscript of Milton's *Lycidas and Comus*; a first draft of *Paradise Lost*; the manuscript of *Esmond; In Memoriam; Poem by Two Brothers* by Charles and Alfred Tennyson; the Canterbury Psalter; a Sarum Missal on vellum; and a fifteenth century *Roll of Carols*, said to be the earliest-known manuscript of musical harmony. Also to be seen is Newton's telescope and a death-mask of his face. The south window shows Fame presenting Newton to George III, as Bacon takes notes. The design is by Cipriani, dated 1774, the window by Peckitt of York who discovered how to colour glass.

To balance the Library, Wren designed another improvement in Nevile's Court, placing in front of the Hall a decorated feature known as the Tribune, a platform, columns, niches and staircases leading down into the Court. The Tribune is sited exactly in line with the centre of the Library and was built in 1682 by Grumbold, the mason used by Wren on the Library.

The long Cloister on the north side is interesting to visitors for it was here that Newton experimented on his theory of sound. Stand at the west end and stamp your foot sharply. The clear echo you hear was what Newton timed to measure the speed of sound. One feature is missing at Trinity: the long avenue of lime trees, planted in 1672, from New Court to the river. The trees were cut down, and although happily now replaced, the effect is still miniature.

Below: Trinity Library designed by Sir Christopher Wren was based on Sansovino's library of St Mark's in Venice. It is called the Wren Library and ranks as one of his most outstanding works

VALHALLA OF TRINITY

The number of distinguished men who can be claimed by Trinity is quite remarkable. No other College in the world has had so many Nobel Prize winners. To turn such facts into personalities, it is interesting to identify some of these great men and refer to their achievements for the benefit of those who visit the College. They are walking across the same courts and paths that inspired these men and in the Library can see further evidence of their work and the death-masks that bring them back to life. They become real people. Some are remembered in the white antechapel where statues are grouped like a Trinity Valhalla.

Bacon reclines in a chair as if reflecting how his hopes for a corporate body of scientific investigators eventually took shape in the Royal Society of London with Charles II as its first patron. He ranks high as a philosopher, even though he could claim no personal contribution to natural knowledge. His precepts nevertheless influenced the promotion of such advances. Whether he was likeable is another matter. Pope described him as "the wisest, brightest, meanest of mankind", Weeks, the sculptor, certainly made him look miserable. The sculptor, Noble, was kinder to Isaac Barrow. Looking at the latter it is not surprising he was able to persuade Christopher Wren to design the Library, which sadly he never saw completed. He died suddenly in 1677, two years after being appointed Vice-Chancellor. His early career was affected through having royalist sympathies in a Commonwealth, but under Charles II he was made a royal chaplain. Not only was he a cleric and poet, but became Lucasian Professor of Mathematics and had produced an edition of *Euclid* before he was 25.

Isaac Newton was eighteen when he matriculated as a sub-sizar in 1661. He became a Fellow at twenty-four and, through Charles II granting Letters Patent, he was eligible to become the Lucasian Professor of Mathematics outside the regulation which required Holy Orders. This great mathematician and physicist, one of the greatest natural philosophers and discoverer of the law of gravity, in 1665–6 discovered the binomial theorem, the basic concept of his method of fluxions (now called differential calculus), inverse fluxions (integral calculus), and the first ideas concerning universal gravitation. He had also begun investigations on light and optics by using a prism to split sunlight into a spectrum to prove that white light is made up of a mixture of rays of different colours, each of which has its own refractive index. In 1668 he invented the reflecting telescope which can be seen in the Library.

His rooms in Trinity were E4 Great Court on the first floor, between the Great Gate and the Chapel. His kinsman, Humphrey Newton, left personal details of his stay: "He very seldom sat by the fire in his chamber excepting yt long frosty winter, which made him creep to it against his will. I can't say I ever saw him wear a night gown, but his wearing clothes that he put off at night, at night do I say, yea rather towards ye morning, he put on again at his rising. He never slept in ye day-time yt I ever perceived; I believe he grudged ye short time he spent in eating and sleeping . . . He kept neither dog nor cat in his chamber, wch made well for ye old woman his bedmaker, she faring much ye better for it, for in a morning she has sometimes found both dinner and supper scarcely tasted of, wch ye old woman has very pleasantly and mumpingly gone away with." A painting by Thornhill in 1710 shows him in dressing-gown and wigless, reserved and serious, with sharp features.

ISAACUS BARROW

The statue of Newton in the antechapel by Roubiliac is a masterpiece. It inspired Wordsworth's lines in the *Prelude*:

> Near me hung Trinity's loquacious clock,
> Who never let the quarters, night or day,
> Slip by him unproclaimed, and told the hours
> Twice over with a male and female voice.
> Her pealing organ was my neighbour too;
> And from my pillow, looking forth by light
> Of moon or favouring stars, I could behold
> The antechapel where the statue stood
> Of Newton with his prism and silent face,
> The marble index of a mind for ever
> Voyaging through strange seas of thought alone.

The visitor should study this famous statue, read Wordsworth's lines, then gaze on Newton's death-mask in the Library. He left Trinity at the age of fifty-three and ended the academic period at Cambridge, but in one sense in that room he has never left.

Trinity fame has not always been academic. I think of A. A. Milne, the essayist and children's writer who created the world of Pooh Bear with tales about his son's toy animals and adapted Kenneth Grahame's *Wind in the Willows* as *Toad of Toad Hall*, which proves that Cambridge influences can be gentle and fanciful. Another was Jawalharlal Nehru, the Indian statesman, who became the first Prime Minister of India following independence. Nehru joined Gandhi's non-violent Nationalist Movement and was repeatedly imprisoned by the British for his political activities, later co-operating with the last viceroy, Mountbatten, in the partitioning of the sub-continent into India and Pakistan, and in the transfer of political power. On a return visit to Cambridge he recalled the formative years at Trinity during a Union Society debate.

The Great Gatsby, written in meticulous prose by Scott Fitzgerald, examines the division between possessions and ideals, wealth and youth, and could have been inspired by the American novelist's period at Trinity. The College can claim a fleeting link with William Thackeray, who entered Trinity in 1829, went through the motions of studying, but left the following year without a degree. His rooms were incorporated into the Porter's Lodge. His first inclinations were painting and literature, but becoming short of money, he turned to journalism. His early pieces and stories made little impression, but fortune changed with the publication of *The Book of Snobs* and *Vanity Fair*.

George Herbert, English churchman and metaphysical poet, became a Fellow in 1616 and Public Orator from 1619 to 1627. Very conscious of his position, he carried out his duties "with as becoming and grave a gaiety as any had ever before or since his time; for he had acquired great learning, and was blessed with a high fancy, a civil and sharp wit, and with a natural elegance, both in his behaviour, his tongue, and his pen." He sounds somewhat pompous. Another evaluation was equally revealing: "Herbert speaks to God like one that realy believeth a God, and whose business in the world is most with God."

George Macaulay Trevelyan was an impressive figure. In an age in which scholars are plentiful and artists rare, he occupied a unique place in the history of English letters. Although Gibbon, Macaulay and Clarendon were his superior as stylists, and some ranked R. H. Tawney above him on the same score, Trevelyan stood out as the poet of English history. Innumerable passages of lyrical beauty in his books reflect the workings of a poet's mind. His imagination pursued facts, and being that rare phenomenon, a natural story-teller, he focused them with exquisite feeling. Had he wished,

Opposite: The antechapel of Trinity has several striking figures of Victorian and Edwardian sculptural style. Isaac Barrow is sympathetically depicted by the sculptor Noble

Trevelyan could have used this gift of imagination in poetry rather than in history. That he did not do so may well have been due to the richness of his inherited tradition, for his great-uncle was Lord Macaulay who, with Gibbon, reigns supreme in English historical writing, whilst his father, Sir Otto Trevelyan, was also an eminent historian. It was not surprising to find that his sense of duty as a historian was highly developed. He roamed over all centuries with equal ease and zest, from Garibaldi to Wyclif, from Queen Anne to Sir Edward Grey, and never failed to bring the past to life. He was a historian in the Whig tradition.

It is impossible to comment on each of Trevelyan's works, but I must mention *History of England*, which took three years to write. His own comment was unnecessarily modest: "In April 1926 my *History of England* came out. It has been, as regards sales, the most successful of my books, except the *Social History*, because it treated so necessary a subject as the history of England at the length, and to some extent in the manner, which suited a large public, including schools and Universities. Some day, very soon perhaps, it will be replaced, but it will have served its generation."

That was an understatement. The book's social value has been incalculable. Millions of Englishmen garnered from it the little history they will ever know. Well over 200,000 copies were sold, and in schools copies were used innumerable times, whilst many schoolmasters based their courses on it. Before the last war Trevelyan was working on a social history of England to serve as a companion volume to his *History of England*, which mainly dealt with war and politics. In 1940 he decided to omit the early

Below: George Macaulay Trevelyan with the author. He was an impressive figure and occupied a unique place in the history of English letters. He stood out as the poet of English history

part of the work and begin with Chaucer. It was published in 1944 under the title of *English Social History*. The sales were remarkable. In seven years more than 400,000 copies were sold, a record among history books.

History for Trevelyan had a literary and moral purpose. He was absorbed by the mystery of time, by the mutability of all things, by the succession of the ages and generations. He maintained that the present only takes us by surprise because we do not sufficiently know and consider the past. With Trevelyan as our guide the story of man became far more wonderful than the wonders of physical science. It also provided insight into the historian's thinking and cast light on many aspects of his personal beliefs. As he once said, the proper study of mankind becomes man.

At the time of his citation for the Nobel Prize for Literature, Bertrand Russell was described as "one of the time's most brilliant spokesmen of rationality and humanity and a fearless champion of free speech and free thought in the West." In another field he made greater original contributions to philosophy than any other writer in this country since Hume. And yet, his long life was marked by contradictions. It was remarkable that the man who sat in Brixton Prison at the end of the First World War should have received at the end of the Second World War the blue and crimson ribbon of the Order of Merit, the greatest honour that the Monarch and Government can bestow on a distinguished citizen.

It is easy to describe Russell as a great man but more difficult to explain why. He was one of the most brilliant mathematicians of the century. His *Principles of Mathematics* and *Principia Mathematica*, both published before the First World War, determined the direction in which modern philosophy was going to move, yet many people have read the *Principia* and of that number only a handful have understood it. Assessment of the contents needed the competence of Whitehead or Wittgenstein to pass a judgment. It was brilliance in a rarefied atmosphere, yet Russell's name was known and respected by a cross-section of ordinary people in Europe and America. He fascinated the most unlikely people and often did the most unlikely things. Not many men of eighty-eight are imprisoned for identifying themselves with a campaign of civil disobedience against a government's defence policy. At that age most people are unmoved by threats to the future of humanity.

Somehow incarceration and death never greatly bothered the third Earl of Russell. He was the product of one of the strongest hereditary strains and most dominating traditions that have existed in Europe. He was an unmitigated Russell, an aristocrat and a Whig. His grandfather was Lord John Russell of the Reform Bill. He had a superb intellect and a passion for freedom, yet somehow he never wholly understood politics. None of his political writings could compare with those of his godfather, John Stuart Mill. His parents died when he was a child and he was brought up by his grandmother, who had him educated privately at home and earmarked for politics. The prospect did not appeal to this shy and lonely boy who preferred mathematical and philosophical speculation. He used to say that he was ten years old before he met anyone who hadn't written a book. The habit was catching for over fifty learned books stand to his credit. He blossomed at Cambridge where he got a First in Mathematics, was elected a Fellow of Trinity and became a leader of that brilliant circle of intellectual young men so disliked by D. H. Lawrence but approved by Maynard Keynes.

Physically he was small – Lytton Strachey used to say that be belonged to the dangerous class of great gnomes – but he was never overlooked. Women found him attractive. With four wives to his credit, it was clearly mutual. At any party he was always surrounded by the prettiest women fascinated by the charm of this white-haired man with bird-like head and a laugh like the yaffle of a woodpecker. His talk was usually dry but passionate, his voice slightly donnish and clipped. He sparkled more wit and gleamed with malice, as might be expected from an advocate of free love, the rights of women, trial marriages and new methods of education that included a personal experiment aimed at proving the value of the utmost freedom for every human being. With his wife they had a school for children who could do whatever they pleased. In an intellectual free-for-all conversation, there were invariably flashes of Russell's dislike of parents, policemen, schoolmasters, judges and the English public school system prefaced by a dry pleasant smile.

An interesting point about Bertrand Russell was that the thought of death never seemed to bother him. Such was his mental and physical energy that age was ignored. Maybe his atheistic conviction made it seem irrelevant. There was no last minute conversion. Even at ninety-six his views had not changed; if anything, they had hardened. He regarded all forms of religion as false and harmful. He did admit that the thought of dying loomed large when a plane in which he was travelling to Norway crashed and ditched him in an icy sea. He was indignant at the thought of his demise at the early age of seventy-six. Towards the end he almost welcomed death as the final confirmation of his theories and an opportunity to prove the bishops wrong, though a wistful aside hinted that it would be comforting to make contact in a future state when possibly memories might survive, but at heart he was content, like the young Newton, to wander through strange seas of thought, alone.

Influence of a different kind came from James Clerk-Maxwell, who entered Peterhouse in 1850 but changed to Trinity in the same year. Elected Fellow after taking a degree as Second Wrangler, he became the first Cavendish Professor of Experimental Physics. His research had far-reaching effects. He was the first to prove by mathematical or theoretical reasoning "that light consists in the transverse undulations of the same medium which is the cause of electric and magnetic phenomena." Faraday had conceived the idea of light as an electro-magnetic effect, but it was on Maxwell's philosophic basis that experiments led to the results now so familiar in communication with all parts of the world by means of electro-magnetic waves.

From its foundation in 1871, the Cavendish Professorship has invariably been held by a Trinity man. Rayleigh took over from Clerk-Maxwell, J. J. Thomson succeeded Rayleigh, Rutherford carried on from Thomson, Lawrence Bragg followed Rutherford. Scientists are very much a race apart. One such figure was J. J. Thomson, physicist and Master of Trinity, a significant influence in world history through his discovery of the electron. When he isolated at atom of pure electricity, he set in motion the theory of nuclear as well as atomic structure. Under his guidance the Cavendish became the leading research school in experimental physics. The reward for this revolutionary finding was the Nobel Prize for Physics, honorary degrees from twenty-three universities, a knighthood, and the Order of Merit. Achievements and honours on this scale conjure up a mental picture of an international scientist conscious of status and overbearing in manner, if not conceit. Nothing could have been farther from fact. "J.J." was brilliant, but he was always approachable and helpful to those who worked for him. I only knew him in the last year of his life so I cannot assess what he was like during his prime, but stories about him, many from his wife, Rose Elizabeth, the daughter of Sir George Paget and a first-class mathematician in her own right, create a composite word-portrait of a kindly family-man with many idiosyncrasies and a tendency to be absent-minded.

Her favourite story was about an evening when "J.J." changed for dinner in Queens' College. After he left she went into the bedroom and found his trousers lying on the bed. Fearing the worst she rang the porter's lodge to enquire if they had seen the Master leave. She was told he had gone past their windows fifteen minutes earlier. She next rang Queens' and asked the President's wife if her husband had arrived safely and was he looking all right. She was assured he seemed in good spirits with a slightly odd touch: he was dressed for dinner with black-tie, but appeared to be wearing well-worn gardening trousers, no doubt a Trinity eccentricity – an absent-minded gaff for long a source of family amusement.

Opposite: In the realm of letters is this meditative figure of Macaulay by Woolmer in the antechapel

68

In the realm of letters, Macaulay is another in our list of famous Trinity men. (There is a figure of him by Woolmer in the antechapel.) He went to school in Little Shelford, entered College in 1818, gained the Craven Scholarship, and became a Fellow. His nephew, Sir George Trevelyan, has left a picture of his life in the College: "I can never remember the time when it was not diligently impressed upon me that, if I minded my syntax, I might eventually hope to reach a position which would give me three hundred pounds a year; a stable for my horse, six dozen of audit ale every Christmas, a loaf and two pats of butter every morning, and a good dinner for nothing, with as many almonds and raisins as I could eat at dessert."

More melancholy was A. E. Housman, the English classical scholar and lyric poet, probably best known for the poem, "A Shropshire Lad". More sharply-reasoned was the passionate verse of John Donne, the clergyman who became the outstanding poet of early seventeenth century English literature. He entered Trinity in 1587, but took no degree. He was named by Ben Jonson as "the first poet in the world in some things", whilst Thomas Carew described him as:

> a king who ruled as he thought fit
> The universal monarchy of wit.

He epitomised the new age, with colloquial language that made lyrical poetry modern with audacious imagery and complex rhythms. With such an individual outlook he must surely have enjoyed his student days. Equally outstanding was Abraham Cowley, scholar and Fellow, who entered Trinity in 1637. He must have been precocious. At the age of ten he composed an epical romance of *Pyramus and Thisbe*, whilst most of *Davideis*, an epic in decasyllabic couplets on the biblical history of David, was written in Trinity. Contemporary with Cowley was Andrew Marvell, poet and politician, who was assistant to Milton at the Latin Secretaryship to the Council of the Commonwealth. He wrote several poems in praise of Cromwell and later powerful satires, like the *Last Instructions to a Painter*, on Charles II's policies. John Dryden came to Trinity as a scholar in 1650 at the age of nineteen. Little is known of his career in Cambridge except that he was "discommuned for contumacy to the Vice-Master". It is better to remember him as a poet, dramatist and essayist who was the driving force of a literary movement that began with the Restoration in 1660, and for his comedy *Marriage à la Mode*. It would seem that temperamentally he was out of humour with life in Trinity.

Alfred Tennyson, born 1809 in the Lincolnshire Wolds village of Somersby, had a traumatic childhood. His father, a country parson, found the burden of raising a family of twelve on a meagre income too much of a strain. Excessive drinking, violent outbursts of temper and black melancholy forced Alfred to leave home. He went to 12 Rose Crescent in Cambridge. Two brothers were already at Trinity College. Somewhat surprisingly he was accepted as a student in mid-term. The formative years at Trinity were acknowledged by the poet. Among his friends were Edward Fitzgerald, James Spedding and Monckton Milnes, but it was Arthur Hallam who played a significant part in his life. He died in 1833 and Tennyson, in an attempt to express his grief, began *In Memoriam*:

> The same grey flats again, and felt
> The same, but not the same; and last
> Up that long walls of limes I past
> To see the rooms in which he dwelt.

Another name was on the door;
　I linger'd; all within was noise
　Of songs, and clapping hands, and boys
That crash'd the glass and beat the floor.

Ring out the grief that saps the mind
　For those that here we see no more:

The coveted Chancellor's Medal for English verse was won thirteen times by Trinity men between 1814 and 1833. Alfred Tennyson gained it in 1829 with a mystical poem that had little connection with the set subject, but emphasised his mastery of the rhythmic qualities of the English language.

In the antechapel, the statue by Thornycroft of Tennyson in a theatrical pose holding a book has a feature usually overlooked. It is linked with the poet's addiction to tobacco. Fitzgerald described him as "something like the Hyperion shorn of his beams in Keats' poem: with a pipe in his mouth". Smoking at that time was socially unacceptable and forbidden in academic dress, restrictions that the poet ignored. He insisted on smoking strong tobacco in an old stained pipe. The statue was erected during the Mastership of Montague Butler, who abhorred smoking. The sculptor, anxious to add an authentic touch, obtained permission from the donor, Harry Yates Thompson, to insert in the laurel wreaths on the bas-relief the bowl of Tennyson's pipe. In the Hall is a portrait of the Poet Laureate by Watts, whilst a bust of a beardless Tennyson by Woolner is in the Library.

In case it is thought that the poet's views on Cambridge were dewy-eyed, this excerpt from a letter to his aunt, Mrs Russell, from lodgings at 57 Corpus Buildings, Trumpington Street, where he stayed during his academic career, suggests there were moments of boredom: "I am sitting owl-like and solitary in my rooms (nothing between me and the stars but a stratum of tiles). The hoof of the steed, the roll of the wheel, the shouts of drunken Gown and drunken Town come up from below with a sealike murmur. I know not how it is, but I feel isolated here in the midst of society. The country is so disgustingly level, the revelry of the place so monotonous, the studies of the University so uninteresting, so much matter of fact."

Ralph Vaughan Williams' background was a major factor in shaping his outlook. Born in Down Ampney, he retained traces of a Gloucestershire accent; in fact, the West Country influence never left him. It went with him to Charterhouse, to Trinity College and to the Royal College of Music in the same way that Dvorak took Bohemia to New York. In this respect Vaughan Williams could be likened to Thomas Hardy. Both found that independence of vision was first generated by locality rather than personality. Vaughan Williams used to say that his time at Trinity and the unique setting of Cambridge in the fens helped him as an Englishman to compose music serenely and simply. Artistic tranquillity came easily to him. His difficulty was, perhaps, in finding sufficiently strong feeling to remember. All his life he was more interested in examining the wrinkles left in the sand by the tide than in bathing in the sea. At Trinity he found his genius was a genius for reverie.

In October 1908 a student entered Trinity College as a Westminster Exhibitioner and a Major Entrance Scholar in Natural Science. That undergraduate was Edgar Douglas Adrian. His student-days were exceptionally brilliant and he was elected to a Fellowship in 1913. He had pursued Natural Science as a student of Medicine, completed the clinical part of his training at St Bartholomew's Hospital, and took his M.D. degree in 1919. During the First World War he was mainly occupied in the treatment of shell-shock, first at Queen's Square in London, and then at Farnborough.

Though Adrian could have been an able and successful physician, his predominant interests were in teaching and scientific research on the physiology of the brain and

nervous system. After the war he accepted the invitation of Trinity to return as a College lecturer. He came back to staircase E, Great Court, where he had lived as an undergraduate, merely ascending one flight from E1 to Newton's room in E4. In 1929 Adrian became Foulerton Research Professor of the Royal Society, and relinquished his College lectureship. He held this post until 1937, when he became Professor of Physiology in the University and a professorial Fellow of the College. Members of Trinity received with satisfaction the news that the Crown had appointed Adrian to the Mastership of the College upon the retirement of G. M. Trevelyan in 1951. It would be tedious to enumerate the many honours showered upon the Master. He was elected Fellow of the Royal Society in 1923, became President in 1950, but it was the Nobel Prize in 1932 and the Order of Merit in 1942 that endorsed his reputation as one of the greatest scientists. One further honour was conferred when he became Chancellor of Cambridge University.

Lord Byron entered Trinity from Harrow in 1805, a youth of "tumultuous passion", uninterested in academic studies, and over-sensitive to criticism, as when his *Hours of Idleness* was savaged in the *Edinburgh Review*. Various attempts to cure his lame foot failed, but did not prevent him from swimming by the weir above Grantchester still known as Byron's Pool. He engaged "Gentleman" Jackson, one of the most celebrated figures of the prize ring, to give him lessons in the Noble Art of Self-Defence in his boxing school in Bond Street, London. Riding was popular, also shooting with pistols. Annoyed by the ban on keeping a dog in his rooms, he argued that as the College made no mention of bears, he could install one in the tower-attic at the south-east corner of the Great Court and he proceeded to flaunt the dons by taking the animal for walks on a chain. Moore's *Life of Byron* includes a letter to a lady referring to the incident:

> I have got a new friend, the finest in the world, a tame bear. When I brought him here, they asked me what I meant to do with him, and my reply was 'he should sit for a fellowship'. This answer delighted them not. We have several parties here, and this evening a large assortment of jockeys, gamblers, boxers, authors, poets and parsons.

Another letter dated the 26 October 1807 is not so enthusiastic:

> My Dear Elizabeth,
>   Fatigued with sitting up to four in the morning for the last two days at hazard, I take up my pen to enquire how your highness and the rest of my female acquaintance at the seat of archiepiscopal grandeur go on.
>   This place is wretched enough, a villanous chaos of din and drunkenness, nothing but hazard and burgundy, hunting, mathematic, and Newmarket, riot and racing. Yet it is a paradise compared with the eternal dullness of Southwell. Oh! the misery of doing nothing, but make love, enemies and verses.

To correct the balance, an extract from another letter:

> I like College Life extremely. I am now most pleasantly situated in Super-excellent Rooms, flanked on one side by my Tutor and on the other by an Old Fellow, both of whom are rather checks to my vivacity.

As a poet Byron was one of the leading figures of the Romantic movement. His writings embraced satire, cynicism, and sometimes a bleak, despairing view of human nature.

Opposite: The statue by Thornycroft of Alfred Tennyson in a somewhat theatrical pose holding a book

He caught the imagination of the public as no other poet of his time. He died of fever at Missolonghi, Greece in the fight for Greek independence.

On final name. All lovers of elegant writing appreciated the pen of Bernard Darwin. He wrote on the game of golf in *The Times* for over forty years, with the touch of Lamb and the vividness of Hazlitt. But there was more to Darwin than his essays. Eton, Cambridge and the Temple formed his early background. In World War I he spent two-and-a-half years at Salonika. Although a barrister and a fully qualified solicitor, he found the lure of golf too strong, not solely as a scribe, but as a performer. He was in the England team against Scotland on eight occasions, played for England against the United States in 1922 at Long Island, was twice semi-finalist in the Amateur Championship, won the President's Putter in 1922, and the Worplesdon Foursomes in 1933 with Joyce Wethered. By any standard it was a proud record. What was so refreshing was his attitude to University golf, rugby football and the Boat Race. He was partisan and unashamed. "I am at Trinity," said a Cantab to a Londoner. "Trinity, Cambridge or Trinity, Oxford?" asked the latter. The former, with insolent calm, replied, "Trinity!" In like fashion Darwin eyed the *other place* ever since he was *in statu pup* in 1894. Some people regarded such bias as madness, but it was an honest frenzy and in your own kingdom you had the right to be mad. The Darwinian kingdom was a world on its own.

A. E. HOUSMAN (Trinity College)
1859–1936

As a memorial to A. E. Housman an avenue of cherry trees was planted at Trinity from the bridge to the Backs.

> *Loveliest of trees, the cherry now*
> *Is hung with bloom along the bough,*
> *And stands about the woodland ride*
> *Wearing white for Eastertide,*
>
> *Now, of my threescore years and ten,*
> *Twenty will not come again,*
> *And take from seventy springs a score,*
> *It only leaves me fifty more.*
>
> *And since to look at things in bloom*
> *Fifty springs are little room,*
> *About the woodlands I will go*
> *To see the cherry hung with snow.*

ST JOHN'S COLLEGE

St John's College stands on the site of a much earlier foundation, that of the Hospital of St John, founded in 1135 by Henry Frost, a rich burgess, for care of the poor and infirm by a community of Augustinian canons. In 1280 Hugh de Balsham, Bishop of Ely, obtained a licence from Edward I to admit a number of scholars into the Hospital under the rule applying to the scholars of Merton. In that way the scholars and canons became one College. Unfortunately the experiment failed, possibly because the scholars were too wise and the brethren too good. The Bishop transferred the scholars to Peterhouse in 1284. To compensate for the loss of St Peter's Church, the Master and Fellows of Peterhouse had to pay twenty shillings annually to the Brethren of St John.

The Hospital flourished and in 1471 full University privileges were granted and members took part in University ceremonies. Then, under the Mastership of William Tomlyn, everything went wrong. Lack of discipline and finance plus sacrilegious acts brought the College down. Only two brethren were left at the beginning of the sixteenth century. At this point John Fisher, Bishop of Rochester and Chancellor of the University, suggested to Lady Margaret Beaufort, mother of Henry VII, as her spiritual adviser, that the Hospital of St John be refounded as a new College. The proposal was approved. Her stepson, James Stanley, Bishop of Ely, agreed to co-operate if she obtained the Papal Bull and the Royal Licence. Unfortunately Henry VII died on the 21st April, 1509, and Lady Margaret two months later. The wishes in her Will were not approved by Henry VIII, who was reluctant to see monies from her estate spent in such a fashion. Cardinal Wolsey and Bishop Stanley being of like mind, the college bequest was ignored. Fisher did not abandon the project and eventually succeeded in obtaining the King's licence, the papal bull and the Bishop of Ely's approval. Among the records of St John's is a letter to Fisher which states that the "Brethren, later of St John's House, departed from Cambridge toward Ely the 12th day of March at four of the clokke at afternone by water." In such a way was St John's College founded. The Charter, signed by Lady Margaret's executors, is dated the 9th April, 1511 and Robert Shorton was appointed Master with thirty-one Fellows.

So much for the past. Today the College is a showpiece of Cambridge, visited every year by thousands of visitors, many of whom are bemused by its size and magnificence. With so much to assimilate, I have listed some of the features that should be noted.

The Gatehouse is more eloquent in its proportions than the massive Great Gate of Trinity. It commemorates Lady Margaret Beaufort and was built, after her death, of red brick and stone between 1511 and 1516. The heraldic display is magnificent. A shield bears the arms of England and France quarterly supported by the strange mythological animals called yales. Above it is a crown beneath a rose. On either side are the portcullis of the Beauforts and the Tudor rose, both crowned. Alongside are daisies and marguerites, the badge of Lady Margaret, and other flowers identified as "sophanyes", the old English name for the Christmas rose. In a niche above is the statue of St John set there in 1666 to replace the original figure removed during the Civil War.

The First Court is somewhat disappointing. Its appearance was hardly improved when the south range was modified and ashlar-faced by Essex in 1772–5, and finally spoilt by Sir Giles Gilbert Scott's clumping Victorian-Gothic Chapel, built in 1864–9, with 16 feet high tower and a length of 193 feet. The original design should have had a slender spire, but critics caused it to be changed to a tower at an additional cost of

Opposite: *The Gatehouse of St John's College that commemorates Lady Margaret Beaufort with a magnificent heraldic display. It was built, after her death, between 1511 and 1516*

Left: *The oriel windows of St John's Library overlooking the river. It was described by John Evelyn in 1654 as "the fairest of that University"*

£5,000. In view of the adverse comments on the structure, it is interesting to read Scott's remarks on the choice of style and shape which he outlined in this memorandum to the College: "In selecting the style to be followed, we may either adopt the best variety of pointed architecture, irrespective of the history of the College, or we may choose between the date of the College itself and that of the preceding establishment. Had the date of the College itself coincided with that of the highest perfection of pointed architecture, there would have been no room left for doubt; as, however, this was not the case, it is satisfactory that such a coincidence does not exist as regards the date of the older chapel, which belongs to the latter half of the thirteenth century. I have therefore adopted that period as the groundwork of my design. The type of Chapel I have chosen is that so frequent at Oxford, having an ante-chapel placed in a transverse position, something like a transept, at the west end. . . . In adopting this type, I have not been actuated by my desire to introduce an Oxford model, but have done so because it happens to be particularly well suited to the position."

Among features to be noted in the Chapel are the double piscina in the apse that was in the walls of the Infirmary and the heads of Henry VIII and Victoria on the outer arch of the main door, which symbolise the foundation date of the College and the date of erection of the Chapel. The plan of the original chapel is still marked on the lawn. Since 1902 it has become traditional on Ascension Day for St John's choir to sing Palestrina's *O Rex Gloriae* after Morning Service from the top of the Chapel tower.

The Second Court is an attractive example of Tudor domestic architecture. The warm brickwork has mellowed to that rich plum colour so esteemed by Ruskin. It was built in 1598–1602 with money given by Lady Mary Cavendish, Countess of Shrewsbury, whose statue is in an arched recess above the gateway. The original drawings for the Court, small and almost primitive, are in the College Library, and are the oldest collegiate drawings to have survived in either Cambridge or Oxford.

The Hall has a magnificent hammerbeam roof, part-Tudor, and superb linenfold panelling. It was lengthened by forty feet in 1862–5. On the walls hang portraits of Lady Margaret and Bishop Fisher as well as a long gallery of distinguished men including Herrick, Wordsworth, William Cecil, Herschel the astronomer, Lord Palmerston and Wilberforce.

The Combination Room, built as the Long Gallery of the Master's Lodge, is 100-feet long with transommed windows and richly-decorated plaster ceiling executed by the Italian craftsmen who built the fountain at Trinity College. Over the mantelpiece, in a smaller chamber, is a Holbein crayon sketch in red chalk of the only authentic likeness of John Fisher. It was in this room that plans for landing in France during the Second World War were formulated by Eisenhower, Montgomery and their staff.

The Library, built in 1624, occupies the northern side of the Third Court. Originally the intention had been to build it on pillars, like Trinity, but the design was not approved by the donor, Bishop John Williams of Lincoln, Lord Keeper of the Great Seal. Instead it became very Gothic-looking. Its splendid oriel windows overlook the river. The date 1671 on the gable is when the exterior work was completed: the initials ILCS are those of the Bishop, *Joannes Lincolniensis Custos Sigelli*. The two-storeyed building was described by John Evelyn in 1654 as "the fairest of that University". The bookcases are original, richly carved and panelled. The staining with bullock's blood left a rich, deep tone of exceptional beauty. The bookcases had to be heightened by eighteen inches to take the folios left to the College by Thomas Baker. The many treasures include the service-book used by Charles I at his coronation as well as the book used by Laud on the same occasion with comments in his handwriting: 'The day was verye faire, and ye ceremony was performed without any interruption, and in verye good order." An unusual item is a royal promissory note, an IOU of Charles II to John Barwick, a Fellow of St John's and later Dean of St Paul's: "I do acknowledge to have received the summe of one hundred pounds, by the direction of Mr B., Brusselles the first of April 1660, Charles R." Another rarity is the mortuary roll of Amphelissa, Prioress of Lillechurch in Kent, who died in 1299. Only two owners have held this document throughout the centuries, the Priory of Lillechurch and the College. It consists of nineteen sheets of parchment stitched together, 39 feet 3 inches in length, with a width of about 7 inches. On it the Lillechurch nuns record the death of the Prioress, extol her virtues, ask for the prayers of the faithful for her soul. To this end, 372 religious houses were visited in all parts of these islands, each house giving a prayer ending with the words, *Oravimus pro vestris: orate pro nostris.*

The cloister walk of the New Court

The New Court was built in Neo-Gothic style in 1825–31. It is like a mirage in stone, a nineteenth century vision of the Middle Ages, with pinnacles, cloisters, turrets, flying-buttresses, and pinnacled lantern crowned with a Gothic cupola and known as the "Wedding Cake". The building is linked to the Third Court by the Bridge of Sighs, built in 1831 at a cost of £5266.6s.3d. It bestrides the river with a single span, the five unglazed Gothic windows and traceried openings making it resemble a pontine cloister. The iron bars are there for a purpose, to prevent undergraduates getting in at night from the river. The comparison with its Venice counterpart is understandable, though the Italian structure is only a fly-over from the old prison to the ducal palace. Had it not been for Byron, the sighing would probably only have been caused by the delays in building. Beyond the Bridge of Sighs is the graceful bridge built in 1709–12 by Robert Grumbold and based on Sir Christopher Wren's designs. The Cripps Building, a new range behind the New Building, won the RIBA bronze in 1968. Designed by Powell and Mays, it forms a three-sided court for 100 undergraduates and has a large punt lake near the river. It is considered to be one of the best examples of modern architecture in Cambridge.

Below: New Court is linked to the Third Court by the Bridge of Sighs. It bestrides the river with a single span, the unglazed Gothic windows and traceried openings resembling a pontine cloister

The New Court built in Neo-Gothic style is like a nineteenth century vision of the Middle Ages, with pinnacles, cloisters, turrets, flying buttresses and pinnacled lantern crowned with a Gothic cupola known as the "Wedding Cake"

MAGDALENE COLLEGE

The most interesting feature of Magdalene College is the Pepysian Library. The building itself is a fine example of seventeenth century architecture giving the feeling of a Tudor manor house embellished with an Italianate colonnade. Purists may criticise, but the effect is pleasant. It bears the Pepysian arms with his motto *Mens cujusque is est quisque* and the inscription *Bibleotheca Pepysiana 1724* that is misleading, for it refers, not to the date of the building, but to when the Pepysian books were transferred. When Pepys died in 1703 his nephew, John Jackson, was made heir, with the proviso that on his death, the Library should be given either to Magdalene or Trinity, preferably the former, an instruction that was observed.

The collection consists of 3,000 volumes, a figure kept exact. When a new one was accepted, an old volume was discarded. Stipulations laid down by Pepys were precise. Books could only be moved from the Library to the Master's Lodge with a maximum of ten volumes at a time. Reciprocal checks were carried out by Magdalene and Trinity, "the college in possession of the Library being subject to an annual visitation from the other". The volumes are kept in twelve cases or presses. Each book rests on a block of wood to keep the tops level, each one shaped and coloured to match. Pepys refers to these bookcases in a Diary entry for the 14th August, 1666. The six quarto volumes of the Diary are written in a shorthand cypher that Pepys invented for himself. It was not deciphered until 1819 when a St John's undergraduate named John Smith succeeded after three years' work. The Diary was published for the first time in 1825.

As regards Samuel Pepys' career at Magdalene, the records are sparse. Educated at St Paul's School, London, he records how he "did put on his gown first" on the 5th March, 1650. This reference was to Trinity Hall, not Magdalene. Academic success meant an election to a Spendluffe scholarship, followed two years later by a scholarship that ensured his stay at Magdalene. The College Registrar has this record for the 21st October, 1653 . . . "Pepys and Hind were solemnly admonished by myself and Mr. Hill, for having been scandalously over-served with drink ye night before." A Diary entry for the 25th May, 1668 recalls a visit to Magdalene by Pepys accompanied by his son and two brothers: "And there into the butterys, as a stranger, and there drank my belly full of their beer, which pleased me, as the best I ever drunk: and hear by the butler's man, who was son to Goody Mulliner over against the College, that we used to buy stewed prunes of, concerning the College and persons in it; and find very few, only Mr. Hollins and Pechell, I think, that were of my time. But I was mightily pleased to come in this condition to see and ask, and thence, giving the fellow something, away walked to Chesterton, to see our old walk, and there into the Church, the bells ringing, and saw the place I used to sit in, and so to the ferry, and ferried over to the other side, and walked with great pleasure, the river being mighty high by Barnewell Abbey: and so by Jesus College to the town, and so to our quarters, and to supper, and then to bed, being very weary and sleepy and mightily pleased with this night's walk."

Magdalene College is not architecturally outstanding, but nevertheless has considerable appeal. It was founded in 1428 when the Benedictines of Croyland acquired a building to accommodate members of their Order who, whilst observing their monastic rules, were allowed to study in Cambridge at the same time. They were joined by the Benedictine Abbeys of Ely, Walden and Ramsey. Additional rooms were added to the hostel, but Croyland Abbey was acknowledged as the superior house. The new College received financial aid from Henry Stafford, Duke of Buckingham, and a change of name to the Monks' College of Buckingham, then a hostel called Bokyngham College, and finally Buckingham College in 1482. The evolutionary process continued until, by the Dissolution, the College consisted of a complete Court, Hall and Chapel. It became semi-secular as was shown when Cranmer became a lecturer after resigning his Fellowship at Jesus because of his marriage. In 1539 the College was dissolved along with Croyland Abbey, the property lapsing to the Crown.

Three years later it was refounded, "under the new dedication of St Mary Mag-

Below: The seventeenth century Pepys Building of Magdalene College. It houses the Pepys Library with its original bookcases of red oak made in 1666

dalene, by Thomas Lord Audley of Walden, to whom the King had granted it for the purpose.'' History is not kind to the memory of Thomas Audley. He is labelled a vile man, servile to Henry VIII who made him Lord Chancellor, ''the keeper of the King's Conscience'', and, as Fuller drily remarks, gave him ''the first cut in the feast of abbey lands''. Although benefactor and founder of a College, he showed little interest in the New Learning, but was more concerned with the original statutes of Magdalene College and the autocratic power of the Master that gave vesting nomination of the Mastership within the gift of Audley's descendants. Since 1542 this nomination has been held in the gift of the owners of the Audley End estate. Audley is buried at Walden in an altar-tomb of black marble. Fuller added the epitaph, ''The stone is not harder, nor the marble blacker than the heart of him who lies beneath.''

If time permits, a visit to Audley end, a few miles outside Cambridge, is well worth-while. This massive Jacobean mansion was built by a noble, but regarded as too large for a king. In spite of its enormous size, it is only a section of its former layout. The original structure was erected during the reign of James I on the site of the Benedictine Abbey of Walden, when it came into the possession of Lord Chancellor Audley at the Dissolution. His daughter married the Duke of Norfolk; their son, Thomas Howard, became the Earl of Suffolk in 1603 and Lord Treasurer the next year. Extensive alter-ations to the house, plus two courtyards costing £200,000, led James I to remark on visiting the place before it was completed, that it was ''too big for a king, but might do well for a Lord Treasurer''.

In 1669 Charles II, finding the royal palaces unrepaired after the Civil War, bought the place for £50,000. The money was probably never paid and Audley End reverted to the Earl of Suffolk in 1701. Its size proved unmanageable. The outer courtyard was demolished, followed by the eastern side of the inner court in 1750. The Great Hall was remodelled by Sir John Vanbrugh. A further change of ownership occurred in 1762 when the house and lands went to Sir John Griffin, who became a Field-Marshal, then Lord Howard de Walden, and finally Lord Braybrooke. He made several improve-ments that cost £100,000. Capability Brown landscaped the grounds, whilst Robert Adam left his distinguishing mark. He decorated a suite of rooms, added the Circular Temple to mark the British successes in the Seven Years' Wars, the rectangular Temple of Concord to commemorate George III's recovery from illness in 1789, and the three-arched bridge. The showpiece is the Great Hall with its fine Vanbrugh screen and double stair leading to the Saloon and its unusual ceiling.

The list of distinguished Magdalene men is lengthy. It includes Charles Kingsley, who entered the College in 1838, where the attractions of fishing in the river took pri-ority over studies. As a Christian Socialist, he campaigned against the prevailing poverty and distress, highlighting conditions in his books *Alton Locke* and *Yeast*, though he is perhaps better known for the children's book *The Water Babies*. In 1860 he was appointed Professor of Modern History at the University, became tutor to the Prince of Wales and chaplain to Queen Victoria. In 1873 he was appointed Canon of Westmin-ster. Two yeare later, on the 23rd January, he died from an illness aggravated by over-work. Another Magdalene man who would have had much in common with Kingsley was C. S. Lewis, author of *The Screwtape Letters*, whilst Honorary Fellows included Rudyard Kipling, T. S. Eliot and Thomas Hardy. My final choice would be A. C. Benson, Master from 1915–25, who wrote *Land of Hope and Glory*. The selection is not for scholarship, academic distinction or literary output, but for the College building he caused to be built on the opposite side of Magdalene Street, named Mallory Court after ''his favourite pupil''. This was understandable for George Mallory was a remarkable man remembered by a failure. Only one person is alive who witnessed Mallory's last minutes. He is Noel Odell, geologist, Imperial College of Science, and Honorary Fellow of Clare College. Over a dinner party at the Old Mill House with Sir William and Lady Hawthorne, then Professor of Applied Thermodynamics, later Master of Churchill

College, Sir Frank Adcock, Professor of Ancient History, and Henry Moore, the sculptor, and his wife, Irene, Odell told the story how Mallory died.

In 1924 under the leadership of General G. C. Bruce, a possible route up Mount Everest was discovered on the North Col at an altitude of 23,000 feet. Dr Somervell and Colonel Norton reached a height of 28,000 feet. It was during this attempt that Mallory and Irvine were going strong for the top when a blizzard broke. Noel Odell was at Camp V (25,000 feet), and last saw them climbing strongly at a height shown by the theodolite as 28,227 feet, at that time the highest level ever reached by man. Darkness descended. They never returned, but Odell is convinced they reached the top, but died afterwards. No one will ever know. It remains another of the secrets of Everest. Discussion followed as to whether the bodies might have been preserved in the ice and snow, the only way the argument could be settled. History has shown that the ice can give up its victims.

An example was given of how Tilman and Shipton discovered 21,000 feet up on the Rongbuk glacier the body of Maurice Wilson, the man who tried to climb Everest alone. He had been buried where he lay by Charles Warren in 1935. Twenty-five years later Wilson's body re-emerged from the ice and was found by a Chinese climber. Whether that could happen to Mallory and Irvine seems unlikely. Irvine's ice-axe was found, but Odell thought that both bodies would have been swept by gales over a 12,000 feet precipice and entombed in the glacier below, possibly uncovered occasionally, only to be hidden again by fresh snow. Future expeditions might find them, but the odds are against it. Noel Odell believes that the first conquerors of Everest were Mallory and Irvine. At Magdalene the memory of Mallory's tragic climb is kept by the river and willows that he knew so well.

GASTRONOMIC ACADEMICS

On March 4th, 1869 a collation of academic epicures met in Sidney Sussex College to sample a dish of cooked donkey. Reactions to the meal were mixed as J. W. Clark recorded: "Mr. A. A. Vansittart, formerly Fellow of Trinity College, was moved to buy a healthy young donkey. He fattened it on oil-cake and at a suitable moment had it killed by a butcher. The idea of eating him was warmly taken up by Hardy of Sidney, whose gastronomic tastes were notorious, and under his direction every part of the animal was utilized. Joints were also given to Trinity and to one or two private friends. I dined on all occasions . . . and thought the meat delicious, rather like swan. Among the lower orders the proceedings excited the greatest possible disgust, so much so that the man who usually bought the dripping out of Sidney Sussex kitchen refused to take any that week."

JESUS COLLEGE

Instead of being laid out like other colleges, Jesus College adapted the plan of a medieval Benedictine monastic house. In the twelfth century, the priory of St Radegund consisted of a cruciform church with a central tower, chapter-house, cloisters, dormitory, refectory and kitchen. By means of charters, wills, account rolls, and documents, it is possible to gain an accurate picture of life some 800 years ago in a community of Benedictine nuns on the site of Jesus College.

The nuns received their charter from Nigel, Bishop of Ely from 1133 to 1169. It is written with Norman panache "to all barons and men of St Etheldrytha, cleric or lay, French or English", a rent of twelve pence; in return certain lands would be ceded "to the nuns of the cell lately established without the vill of Cantebruge". About the same time William the Monk gave the nuns a benefaction of two virgates and six acres of meadow and four cottars with their tenure in the village of Shelford – property that is still owned by the Master and Fellows of Jesus College. Other benefactions include tithes, customs, fishing rights and the advowsons of All Saints Church and St Clement Church.

Arthur Gray in his *History of Jesus* went into greater detail about the nuns' everyday life: "The Account Rolls which the departing sisters left behind them in 1496 reveal pretty fully the routine of their lives. Books – save for the casual mention of the binding of the lives of the saints – were none of their business, and works of charity, excepting the customary dole to the poor on Maunday Thursday, and occasional relief to 'poor soldiers disabled in the wars of Our Lord the King', scarcely concerned them more. The duties of hospitality in the Guest House make the Cellaress a busy woman. They cost a good deal, but are not unprofitable; the nuns take in 'paying guests', daughters of tradesmen and others. Being ladies, the sisters neither toil nor spin; but the Prioress and the Grangeress have an army of servants, whose daily duties have to be assigned to them; carters and ploughmen have to be sent out to the scattered plots owned by the nunnery in the open fields about Cambridge; the goatherd has to drive the cattle to distant Willingham fen; the crewer has instructions for malting and brewing the 'peny-ale' which serves the nuns for 'bevers'; and the women servants are despatched to work in the dairy, to weed the garden, or to weave and to make candles in the hospice. Once in a while a party of nuns, accompanied by their maid servants, takes boat as far as Lyn, there to buy stock-fish and Norway timber, and to fetch a letter for the Prioress."

It all sounds very business-like, but there were problems. Scandals and misdemeanours led to a visitation from Bishop Alcock in 1487. As a disciplinary measure he appointed an outsider, Joan Fulborn, to act as Prioress of the nunnery. Matters worsened. By 1496 only two nuns were in residence, services were spasmodic and the fabric of the nunnery was dilapidated and decaying. The Bishop took action, petitioned the King for authority to suppress the nunnery, appropriate the revenue and buildings, and replace it with a college. The sequel came in 1497 when the College of the Blessed Mary the Virgin, St John the Evangelist, and the glorious Virgin St Radegund was founded by Royal Charter and became Jesus College with a Master, six Fellows and a limited number of scholars.

Instead of demolishing the nunnery and rebuilding afresh, Alcock decided on adaptation. The Prioress's chambers became the Master's Lodge: the refectory was made the Hall; the cloisters were restored and the chapter-house arches walled-up. The church, some 200 feet in length, was too big for a college chapel so the aisles and four bays at the

Opposite: Jesus College was laid out along the lines of a medieval Benedictine monastic house. It impressed James I during a visit to Cambridge to such an extent that "Were he to chose, he would pray at King's, dine at Trinity, and study and sleep at Jesus"

end of the nave were demolished. The western part of the nave was converted into a three-storeyed block that later became incorporated into the Lodge. The gate tower still preserves the memory of the nunnery gatehouse. Bishop Alcock's coat of arms, an emblem of three cocks, was adopted by the College and is on those parts of the buildings that he altered or built. Over the entrance gateway is a statue of the prelate with his punning crest, a cock perched on a globe. The high-walled path from the street is known as the "Chimney". The Chapel, cruciform with a central tower, is Norman in plan, though predominantly very Early English. Pugin supervised restoration work about 1850 as certain thirteenth century details had to be replaced. Alterations had been significant. The nuns' nave and transept became an antechapel, whilst the Chapel itself was the chancel of the nuns' chapel.

The final result brought pleasure to admirers of the pre-Raphaelites for Morris designed the ceilings, whilst most of the stained glass in the antechapel was also made by him to the brilliant designs of Burne-Jones. The lower scene in the west window of the south nave and the south window on the east side of the south transept are by Ford Madox Brown. It is one of the loveliest chapels in Cambridge.

An alabaster wall-monument shows the head of Archbishop Cranmer, who was a student in 1503 at the age of fourteen. He became a Fellow in 1511, but was obliged to resign through marrying a young woman named Joan who worked at the Dolphin Inn in Bridge Street. Within the year he was a widower. The College forgave the dalliance and restored the Fellowship because of his "towardlinesse in learning". Not so forgiving was the nature of "Bloody" Mary; he perished in the flames because he recanted against his acknowledgement of Catholic doctrines and the supremacy of the Pope.

Also in the Chapel is a tribute to Samuel Taylor Coleridge in the form of a quotation from the *Ancient Mariner*. During his stay at Jesus from 1791 to 1793, he indulged in a foolish whim of tracing the words Liberty and Equality on a lawn in gunpowder and setting fire to it, an action that hardly endeared him to the authorities. He had entered in 1791 as a Rustat Scholar and became a Foundation Scholar in 1793, but took no degree, mainly because of his dislike of mathematics. He was an odd mixture with unconventional habits. In 1793 he enlisted in the 15th Dragoons under the name of Silas Tomkins Comberback, became disillusioned in a few months and returned. The Master issued a caution and told him to translate the works of Demetrius Phalerus into English, but in less than a year his drama *The Fall of Robespierre* was censured by the College.

Laurence Sterne, the great-grandson of Richard Sterne, Archbishop of Canterbury, had a stormy stay at Jesus. Left penniless, he was sent by his cousin as a sizar. He got into debt, took Orders, became vicar of Sutton-in-the-Forest in 1738, and married Elizabeth Lumley. Three years later the unfortunate young woman became insane due to her husband's flirtatious habits. He died insolvent in his Old Bond Street lodgings and was buried in the Bayswater Road cemetery. Two days later his corpse was stolen by resurrection men and sent to Cambridge for dissection, where he was recognised by one of the doctors.

Jesus College is fortunate to have a grove, extensive enough to house its own playing-fields. Beyond is Midsummer Common where the Midsummer Fair is held and by the Cam is the distinctive Jesus boathouse. In every way life at Jesus College is very civilised as James I confirmed after a visit to Cambridge – "Were he to chose, he would pray at King's, dine at Trinity, and study and sleep at Jesus."

SIDNEY SUSSEX COLLEGE

A rchitecturally Sidney Sussex is something of a Cinderella alongside the likes of Trinity, Magdalene and St John's. The reason is partly due to the taste of Sir Jeffry Wyatville, who plastered the original red brick with cement, then embellished the building with Gothic touches. The overall effect is dull, with no hint that it was once part of the Order founded in 1209 by St Francis of Assisi. To be more precise, Franciscans moved to quarters on this site in 1240. This Order, with more than a thousand members in England committed to the rules of chasity, poverty and obedience, had established forty-nine houses. Cambridge was one of the seven senior *custodies*, eventually becoming the main Franciscan house with seventy friars compared to thirty-eight at King's Lynn, forty at Gloucester and forty-seven at Norwich. The six acres at Cambridge were developed to include a church, cloister, campanile, schoolhouse and graveyard. Roger Ascham summarised the picture, "This House was not only a grace and ornament to the University, but presented great convenience for holding Congregations and transacting all kinds of University business."

This agreeable state of affairs ended abruptly. The little community fell foul of the suppression of religious Orders. After nearly 300 years closure came on the 1st October, 1538, when the House surrendered to Henry VIII. Events followed a familar pattern. Officialdom can be outrageous in any century. Three weeks after finishing, the University petitioned the Crown for a grant of the property. The request was ignored. Eight years later the site and buildings were conveyed to the new royal foundation of Trinity College. Grey Friars was destroyed and became a quarry. Records show that between 1556–7 more than 3,000 loads of stone were excavated and used to build the Great Court of Trinity.

The first lessees are known only by name: Ralph Bikerdike, alderman; W. Laing, labourer; William Hedley, yeoman. There seemed reluctance to take a decision as to the use of the ground. The town authorities tried to secure the site for a hospital, but failed. The impasse was finally resolved by Lady Frances Sidney, Countess of Sussex and aunt of Sir Philip Sidney and the Earl of Leicester. In her Will dated the 6th December, 1558, the wishes were explicit. The relevant passage read, ". . . that since the decease of her late lord, she had yearly gathered out of her revenues so much as she conveniently could, purposing to erect some goodly and godly monument for the maintenance of good learning." For that purpose £5,000 and all her bequeathed goods were to be earmarked for the erection of a new college in the University of Cambridge, to be known as the "Lady Frances Sidney Sussex College, and for the purchasing some competent lands for the maintaining of a Master, ten Fellows, and twenty Scholars, if the said £5,000 and unbequeathed goods would thereunto extend."

Her executors, Sir John Harrington and the Earl of Kent, experienced difficulty in carrying out her instructions. Their tactics were recorded by Fuller: "These two noble executors in the pursuance of the will of this testatrix, according to her desire and direction therein, presented Queen Elizabeth with a jewel, being like a star, of rubies and diamonds, with a ruby in the midst thereof, worth an hundred and forty pounds, having on the back side a hand delivering up a heart into a crown. At the delivery hereof they humbly requested of her Highness a mortmain to found a College, which she graciously granted unto them." Five years passed before the consent became fact. An Act of Parliament was made in 1593 allowing Trinity College to sell or let the site of the Grey Friars at a fee farm rent fixed at £13. 6s.8d. In 1596 the Charter was granted. Two years later the building was completed, apart from the Chapel. The architect appointed, Ralph Symons, had already to his credit the Hall in Trinity and the Second Court of St John's. The Statutes of 1598 were based on those of Emmanuel College, with similar aims . . . to be a seminary for the training of ordination candidates. Rules were strict; discipline rigid. Each student had a tutor, who was obliged to have two or more sleeping in his room. The town was out of bounds except for lectures and sermons, whilst the Master, upon election, had to refute Popery . . . *Papismus, Haereses, superstitiones et errores ex animo abhorret et detestatur.* The Refectory of the Friars served as a Chapel until it was destroyed between 1777 and 1780, replaced by a building designed by Essex, and remained unchanged until T. H. Lyons enlarged it in Neo-Wren style in 1912.

The visitor to Sidney Sussex should take note of the portraits in the eighteenth century Hall. Over the high table is that of the founder in a fur-trimmed gown with ruff and a small dog playing at her feet. Others are of Bishop James Montague, the first Master of the College; Lord Montague, resplendent in red-and-white; Sir William Montague, the judge. The curtained portrait of Oliver Cromwell is worth studying in detail. Surprisingly little is known about Cromwell's short stay at Sidney Sussex. Contemporary observers declared that he was "more famous for his exercises in the fields than in the Schools, being one of the chief . . . players at football, cudgels, or any other boisterous sport or game." Educated at Huntingdon Grammar School, he was admitted as a Fellow-Commoner on the 23rd April, 1616. It is probable that academic ambitions were abruptly terminated through having to leave after a year because of his father's death.

Thomas Carlyle added his comment: "Whilst Oliver Cromwell was entering himself of Sidney Sussex College, William Shakespeare was taking his farewell of this world. Oliver's father had most likely come with him; it is but some fifteen miles from Huntingdon; you can go and come in a day. Oliver's father saw Oliver write in the album at Cambridge; at Stratford, Shakespeare's Anne Hathaway was weeping over his bed. The first world-great thing that remains of English History, the literature of Shakespeare, was ending; the second world-great thing that remains of English history, the armed appeal of Puritanism to the Invisible God of Heaven against very many visible devils, on earth and elsewhere, was so to speak beginning. They have their exits and their entrances, and one people in its time plays many parts."

Not everyone agreed with Carlyle. After the entry of Cromwell's name in the College book someone added a more caustic comment; "*Hic fuit grandis ille imposter, carnifex perditissimus, qui, pietissimo rege Carolo primo nefaria caede sublato, ipsum usurpavit thronum, et tria regna per quinque ferme annorum spatium sub protectoris nomine indomita tyrannide vexavit.*" Charles Stubbs added the translation, "This was that arch hypocrite, that most abandoned murderer, who having by shameful slaughter put out of the way the most pious King, Charles the First, grasped the very throne, and for the space of nearly five years under the title of Protector harassed three kingdoms with inflexible tyranny."

The portrait in the Hall is revealing. Lifelike almost to the point of caricature, it emphasises the pronounced forehead, underhung jaw, tight mouth, and gnarled features. The identity of the painter is uncertain. A possible clue was when William Elliston, Master of the College, received a letter in 1776 informing him that "an Englishman, an assertor of Liberty, Citizen of the World, is desirous of having the honour to present an original portrait in crayons of the head of O. Cromwell, protector, drawn by Cooper, to Sidney Sussex College, in Cambridge." A footnote asked that upon receipt of the picture, "the favour of a line might be written to Pierce Delver, at Mr Shove's, Bookbinder, in Maiden Lane, Covent Garden, London."

When the portrait arrived the acknowledgement was sent as requested, but no one knew the identity of the donor. Fourteen years later fresh evidence came to light. Thomas Holles and Pierce Delver were found to be the same person, Holles being a

*Sidney Sussex was built on
the site occupied by
Franciscans in 1240.
After nearly three
centuries, closure came on
1st October, 1538, when
the House surrendered to
Henry VIII*

well-known eighteenth century Republican, but there was still no confirmation about the artist. Some experts pointed to Horace Walpole's anecdote about Cromwell's instructions to Sir Peter Lely, "Mr Lely, I desire you would use all your skill to paint my picture truly like me, and not flatter me at all; but remark all these roughnesses, pimples, warts, and everything as you see me, otherwise I never will pay a farthing for it." On the other hand, the style employed in this portrait is more like Cooper than Lely.

There is a strange postscript. When Charles II ordered that the bodies of the principal Parliamentarians be disinterred and destroyed, the head of Cromwell was removed. In 1960 the College was given this macabre relic. It is buried in the Chapel, but only a few know its exact location.

Below: *Macabre words that speak for themselves*

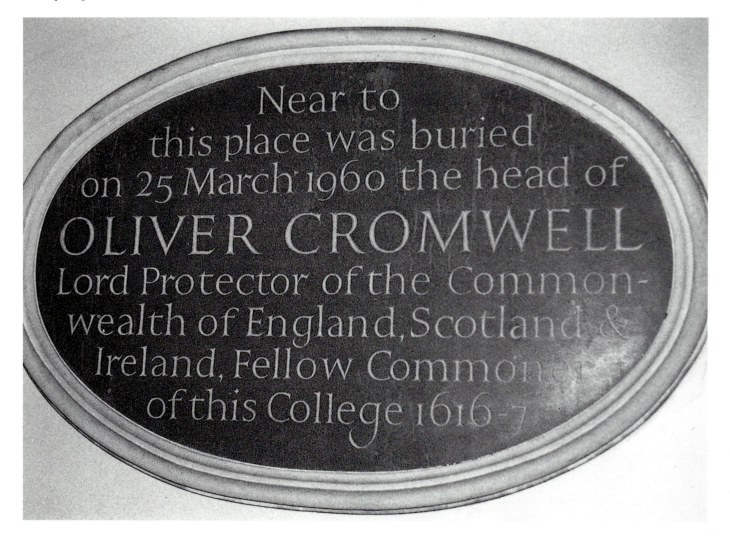

AND SO TO NEWMARKET

The visitor to Cambridge would do well to include Newmarket in the itinerary. It has so much to offer anyone with an eye to history and tradition, as well as an appreciation of the racehorse. Everything is there for the connoisseur, though during the past few years the scene has changed. The sport of kings has become a highly commercial industry, an important part of Britain's national economy. Owner-breeders prominent in the fifties, sixties and seventies have almost disappeared from the scene, crowded out by Middle-Eastern owners. Horseracing is becoming a status-activity of Arab sheikhs. In spite of the world slump in prices, they are oil-rich beyond imagination and indulge in racing which is banned in Arabia by the Muslim law forbidding betting.

Sheihk Mohammed, Defence Minister of the United Arab Emirates, paid 10.2 million dollars for a *Northern Dancer* colt out of *My Bupers*, more than double the previous record set in the same ring a year earlier. Maktoum's purchase fetched more than double its true value. The sire, *Northern Dancer*, had dominated the world classic breeding for a decade. The mother, *My Bupers*, was an exceptional brood mare but had been unimpressive as a racehorse. *Northern Dancer*'s most famous offspring was *Nijinsky*, the 1970 Derby winner. The Gulf State sheikh hoped that the colt would justify the world record price for a yearling by winning the Triple Crown.

One of the dangers of spending money like confetti is that one never knows how long the boom will last and when Arab enthusiasm for acquisition will lose its appeal. This fever of buying horses for astronomical sums will pass, the market will level, and sanity will return. Meanwhile the onlooker can watch with interest the attempts to buy instant success with limitless finance. One thing is constant. The horse mirrors the tradition of Newmarket, a tradition that stretches in unbroken continuity across the centuries to the misty days when Iceni horsemen exercised their mounts on the Heath. In the High Street is a building where past and present receive equal due. In 1777 a writer declared that "it modestly turns its back upon the street, as if to shun the public view in silent retirement." The words still apply. The Jockey Club, as befits the ultimate authority of the racing world, is conservative in habit, exclusive in membership, and dignified in repose. Within its walls are preserved many reminders of the past. Here is "The Whip", alleged to have been given by Charles II, with the wristband woven from hairs taken from the tail of Eclipse. William IV presented another relic, a hoof mounted on a gold salver, but these and many other historic treasures are not for the public eye. Instead, the National Horseracing Museum housed in the old Subscription Rooms a few yards away offers a wide range of items of racing interest. It was opened officially by the Queen in 1983. The brain child of David Swannell, one-time senior handicapper of the Jockey Club, its display areas capture through memorabilia and paintings glimpses of racing over a wide span of years.

Some of the most interesting items on loan are from the Sandringham Museum. They were given by the Queen and include parts of the racing collections of George IV and Edward VII. Unusual is the stuffed head of *Persimmon*, bred and owned by the Prince of Wales and winner of the 1896 Derby and St Ledger. The paintings and bronzes of the horse are outstanding. The Jockey Club has lent the paintings of *Persimmon* by Ernie Adams, whilst the Royal College of Veterinary Surgeons has loaned its skeleton. Veterinary equipment of the last century is on view, like the clipping shears and the crude but effective castration shears. Paintings and bronzes lent by the Queen and the

Queen Mother from Windsor and Buckingham Palace are alone worth the visit, whilst Manchester City Art Gallery has lent Frith's famous *Derby Day*. Any racing enthusiast who visits this museum will not be disappointed, unlike the High Street, which is bleak and uninspiring. There is no glamour about the shops that are functional in a plastic way. It is impossible to visualise the part Newmarket and this street once played in the affairs of State.

Macaulay summed it up when he wrote . . . "it was not uncommon for the whole Court and Cabinet to go down there, posting in a single day." During Charles I's reign, Newmarket was virtually the administrative capital of England. The streets were bustling. Macaulay adds his description: . . . "jewellers, milliners, players and fiddlers, venal wits and venal beauties, learned doctors from Cambridge and fox-hunting squires with their rosy-cheeked daughters." Gwynn House in Palace Street is a reminder that the charm of Nell Gwynn must have countered the chill winds that whistled over the cobbled streets. The gambling-salon of the Duchess of Mazarin, accepted as part of the Court life and noted for the attractiveness of this niece of Cardinal Mazarin, echoed to the gossip and intrigue of the capitals of Europe. Lady Castlemaine, royal mistress of singular beauty, likewise presided over a gambling-house. Pepys referred to it when he wrote in 1668: "I was told tonight that my Lady Castlemaine is so great a gamester as to have won £15,000 in one night, and lost £25,000 in another night, at play; and hath played £1,000 or £1,500 at a cast."

If we want that sort of excitement we are three centuries too late. On the other hand, one aspect of Newmarket never changes. To experience it is easy, but it does mean getting up very early and walking over the Lime Kilns while the morning mists still linger. It is a world apart. One hears only the thud of hoofs from the strings of racehorses as they are exercised. It is worth the effort. Only then will you really know Newmarket.

CHRIST'S COLLEGE

Opposite: The superb Gateway of Christ's College with its heraldic display of arms supported by yales, animals with goats' heads, antelopes' bodies and elephants' tails

With the help of the Master and Fellows of Clare College, William Bingham of St John Zachary, founded a God's House "for the free herbigage of poure scolers of gramer" in 1442. It was to be sited to the south of King's College antechapel, an unfortunate choice for both God's House and the Church of St John had to be demolished in 1446 to make way for Henry VI's College. In compensation, Bingham had a royal licence to rebuild his college elsewhere. The eventual location was where the present First and Second Courts are sited. The new charter was dated the 16th April, 1448. Lack of finance and poor endowments led to John Fisher influencing the Queen Mother, the Lady Margaret Beaufort, to enlarge and endow God's House, the name to be changed to Christ's College.

This refounding took place in 1505, the new benefactors including manors in Cam-

bridge, Essex, Norfolk and Leicester, income that altered Christ's standards. Suddenly the College had become wealthy. The buildings were completed in 1511 at a cost of some £1,000 and occupied the present First Court area. The material used, clunch and red brick, began to deteriorate and had to be ashlared. A degree of continuity was achieved through the last Proctor of God's House becoming the first Master of Christ's. The Foundress had chambers in the College. One of these rooms had an oriel to the Chapel and became a private oratory. This pious mother of Henry VII must have been a remarkable woman at a time when arrogance and insensitivity were the usual qualities of the rich. If Bishop Fisher's sermon at her funeral was not over-exaggerated, the nature described was at variance with the time . . . "Bounteous she was and liberal . . . of singular easiness to be spoken to . . . of marvellous gentleness to all folk . . . unkind to no creature, nor forgetful of any service done to her (which is no little part of very nobleness) . . . All England for her death have cause for weeping."

Fisher became the dominant figure. He watched the College being built, followed the progress through every stage, and drew up the statutes. The palatial Fellows' Building was erected in 1640–43 to ease the demand for accommodation. The Chambers on the right of the Second Court were on the site of a timber structure known as Rat's Hall. John Evelyn described Christ's when he visited Cambridge in August 1654 as "a very noble erection, especially the modern part, built without the quadrangle towards the gardens, of exact architecture." The gardens of Christ's are still famous, though not perhaps for the reason described by George Dyer, the friend of Charles Lamb, when he wrote: "Travellers are here shewn a rich mulberry tree broken down with age, but not deserted, it being propt up with wonderful assiduity and skill, and not merely consecrated to Milton, but planted, we are told, with his own hand. Whether true or not, the fancy may be improved by supposing that Milton here meditated some of his juvenile poems, many of them, particularly his Latin Elegies, having been written by him while a student of this college, and relating to Cambridge." This mulberry tradition may or may not be true. What is established is that the College planted three hundred mulberry trees in the orchard in 1608 and this particular "relic" was a survivor of the exercise.

Of Christ's men of note, John Milton figures high. He was sixteen when he entered as a pensioner on the 12th February, 1625, and resided in the College for seven years. He took a B.A. degree in 1629, the year he wrote *Ode on the Nativity*. In his seventeenth and nineteenth years, he composed the poems *On the Death of a Fair Infant* and *At a Vacation Exercise*, as well as Latin epigrams and elegies. If Aubrey's account is accurate, Milton was flogged in the College Hall for breaking some rule, punishment that was not uncommon. If true, it did not jaundice his outlook judging by what he wrote later: "I acknowledge publicly with all grateful mind, that more than ordinary respect which I found, above any of my equals, at the hands of those courteous and learned men, the Fellows of that College, wherein I spent some years; who, at my parting, after I had taken two degrees, as the manner is, signified in many ways how much better it would content them that I would stay; as by many letters full of kindness and loving respect, both before that time and long after, I was assured of their singular good affection towards me."

Founders, benefactors and eminent members of colleges are remembered in varying ways, but Christ's introduced an unusual idea. The west oriel in the Hall depicts them in the twenty-one lights. They are: William Bingham; Henry VI; John Fisher; Lady Margaret; Edward VI; Sir John Finch; Sir Thomas Baines; John Leland; Edmund Grindall; Sir Walter Mildmay; John Still; William Perkins; William Lee; Sir John Harrington; Francis Quarles; John Milton; John Cleveland; Henry More; Ralph Cudworth; William Paley; and Charles Darwin. Impressed though the visitor may be by such an assembly of great men, the features that might make the most lasting impression is the magnificent Gateway with its brilliantly painted heraldic display, the arms supported by yales, animals with goats' heads, antelopes' bodies, and elephants' tails. It is a glimpse of Lady Margaret's time.

CHARLES DARWIN (Christ's College)

Although, as we shall presently see, there were some redeeming features in my life at Cambridge, my time was sadly wasted there, and worse than wasted. From my passion for shooting and for hunting, and when this failed, riding across country, I got into a sporting set, including some dissipated, low minded young men. We often used to dine together in the evening, though these dinners often included men of a higher stamp, and we sometimes drank too much, with jolly singing and playing cards afterwards.

I also got into a musical set . . . From associating with these men, and hearing them play, I acquired a strong taste for music and used to time my walks so as to hear on weekdays the anthem in King's College Chapel. This gave me intense pleasure, so that my backbone would sometimes shiver. I am sure there was no affection or mere imitation in this taste, for I used generally to go by myself to King's College . . . I cannot perceive a discord, or keep time and hum a tune correctly; and it is a mystery how I could possibly have derived pleasure from music.

EMMANUEL COLLEGE

American visitors to Cambridge put Emmanuel College high on the list. The reason is understandable. In his *Ecclesiastical History of New England*, Cotton Mather paid this tribute to Emmanuel men like Thomas Shephard, John Cotton and Thomas Hooker, who had become Puritan leaders of America. . . . "If New England hath been in some respect Immanuel's land, it is well; but this I am sure of, Immanuel College contributed more than a little to make it so." Further evidence is a brass tablet in the Chapel that commemorates a student who entered the College in 1627 – John Harvard. The *Mayflower* sailed in 1620. He followed in 1636, "emigrating to Massachusetts Bay", but died two years later of consumption. He bequeathed half of his estate – £779.17s.2d. and 320 books to found Harvard College, "that eldest of the seminaries which advance learning and perpetuate it to posterity throughout America". Americans are often curious to identify his rooms. Unfortunately no one is quite sure which were his. At the tercentenary of Emmanuel in 1884, the memorial window in the Chapel was given by Harvard men.

Emmanuel College has many interesting features. Founded in 1584, it is one of the later Colleges that, like Sidney Sussex, was intended to combat popery. The founder, Sir Thomas Mildmay, a courtier of Queen Elizabeth and Chancellor of the Exchequer, was granted a charter empowering him "to erect, found and establish for all time to endure a certain college of sacred theology, the sciences, philosophy and good arts, of one master and 30 fellows and scholars, graduate and non-graduate, or more or fewer according to the ordinance and statutes of the same college."

Three months earlier Mildmay had bought the Dominican site for £500, possibly influenced by the description of the vendor: "All that the scite, circuit, ambulance and precinct of the late Priory of Fryers prechers, commonly called the black fryers within the Towne of Cambrigge . . . and all mesuages, houses, buildings, barnes, stables, dovehouses, orchards, gardens, pondes, stewes, waters, land and soyle within the said scite . . . And all the walles of stone, brick, or other thinge compassinge and enclosinge the said scite."

Opposite: The design for Emmanual Chapel was drawn by Christopher Wren at the request of William Sancroft, then Master and subsequently Dean of St Pauls. It is modelled on the lay-out of Peterhouse Chapel. A tablet in the Chapel commemorates John Harvard, a student who entered the College in 1627. A memorial window was later presented by Harvard men

Left: The site of Emmanuel College was originally the Cambridge house of the Dominicans or Black Friars

The Dominicans had a long-standing link with Cambridge. The Close Rolls has an entry in 1240 recording that the Order of mendicant friars, instituted twenty-five years earlier by the Spanish ecclesiastic, Domingo de Guzman, had a small house outside the Barnwell Gate. As it was closed under the Act of the 1st October, 1536, it is reasonable to presuppose that the community was very small for these officials were only involved with foundations whose income was below £290 per annum. The closure meant that the Prior became Dean of Exeter, whilst one of the Black Friars became Bishop of Rochester. During the next forty-eight years the site again changed hands before Mildmay took possession. His first task was to appoint Ralph Symons of Westminster as architect to convert the Dominican house into a College with the emphasis on Puritan dogma. The results were clear-cut. The old chapel, which ran east and west, became the Hall; the refectory, which ran north or south, became the Chapel, a non-orientation that caused considerable comment, even accusations of black magic. However disturbing, the dissension clearly had no effect on the health of the first Master, Laurence Chaderton, for he lived to be 103.

This Puritan tendency was so pronounced that during the Commonwealth, no fewer than eleven Masters of other Colleges came from this foundation, whilst, with the exception of Henry More who came from Christ's, Emmanuel could claim all the Cambridge Platonists. Narrow Protestantism found expression in the statutes governing student life that must have been irksome. The behaviour of the scholars in Hall and Chapel was noted: playing, feasting and talking had to be stopped – "idle gossip of youths was a waste of time and a bad habit for young minds." At least twice a week and at night two Fellows had to visit the scholars' rooms and carefully examine what they were doing. Their progress "to their lodging and the latrines" had to be checked carefully, and two Fellows were to see that no levity occurred in the College Courts. Others were detailed to note "of such as go often out of the college". Chapel attendance was compulsory and prayers took place every night at 8 o'clock with the tutor. There was "frequent hearing of sermons": every Sabbath afternoon, the Dean lectured on some article of the Christian faith and catechised the students; every form of amusement was frowned upon and offenders were whipped by the Dean-catechist . . . so much for the good old days!

At the Restoration, Dillingham was succeeded by Sancroft as Master. He left after three years to become Dean of St Pauls and it was through his influence that Christopher Wren was invited to build a new chapel. At that time Wren was at the outset of his career. Pembroke Chapel was evidence of what he could do. Emmanuel, built between 1668 and 1674, was less classical, correctly orientated, and pleasing to the eye, particularly when viewed from the gateway with the cloisters at the far end of the First Court, the Gallery extending along the colonnade wings and the Chapel front. The interior is subdued though the woodwork is good. Architecturally, Emmanuel is comfortable rather than distinguished, marred in places by features like the cemented parts whilst the 1959 additions have been likened to a prototype public convenience. But any minor irritations are dismissed by the gardens, that rank among the finest in Cambridge. Walk beneath the cloisters – the arches open out to a delightful setting. The long pool, once the fishpond of the Dominican monastery, is rich with water-lilies. An island dominated by a swamp cypress is flanked by bamboos, flags, seakale and the overwhelming *Gunnera manicata*. Outstanding on the lawns is the great oriental plane, almost 100 feet high and girth 16 feet, one of the great trees of England and some 200 years old. Henry More's bronze "Warrior with Shield" is ideally sited. There are many trees, shrubs and flowers to appreciate, but another tree in particular should be studied. It is the "fossil" tree or *Metasequoia glyptostroboides*, that until discovered growing in China at the end of the Second World War was known only in fossil form. It has grown to its impressive height in under fifty years.

The history of Emmanuel at times has been one of extremes. During the Civil War the students had the reputation for destroying vestments and smashing windows, whilst the Master, Richard Houldsworth, was sent to the Tower for not being loyal to Parliament and holding Royalist sympathies. With the Restoration life became more relaxed, as the Combination Room Betting Book entries suggest: 178–: That Rodney would beat the French before the 30th June, 1781 (lost). 1791: That Hastings would be found guilty (lost). That Marat would be murdered before the end of the Lent Term (won). 1794: That the War would be over in two years (lost). In all the bets, wine constituted the stakes. Then, as reaction to Protestantism, the College Society became High Church.

Like all the Colleges, a lengthy list can be compiled of the eminent men who belonged to Emmanuel, but rather than concentrate on figures of another century, I recall Sir Frederick Gowland Hopkins O.M., who was a biochemist and worked in a less turbulent field of research than the physicists. This first cousin of the poet, Gerard Manley Hopkins, concentrated on the nature of the amino-acids and succeeded in identifying unknown substances so necessary in diet and the chemistry-of-life process, which are now known as vitamins. He was a delightful personality, small in stature, but brimming with enthusiam. He began as a lecturer in chemical physiology at Cambridge, supplementing his income with tutorial work at Emmanual, eventually becoming the first Sir William Dunn Professor of Biochemistry, a post he held for twenty-two years. Among his friends, he was affectionatley known as "Hoppy". His household was enlivened by two bright daughters, one of whom was Jacquetta Hawkes, the wife of J. B. Priestley.

Hopkins always played down his role in the discovery of vitamins and became actively involved in a research programme on the effect of the pigmentation of butterfly wings on the human bloodstream and the former's possible use in the treatment of leukaemia. These experiments were highlighted in an official paintings by Meredith Frampton. The meeting between these two men was interesting. Both were individualistic; neither understood the other. Hopkins thought the artist was self-opinionated and still suffering from the fact that his father, Sir George Frampton, the Edwardian sculptor, was responsible for the Peter Pan in Kensington Gardens, and felt he had been cast by his parents for a similar role. He also thought that Frampton's style was obsessively realistic, concentrating on the detailed rendering of three dimensions with something like *troup l'oeil* accuracy in two. He thought the intensity of his gaze had been given an almost surrealist air like photo-realism. Meredith loved the microscopic finish and particularly any background that featured glass. Hopkins felt that in portrait-study, he came second in importance. The focus was on the test tubes that reflected light and the varied colours of the pigmentation, but Meredith had shown his handwritten note on the pad *Lepidoporphyrin* – plus details of the experimental stages. He preferred to talk about this project rather than make retrospective comments about vitamins. Gowland Hopkins demonstrated that an active mind is never satisfied . . . there is always the challenge of tomorrow.

Overleaf: Emmanuel has one of the finest gardens in Cambridge. The long pool was made shortly after the College was founded in 1584 and may have been the fish-pond of the Dominican monastery. A prominent feature is a swamp cypress and Cornus stolonifera "Flaviramea"

CAMILLE SAINT-SAENS

Abler pens than mine having described the English Universities for Continental readers, I shall not make the attempt; I will merely speak of the pleasure which it gave me to visit the charming town of Cambridge. It is a nest of ogival effects embosomed in verdure, of extraordinary originality with all its 'colleges', which are huge Gothic of Renaissance structures, some ancient some modern in the same style, with immense courts, magnificent lawns, and secular trees; they often abut on one another, and communicating in this way form complications of palaces and vast spaces in which it is easy for the stranger to lose himself.

Each college is furnished with a chapel, if one may so call what elsewhere might pass for a cathedral; and there every days the students take part in the service and sing, clad in surplices. Now the least curious of these universities is their religious character, to which French students would with difficulty adapt themselves.

But the yoke of this English religion is so light! The services, which are very short, consist chiefly of listening to good music very well sung, for the English make admirable choristers.

A SPORTING INTERLUDE

The Boat Race is a national institution, the only instance in this country of a highly specialised sport commanding unprecedented public appeal. For weeks beforehand, people who have never handled an oar in their lives and to whom a sliding seat might mean anything, read with interest Press accounts of the preparations of both crews. Towpath forecasts are unending. By the day of the race the physical likenesses and personal idiosyncrasies of the crews are known, the length and cost of the boats common knowledge, the names of Oxford and Cambridge bandied about with casual informality. It is all so familiar. An annual titillation by methods that never lose their anticipated excitement. Yet in thin Spring sunshine, it is speculative how many in the crowd who sport light or dark blue favours have any idea of the intensive training schedule before the crews reach the tideway.

Three months is a long time for anyone to maintain rigid physical discipline. In practice outings the crews between them row over a thousand miles. An enthusiast can judge for himself. Conditions on the Cam, particularly above Ely, can be Arctic. An east wind with knife-like edge sears across the naked Fens. With temperature at near freezing-point and flurries of snow making visibility difficult, you can watch the cox, coach and a handful of Old Blues in a launch turn Oxford-blue before the warmth of an Ely boathouse is reached. Training for the Boat Race is a spartan business, a seasonal challenge that follows a recognised pattern. The sight of an eight cleaving the water with oars hissing always seems in harmony with the surroundings whatever the temperature.

It is interesting to recall how the Cambridge "blue" originated. When the race was inaugurated in 1829 there were several outward differences. The Oxford uniform had been chosen by Wordsworth and Garnier. The crew appeared in black straw hats, dark-blue striped jerseys, blue handkerchiefs and canvas trousers, which were the colours of Christ Church. Cambridge wore pink sashes as a compliment to their Johnian captain. Seven years later Cambridge dressed in white. Legend declares that just before the start of the race, R. N. Phillips of Christ's rushed to a shop and bought a piece of Eton blue ribbon, which was fastened to the bows. The historicity of this incident may be suspect, but at least it makes a charming preface.

The first Boat Race was the result of a challenge issued by a Mr Stanniforth of Christ Church, Oxford, to a Mr Snow of St John's, Cambridge, and took place on the 10th June, 1829, on the Henley reaches and was watched by a crowd estimated at 20,000. The race over a course of two miles was won by Oxford in a time of fourteen minutes. From then on there was never a shortage of incident. In 1843 an exciting race went in favour of Oxford who were reduced to seven men. It is commemorated in practical fashion: the chair used by the President in the O.U.B.C. rooms at Oxford was made from a section of this boat. That same year the picturesque College "barges" appeared at Oxford. In 1845 the race moved to Putney. The following year outriggers were used for the first time. The year 1849 was noteworthy for two unusual incidents: Oxford and Cambridge crews met twice on Putney waters; and the race was awarded on a foul. 1852 produced the famous "Chitty" crew, the equivalent in perfection to "Cobden's over" of 1870. The 1857 race hit the headlines. Oxford, using the new Matt Taylor boat, rowed the course in 19 minutes, 50 seconds, which remained the record until 1873, when the first sliding seat was introduced. 1863 made different news. A long-running dispute with owners of steamers that followed behind had almost ruined the race. This time fourteen paddle-steamers left Mortlake. They refused to get behind the umpire. In protest, the crews refused to start.

Other exciting occasions include the unfortunate year when the Cambridge boat sank off the White Hart; the much-debated dead-heat of 1877 when "Honest John" Phelps' ruling was the subject of controversial argument; the 1880 race which had to be postponed due to thick fog; and the 1883 race which was rowed in a snowstorm. The most exciting moment of the 1886 race came when the coxswains steered under the arch of a temporary structure at Hammersmith Bridge, the bows of both boats clearing the obstacle by a narrow margin of inches. In 1903 Cambridge had a flying start – about a third of a length – through the starter's pistol sticking at half-cock for several seconds. Considerable comment was caused by the style introduced by D. C. R. Stuart, the Cambridge stroke, in 1906. Aeroplanes followed the race for the first time in 1911 when the Prince of Wales and Prince Albert watched from an Oxford launch. The following year both boats sank. Oxford managed to get theirs to the shore, refloated it, and completed the course, but the race was ordered to be re-rowed. In 1934 the Cambridge boat produced the record time of 18 minutes, 3 seconds. A new all-time record was set-up in 1948 by the Light Blues in 17 minutes, 50 seconds, conditions being ideal for 18 minutes to be broken for the first time. There was an exceptionally close finish in 1949 with Cambridge winning in the last few yards.

In 1951 the Oxford crew proved they could swim as well as row. Before the start, E. H. Phelps, the former professional sculling champion, observed that the conditions were as bad as any he had seen for twenty years. Terrific gusts of wind had demolished three chimney stacks in Chiswick. Experts predicted that the flood tide would not be so

Opposite: The Light Blues crew that covered the Boat Race course in 17 minutes, 50 seconds, and won by four lengths. It was the first time the 18-minute barrier had been broken

strong as previous years through so much water flowing down from the upper reaches. Oxford won the toss and chose the Surrey side. It gave little advantage. With the wind head-on, neither crew could gain any shelter. Only when they reached the inside of the long Surrey bend after Hammersmith would the choice show a dividend. The umpire, Dr Ellison, then Bishop of Willesden, set the stake-boats in mid-stream, but conditions deteriorated so much that the odds were against the crews escaping disaster. The Dark Blues shipped water so rapidly that their rate of striking laboured as the boat sank lower. The rate of striking had been slow from the start: Cambridge at thirty-four; Oxford at thirty-two. Cambridge gained an immediate lead. They reached the London Rowing Club almost two lengths up. Oxford, meanwhile, had their riggers awash. The precaution they had taken of having wash-boards down the length of the boat was not as satisfactory as the Cambridge device of a double-width of their protection to stop waves splashing over the riggers. Before Beverley Brook was reached Oxford had foundered. Nine men sat until the water reached their waists before giving in. Cambridge by then were five lengths ahead, having crossed over to the Surrey shore. The umpire's launch accelerated and the Light Blues were recalled. The race was declared void. The Port of London agreed that the race should be re-rowed on the Bank Holiday afternoon. Conditions were better, although the flood water was heavy. In the first minute Cambridge were 9, 19 and 37½, Oxford 9, 18, 37. From that point the race turned into a procession. Oxford were outclassed.

Every race takes its place in this long line of tradition. To highlight one in particular, my choice would be 1949. Oxford had Christopher Davidge, who had stroked Eton to win the Ladies Plate at Henley the year before. Throughout training Oxford appeared a very fine proposition, whilst Cambridge were distinctly poor. A couple of weeks prior to the race, Oxford had a food poisoning scare and took time to regain their form. Credit for this was largely due to their coach, H. H. A. Edwards, the last man to win three finals at Henley in one day. His personality was ideal for the strain of the days before the race. Meanwhile, Cambridge, who had seemed so backward, suddenly struck their peak and they, too, were superbly coached by H. N. Rickett, one of the finest coaches of his day.

Oxford won the toss and went into the lead. Cambridge began to come up in the Chiswick Reach, where they attacked with spirit. If Oxford reached Barnes Bridge in the lead, victory was almost assured. Any crew who has the wrong station at this point rarely catches up. The climax of the race was the final row-in from Barnes. David Jennens, the Cambridge stroke, had shown no signs of racing genius in training, but now held his crew together magnificently with two Olympic oars, Paul Massey and Paul Bircher, behind him giving stupendous support. With 100 left the crews were dead-level. It beame a question of whose oars were in the water as the boats crossed the line. When the moment came, the result was in doubt until the judge announced that Cambridge had won by six feet, the narrowest margin by which the race had ever been decided and the nearest to the dead-heat recorded in 1877. Cambridge had trailed behind for something like 600 strokes and was in front for only one, but that was the all-important one.

At times, pre-race publicity settles on the cox. In a way such attention is overdue for these little people are a race apart. Sitting motionless, like frozen martyrs, in an unprotected boat, lashed by rain, wind and the rough water of an English winter, they are neither full-blooded nor deep-chested, yet are expected to avoid chills and look as robust as the men who row twice a day. They are like cricket umpires. Laden with sweaters which are passed on to them, they can wear as many as they like whilst the others are sweating until, at the critical moment, these fellows want them all back and the cox is stripped nearly naked in a biting wind.

They are not chosen to steer just because they are small. Above all they are pilots. There is much to learn about the Thames between Putney and Mortlake: eddies, currents, shallows, bends and bridges come into the reckoning as do wind and tide. The best course takes a deceptive and astonishing pattern, whilst it can be fatal to cut a corner. On race-day the cox has to get his crew into position, as tricky a manoeuvre as coaxing a truculent horse into a starting-stall, whilst approaching the stake-boat with a strong tide running is like reversing a lorry into a difficult gateway when both are swinging. The one-hundred-and-third Boat Race was a classic example of how important the cox can be. Before the race Said, the Oxford man, was regarded as the better pilot, yet, in the race, he never had a chance. Hilton steered for Cambridge a course that remains an inspiration for all coxes. He used every legitimate advantage to embarrass Oxford. It was tactics at their best.

Tradition was broken in 1981. Oxford decided that the best coxswain was the diminutive 22-year-old Susan Brown. Only seven stone in weight, she became the first woman to steer a man's Boat Race. Her presence in the stern was merited. She earned the trip through experience gained by steering on the Tideway with Britain's women team and going to the Moscow Games with the women's four. The race was a Dark Blue monopoly. Everything went in their favour. A stronger crew aided by Dan Topolski's brilliant coaching overpowered Cambridge by the most decisive margin of the century. The performance did not live in Cambridge memories. Neither did 1984 when the Cambridge cox discovered a fresh hazard before the race started. He rammed the Light Blue boat into a barge and the spare boat had to be used. A reminder of that unfortunate mistake can be seen on the wall of the Cambridge Blue pub in Gwydir Street. The remains of the boat, signed by the crew, hangs on the wall with a postscript written by the cox – "all my own work". Two years later, Cambridge again triumphed after a run of defeats. In the Boat Race, predictions can be unreliable. It is safer to close with the comment of a Cambridge coach at the end of last century. Lost for words of criticism about his crew after a ragged Cam outing, he leant towards them and said as confidentially as a magaphone would allow, "Well, if you *must* row like that, then at least make it look dignified," advice that never dates, be it lost courses or causes.

There are variations in Cambridge river sport. Every February, June and July the "Bumps" take place. To the uninitiated the exercise seems pointless. The University Bumps – Lents in February and Mays in June – attract an entry of over 150 college crews. They start one behind the other with 15 to a race and a one-and-a-half-length gap between each. The first crew is the Head of the River. The object is for a boat to bump the one in front, the successful boat moving up in the starting-order in the next race. The course is between Post Reach, below Baits Bite Lock, and finishes at Long Reach, near Fen Ditton. The tow-path looks the ideal spectator viewpoint, but not for the inexperienced. They can literally be swept away by the wave of followers on bicycles shouting encouragement to the crews. Pedestrians are ignored. It is safer to retire to the garden of the Plough Inn at Fen Ditton for a grandstand view. The same applies to the Town Bumps in July when town boat clubs compete with equal vigour and expertise.

Golfers in Cambridge have a somewhat limited choice. The Fens have no natural golfing country with Nature as the architect like Sandwich where there is solitude without loneliness. There are no terrors of the likes of Hoylake or Birkdale, or championship examinations like Turnberry and St Andrews. Instead we have a light-hearted test of golf at the friendliest of courses at Gog Magog and a comparatively new lay-out that is establishing itself at Bar Hill, but close at hand is the best nine-hole course in the country at Royal Worlington and Newmarket. In some respects it is contradictory – a first-class sea-side links inland with every hole on light sandy soil. It was as long ago as 1895 that Queen Victoria pronounced it "Royal". King George VI was its Patron and the Duke of Gloucester its President. Future champions from the Universities have enjoyed its holes, particularly the short fifth, that ranks among the finest short holes in the game. The social side of the Club is heartwarming. The miniature pink jug on the Club tie against a dark blue background is inspired by their champagne cocktails.

Those who enjoy chasing an inflated piece of leather are well catered for in Cambridge. Association football is alleged to have been introduced by Cambridge University in the middle of the nineteenth century. Devotees of rugby must look to the Close of Rugby School where is enshrined the beginning of the code in 1823, when one, William Webb Ellis, in his teens, caught the ball in his arms and instead of running back as far as he liked without parting with it, as the rules of the day permitted, headed for his opponent's goal with the ball still in his arms – a revolutionary seed that bore fruit. It matters not. Both codes attract a distinctive following. I find a rugby crowd more self-controlled, due maybe to the complicated nature of the game that requires keener powers of observation than Association football. Grange Road is a rugby ground without the spaciousness of the London clubs. No spectator is very far from the players. The playing area is invariably in good condition with springy turf. The place is friendly and hospitable, a delight to visit. It is the testing-ground for the University Match at Twickenham and often brings recognition for international honours. To many enthusiasts the University Match is the game of the season. The football is not always of the highest class, but always desperately keen. Players rise to heights which they have never previously approached, which is one reason why form can be misleading and wise selectors do not allow themselves to be unduly influenced.

Every 'Varsity Match has its quota of excitement and incident with reputations made and lost. I have seen and suffered many, but among them I recall one, not because of the result which went in favour of Oxford, but for the rugged determination shown by the losers. It was a December afternoon in 1937, cold and raw with murky fog swirling thinly around the grandstands. The players were presented to the King. The

Below: The Grange Road rugby ground is the testing-ground for the University Match at Twickenham and later international honours

Light Blue shirts looked startlingly light in the murk, likewise Cyril Gadney's red shirt as referee. On paper Cambridge should have won decisively. Instead Oxford scored five times and restricted Cambridge to a dropped goal, a magnificent effort by Bruce-Lockhart from twenty yards out. Other details have faded, but it was a match of magnificent tackling and missed opportunities. For Oxford Renwick, Freakes, Mayhew, Cook and Obolensky were inspired, particularly Mayhew who, like Cooke, scored two tries. Cambridge would have won had they wheeled and shoved. Occasionally Bruce-Lockhart showed glimpses of his skill but found the Oxford defence superb. What I do remember was the magnificent tackling by the Light Blue forwards. Newton-Thompson, Parry, Young and Chadwick were outstanding. The result was a shock, but like many University clashes, it was a remarkable match. W. O. Chadwick went on to achieve academic distinction, crowned with the ultimate honour of the Order of Merit, but he never lost his keenness for the game and continued, after playing days were over, as a referee, that most difficult role only noticed when mistakes are made. The technique is not easy. It can be acquired by practice and experience, involves a deep knowledge of the rules and their application, physical fitness to enable the play to be followed or anticipated, speed of eye and fleetness of foot. Chadwick also had an extra sense that differentiated between the trivial and the important. He knew when a loose scrum was about to become dangerous; when a technical fault could be ignored or should be dealt with firmly. It sounds simple, but does not often happen. Too frequently there is whistling for every possible offence and innumerable penalty kicks to impress by imposed authority. Chadwick was fair and impartial. Like all Old Blues, and men whose student days are but a distant memory, he must look back to the Grange Road days with affection.

In the same way cricketers look to Fenner's. The opening of a new season is always full of promise. Early days are exciting. Form is uncertain with new names, new faces. Freshmen are unknown quantities, but potential talent is encouraged. It has always been a nursery for recruits to county and often England status. Success at Fenner's can be a passport to Test recognition, a short cut denied those who graduate by the usual route.

Fenner's has continuity of purpose and tradition. As a cricket ground it transcends the bounds of cricket ties. The parochial dourness of Trent Bridge or Old Trafford is absent. Last century it was claimed that a stump could be put on any part of the ground, twenty-two yards measured, and a first-class pitch would result. That boast can still be made. From the pavilion it looks vast, the impression being helped by the method of grass-cutting in wide longitudinal stripes, the nap leaving wide bands of light and darker green in striking pattern.

Theoretically, the morning of the opening day should have dew on the grass and trees delicate green in the sun. Everything should be nostalgic. Reality is usually harsher. A few years ago the cold was so intense the players had to seek refuge in the pavilion. There can be rain, incessant rain, and biting winds that leave cricketers huddled together indoors like coveys of disgruntled rooks. Leaden skies make a mockery of the game, but layers of sweaters launch just as effectively another University season. From the comparative comfort and shelter of the pavilion there is opportunity to recall outstanding players moulded by this tradition. One thing is clear. There is little in Fenner's to encourage bowlers. Only rarely is there life in the pitch, a hint of greenness to assist the new-ball bowler for a couple of hours in the morning. Even after rain there is not much help. The ball turns so slowly that batsmen have plenty of time to vary their strokes. Some earlier matches prove the point. In the West Indies match of 1950, three days' play saw seven wickets fall for a total of 1,324 runs. John Dewes and David Sheppard shared an opening partnership of 343, the University eventually declaring at 594 for 4. The West Indies retaliated by dominating the rest of the game with 730 for 3.

In 1901 the South Africans found the pitch to their liking to the tune of 692 runs.

Some thirty years later Tom Killick and W. H. Harbison scored 331 for the second wicket against Glamorgan. In the same match Harbison had 130 in the first innings and became the first batsman to score two centuries in a match for Cambridge. N. F. Druce almost had the same distinction: he made 199 not out, and later missed the double century by the same margin. It would be wrong, however, to suggest that Cambridge batsmen only excel at Fenner's. In 1890, under the captaincy of S. M. J. Woods, the University made 703 for 9 against Sussex at Brighton with three centuries by Cambridge men – F. G. J. Ford 191, C. McGregor 131, and C. P. Foley 117. Sussex that year was captained by C. Aubrey Smith. Again at Brighton in 1919, John Morrison and his men scored 611 at the expense of the Sussex bowlers, whilst at the Oval in 1930, Surrey scored 565. Cambridge replied with 572, Freddie Brown making 150 and J. T. Morgan 110.

Taking stock of the talent at Fenner's is interesting. In 1948 Hubert Doggart had in the Cambridge side such men as Trevor Bailey, Douglas Insole and John Dewes. Their appeal, along with Oxford men like C. B. van Ryneveld, H. A. Pawson and P. A. Whitcombe, drew a crowd of some 10,000 to watch the Light Blues win by an innings and eight runs at Lords. In 1949 Doggart included John Warr, who loved cricket and expected some fun in return. He was a born showman. As a bowler, he had a beautifully high and easy action. In 1950 Doggart awarded Blues to Peter May and David Sheppard. The years passed and in the eighties, Hubert Doggart returned to Fenner's to watch his son, Simon, bowling off-breaks to great effect. Peter May continued the promise he showed at Cambridge. He is remembered for many flowing, well-timed, elegant innings. He had that rare ability to make a devastating delivery appear inconsequential. He captained England for a record forty-one Tests before his early retirement at thirty-three, but in that comparatively short space of time he scored 4,537 runs with thirteen centuries. His peak was in 1951 when, appearing both for Cambridge and Surrey, he scored 2,339 runs with an average of 68.79. Surrey could do with another such talented undergraduate. Whilst with that county, the Championship was won seven years in succession, and eight times in nine years. From 1953 until he went to Australia, Peter May never finished on the losing side in a Test series.

Another Cambridge man who bears comparison with May was F. S. Jackson, the second son of the first Lord Allerton, and one of the greatest all-rounders to come from Fenner's. He was awarded his Blue on the strength of his bowling which was brisk medium with a difficult out-swerve varied by a cunningly concealed break-back. As Cambridge captain he invited Ranjitsinhji to play against Oxford and was himself invited to play for England while still a student, scoring 91 in his first Test innings against Australia. Jackson went on to captain England in the 1905 Test series at home. England were undefeated. He beat the Australian captain, Darling, all five times with the toss and topped the batting and bowling averages.

Fenner's came to know two of India's greatest batsmen, K. S. Ranjitsinhji and his nephew, K. S. Duleepsinhji. When Ranji first arrived at Trinity, he could not make the College Eleven so he joined the Cassandra Club, who played their matches on Parker's Piece, an expanse of public land in the centre of Cambridge where anyone and everyone plays cricket. Before Fenner's was opened in 1846, University fixtures were played there. Few of those who play on Parker's Piece today – and on summer evenings there can be as many as half-a-dozen games in progress – realise that on this turf Ranji practised his classic strokes, Jack Hobbs learnt the game, and David Sheppard used to coach the town lads. It was during this period at Cambridge that Ranji wrote his classic book on the game. Duleepsinhji's cricketing career was regrettably short. In 1925 he was awarded his Blue, and eight years later he had retired through ill-health, but in that short time he dazzled with rare displays of batting fluency. His Cambridge period was marked by a brilliant century against Yorkshire, followed by 254 not out against Middlesex.

The new pavilion at Fenner's, the official home of the Cambridge University Cricket Club; a nursery for county and England cricket. Veterans still talk of the match when John Dewes and David Sheppard shared an opening University partnership of 343, the innings being declared at 594 for 4 wickets. The West Indies replied with 730 for 3. Somewhat different to the opening match of the 1987 season when Essex bowling captured 7 University wickets for 20 runs!

Of the older players who graced Fenner's there was S. M. J. Woods, the fastest amateur bowler of his time, and Gregor McGregor, the wicket-keeper, who stood up to his sizzling deliveries as if they were mild spinners. Gilbert Jessop was a Freshman in 1896 when Frank Mitchell was captain. Even in those days the "Croucher" had the reputation of being a slogger. He went on to score fifty-three centuries in first-class cricket. Other Blues included the Hon. Ivo Bligh, later Earl of Dudley, who was Cambridge captain in 1881, and later played in nineteen Tests for England, becoming President of the M.C.C. in 1900; the Hon. Alfred Lyttelton, captain in 1879, who played in four England Tests and became M.C.C. President in 1898; Lord Hawke and A. G. Steel, both Test players and former Presidents; and outstanding men like "Gubby" Allen, A. P. F. Chapman, A. E. R. Gilligan, F. G. Mann, R. H. V. Robins and Norman Yardley.

Among more recent brilliant players were men like Trevor Bailey, who was dour even as a student. He always looked cool and calm. When beaten by a bowler who threw up his arms invoking the heavens because of his wretched luck, Bailey would be unimpressed, never look round to see if the bails were still on, and acted as if he had scored several boundries. No Fenner's roster could be complete without Mike Brearley, a First Class Honours man, whose Test record was equally noteworthy, former Cambridge captains like Phil Edmonds and Derek Pringle who have made their mark in Test history' or Robin Marlar and Tony Lewis as fluent with bat and ball as they are now with words. One man whose name is engraved in Fenner's history is Cyril Coote, the master-groundsman, now retired after many years tending the immaculate grounds and its youthful players.

One of the most brilliant cricketers from Cambridge was Ted Dexter. He was something of a temperamental enigma. His problem was having the potential to shine at so many things. As a cricketer he was a joy to watch. His personal dilemma was summed-up by Neville Cardus: "Apparently Dexter is undecided at the age of 28 whether he is (a) a great batsman, (b) an unpredictable bowler, (c) a journalist, (d) a television star (in Australia), (e) a potential golfer, or (f) a future leader of the Tory Party . . . it is beyond me that Dexter, a young man with his talents as a great cricketer, should think for a moment of giving up any of his days or nights to Westminster and politics."

Years later Cardus might still have said that it was not clear how Dexter saw himself. It is sad that such rich promise has never fully developed except in cricket. Dexter led England in thirty of his sixty-two Tests. At times his style of captaincy invited criticism, but nothing dimmed his reputation as a batsman. Dexter was the most exciting discovery of the post-war era. After retiring he has developed the habit of backing into the limelight like a peripatetic one-man cricket delegation. At times, aspects of the current cricket scene give him the bellyache. He is honest enough to feel it, to show it, and to express it. With such a temperament, it is inevitable. When an obstinate man with ability to match becomes dogmatic, he is bound to collect critics on the way, but the point is made.

As a young man, Dexter could be naive. I remember a conversation in a London hotel, when he asked if I could suggest a commercial outlet for his skills. When I asked if he had anything specific in mind, he replied that all he wanted was a job that would give him time to play cricket in summer and probably tour in winter. When I said that a would-be employer might not be over-joyed by the prospect, the reply was that the fellow would have the benefit of his name. Such is the optimism of youth. On another occasion at a dinner-party, I sat him next to Barbara Thorpe. True to form, Dexter rattled away to a seemingly impressed female. During a lull in the performance, she enquired what his subject was. On being told he was at Jesus College reading Modern Languages and specialising in Italian, Barbara, as Professor of Italian, remarked that she had never seen him at any of her lectures, but no doubt might expect him in the future. The subject was quickly shelved. Dexter now enlivens the television screen with authoritative comments during Test Matches. He is always good value and a reminder of how he might have fared had he pursued the early ambition to become a Member of Parliament.

Fenner's has its own appeal. No ground is quite like it. Many are larger, more pretentious and comfortable, but few can equal its quiet dignity. It is a storehouse of the past. Glance at the panels in the pavilion – there are the names of men who have represented the University for over a hundred years. You are literally surrounded by cricketing tradition. Fenner's is more than a cricket ground: it is a meaningful institution. As the years go by and fresh generations of undergraduates tread its turf, they too will come under the spell that lasts a lifetime.

A UNIQUE ROYAL MEMORIAL

Within easy reach of Cambridge is Bury St Edmunds where in the Lady Chapel of St Mary's Church is the only memorial erected by a Queen of England to a Queen of France. In 1881, Queen Victoria presented the window which depicts scenes from the life of Mary Tudor, Queen of France, who is buried in the north corner of the sanctuary. Mary was the younger daughter of Henry VII and sister of Henry VIII. As a small child, she was betrothed to Prince Charles of Castile, who was her junior by five years. Through the illness of her father, the marriage was postponed. Henry VII died in 1509. In the meantime Mary had become attracted by Charles Brandon, whose father had been standard-bearer to Henry VII at the Battle of Bosworth and was often at Court in attendance upon Henry VIII. Through the influence of Henry VIII, the engagement with Prince Charles was broken and the Princess was ordered to marry Louis XII, the decrepit King of France. The marriage was celebrated on the 9th October. On the 5th November she was crowned Queen of France in the Cathedral of St Denis. Three months later the King died. Charles Brandon was sent to escort the Queen home, but secretly married her in France. The anger of Henry was only appeased by the payment of a dowry of £200,000, together with her jewellery and plate, plus a further sum of £24,000. Cardinal Wolsey acted as mediator. The King granted them his pardon, and the marriage was celebrated at Greenwich on the 13th May before the whole Court. For the remaining years of her life Mary lived with her husband at Westhope, Suffolk. Her eldest daughter, Frances, became Marchioness of Dorset and mother of the ill-fated Lady Jane Grey. Mary died on the 25th June, 1533. Her body was embalmed, and buried with great pomp in the Abbey of Bury on the 21st July.

On the Dissolution of the Abbey, the body was removed to St Mary's. The grave was opened in 1784. The leaden coffin, 6ft 2in long, was shaped like a body, with a representation of a face upon it and the inscription: "Mary Quene of Ffraunce 1533. Edmund H." The coffin was then opened and exposed. The hair was found to be nearly 2ft long. A lock can be seen in the Moyse's Hall Museum.

Near to Cambridge, in the Lady Chapel of St Mary's Church in Bury St Edmunds, is the only memorial erected by a Queen of England to a Queen of France

DOWNING COLLEGE

The founding of Downing College was marred by litigation. The founder, Sir George Downing, a wealthy landowner with estates at Gamlingay and Dunwich, was no stranger to dissent. In 1700 as a youth of fifteen, he married his cousin, Mary Forester, a girl of thirteen. On the wedding-day, he instructed his wife to stay at home, whilst he left for an extended continental tour. Two years later the girl was invited by Queen Anne to become a Maid of Honour at Court. Her acceptance was not popular with the absent husband: he refused to have anything to do with his wife when he eventually returned. An attempt to have the marriage annulled was rejected by the Bishops. In 1734 Lady Downing died. Sir George survived her by fifteen years. His will, dated more then thirty years earlier, left the estate to a collateral branch of the family. Three others were named as successive legatees if the previous one became extinct. Should all four branches fail, the properties were to be realised and the money used to form a college "to be named Downing Colledge". By 1764 all four cousins had died heirless. Thirty years of litigation in Chancery followed and it was not until 1800 that the charter was granted.

There were difficulties about the site. The town agreed that Pound Hill at Castle End, Parker's Piece, or Doll's Close near Maid's Causeway could be available. The trustees chose the last named, then changed their minds, preferring instead thirty acres of marshy meadowland by Regent Street, known as Sir Thomas' Leys, open country where, as Gurney records, "you generally got five or six shots at snipe".

The trustees were over-ambitious. They wanted a College that would outshine all other Colleges with a court on a par with the Great Court of Trinity. Financially, such grandiose dreams were out of the question, quite apart from the burden of maintaining so large an establishment. Plans were drawn up as early as 1784 by James Wyatt who, influenced by George III, avoided any suggestion of Gothic style. Further plans were submitted in 1804, but all were rejected. Designs were then requested from George Byfield, Lewis Wyatt and William Wilkins, a Fellow of Christ's. Those by Wilkins were approved and building began in a Neo-Grecian style with a Greek Doric Propylace. There were to be no enclosed courts. College buildings concentrated round a large lawn-area, a plan that anticipated the campus idea later adopted by the first campus university in Virginia. The overall effect was to be a large Keton stone-faced quadrangle, more spacious than Trinity with the south side 500 feet long. The Master's Lodge would be a striking example of the Ionic order, the College entrance Doric, both orders to persist through the whole quadrangle.

The worst happened. Work was stopped at the halfway stage because of lack of finance. Progress became slow. By degrees the plan was completed as money was provided with architects like Edward Barry in 1873, Sir Herbert Baker in 1929, and A. T. Scott greatly modifying the original concept. This mixture of architectural finger-prints has not been successful, some being irritating and fussy in design, though not detracting too much from the College's main appeal: the extensive grounds and lawns retain something of the original spacious restfulness that prevailed when the College was begun some 180 years ago.

Like all the Colleges, Downing can claim many distinguished personalities, like Lord Cranworth, twice Lord Chancellor, W. P. Schreiner, Premier of South Africa, Lord Collins, Master of the Rolls, and Professor Maitland, but none can equal Dr Frank Leavis, the problem figure of the University, equally disliked and praised, the centre of

Below: When the original plans for Downing College were being drawn up, George III advised against anything suggesting Gothic style. A plan submitted by William Wilkins, a Fellow of Christ's, won approval. There were to be no enclosed courts, and College buildings would be around a large lawn-area, anticipating the campus idea later adopted by the first campus university in Virginia

a controversy that continued for years in the common rooms. He split the English Faculty into two camps like civil war in the world of literary criticism. According to some academics, Leavis was anathema and a damned nuisance; to other members of the Faculty and generations of students, he could do no wrong. To them he was the leading critic of his age, the greatest since Matthew Arnold. Only on one point did both sides agree. Leavis would never run away from controversy, retreat was out of the question. This was highlighted in the famous attack on C. P. Snow that created the biggest upset in English literature since the eighteenth century.

In action Leavis was abrasive: his intellect had the cutting edge of a razor. He revelled in the glare of publicity, yet in private life the image was quite different – there was no hint of basking in the reflected aura of an international reputation. In appearance, Leavis never varied. He disliked ties and always wore an open-necked shirt. In warm weather a frayed pair of khaki shorts were resurrected. Sandals were preferred to shoes. Lean, sinewy, and suntanned in summer, he carried books and papers in a knapsack slung over his shoulder. His mode of transport was a creaking bicycle with suspect brakes. It was a familiar sight to see him making heavy weather of the slight incline in Trumpington Road, spurning the luxury of a three-speed gear, pedalling away, giving a helpful shove to one of his children who cycled slightly ahead. A favourite habit when he called at the Old Mill House was to sink into an armchair sideways so that his legs rested across the arm. Our youngsters were at the age when knees had to be scrubbed. It was difficult to insist on this when the knees of this eccentric don had avoided soap for some considerable time. He had another quirk that must have been a nuisance at home,

but even more tiresome for a host: he declined to eat anything after lunch with the result that whoever sat next to him at dinner became conscious of eating whilst he stared at an empty plate.

In many ways Frank Leavis was a typical product of East Anglican stock, somewhat puritanical in outlook and deficient in humour. His father was a tradesman in Cambridge who sold musical instruments in a shop near Parker's Piece. His grandfather had been a piano-tuner at Denver, his great-grandfather a basket-maker, whilst Uncle Frederick was landlord of the Six Bells off Mill Road. After the First World War, in which he served as a stretcher-bearer, he went to Emmanuel College on a scholarship and read History, but only scraped an indifferent Second in the first part of the Tripos. He switched to English under Richards, and finished with a First. His ambition was to be a teacher. Little did he think that years later he would make Downing College world-famous for its English studies.

The feud between Sir Charles Snow and Dr Leavis had been brewing for some time. If conversation lagged, it was only necessary to mention Snow's name to get things moving. In his eyes, Snow represented the superficial culture and introverted snobbery of High Table complacency. It came to a head when in his Rede Lecture entitled *The Two Cultures and the Scientific Revolution*, Snow attacked the universities and the educational system for not placing sufficient emphasis on the new scientific cultures. Leavis interpreted the comparison as a rejection of literary and historical traditions. The lecture received tremendous publicity and went through innumerable editions, building-up in the process Snow's reputation particularly in America where a college in the University of Buffalo had been named after him.

The counter-blast was planned with care. Leavis chose the Richmond Lecture, founded during the Second World War by Sir Herbert Richmond, Master of Downing, and delivered in the Hall of the College under the title *Two Cultures – the Significance of C. P. Snow*. No punches were pulled. The opening set the tone. . . . "If confidence in oneself as a master-mind, qualified by capacity, insight and knowledge to pronounce as authoritatively on the frightening problems of our civilisation, is genius, then there can be no doubt about Sir Charles Snow's." Leavis went on to attack the *Two Cultures'* theory. He referred to its utter lack of intellectual distinction and embarrassing vulgarity of style, calling it a document for the study of the cliche. Of Snow's authoritative tone on science and literature, he said that while only a genius could justify it, one couldn't imagine a genius adopting it, and Snow was not a genius. His superficial literary culture was something which people who loved literature could only regard with contempt. As a novelist Snow was without a glimpse of what creative literature was or why it mattered. There was no more significance in his completed books than there was drama or life. The thinking was representative of a shallow materialistic philosophy. The "literary intellectuals" were merely *New Statesmen* scribblers and Sunday newspaper reviewers. Snow was as intellectually negligible as it was possible to be. To call his argument a movement of thought was to flatter it. The comparisons between scientific and literary values were meaningless. Worst of all, Snow's insistence that material progress was the world's first priority was a pernicious untruth. There were higher values at stake.

When the smoke cleared, little of Sir Charles or his theories had survived the broadside. He was badly shaken, but decided not to reply. He believed that the adverse publicity that followed killed any chance of a Nobel Prize. He accepted the Downing undergraduates offer to deliver the following year's Richmond Lecture, but made no reference in it to Leavis.

A great deal has been written about Leavis's criticism, his dogmatism, his roughness in controversy and his puritanism, but it nevertheless established him as one of the greatest of literary critics, reinforced by the output of some twenty books. At times, though, it was a pity that dogmatism and an uncompromising style were over-emphasised – but that was Leavis and a leopard cannot change its spots.

His principal weapon was a periodical called *Scrutiny*, the most remarkable critical quarterly in the history of English letters. It began in 1931 when a group of research students founded it in Leavis's house. Contributors and staff were unpaid. In the thirties 750 copies were printed and its circulation at the end of its life in 1953 only totalled 1,500. Leavis was its principal editor throughout. Its influence was immense because he used it as a sounding-board for a wide range of cultural issues. He was never afraid of stepping out of line and making controversial statements, but on one occasion he ran into unexpected trouble. He wanted to quote from *Ulysses* in his lectures. As it was a banned book he wrote to the Home Office for permission to import a copy. Shortly afterwards he was summoned to see the Vice-Chancellor, who showed him a letter from the Public Prosecutor, saying that the Cambridge police had been monitoring his lectures. He concluded with the recommendation that Leavis should be suitably and firmly dealt with.

After he retired I asked Leavis whether he had many regrets when looking back on his academic career. There was only one discordant note: he was still bitter about the manipulations of some members of the Board, who, disliking his attitude to literature and criticism, had persistently blocked his programme in the English Faculty. On a personal basis he admitted disappointment that, after being nominated for the Chair of Poetry at Oxford, the election went in favour of Robert Graves. Had he been successful, the experience might have had a mellowing effect . . . on the other hand, it made no such impact on Graves.

Dr Frank Leavis of Downing became the problem figure of the University. He was the focal-point of a controversy that continued for years in the common rooms and split the English Faculty into two camps, like civil war in the world of literary criticism

THE SCOTT POLAR RESEARCH INSTITUTE

The Scott Polar Research Institute in Lensfield Road is packed with interest. Over the main entrance is a bust of Scott, modelled by his widow, Lady Kennet. Along the roof balustrade is the inscription *Quaesivit arcana Poli videt dei* – "He sought the secrets of the Pole: he found the hidden face of God". On the left of the entrance, as a memorial to Scott's polar party, is another statue by the same sculptor of a boy with arms outstretched, titled *Aspiration.* "The front of the building is composed of two large arches suggesting the two poles. Small balls lie behind the arches vaulted with domes of the same arc as the polar regions of the globe" – such was the description of the architect, Sir Herbert Barker. Inside, coloured diagrammatic maps of the two polar regions are encircled by the names of their explorers. Below the domes, stars are set in the marble floor in the polar constellation, the Southern Cross for the Antarctic, the Great Bear for the Arctic.

The Institute was founded as a memorial to Captain Robert Falcon Scott and his companions who perished on their return from the South Pole in March, 1912. The emotional reaction of that tragic journey and Scott's last letter led to the Lord Mayor of London opening an appeal fund at the Mansion House. The response was so overwhelming that, after the needs of the surviving dependents had been met, a substantial balance remained. Frank Debenham, a member of Scott's last expedition, and the first Professor of Geography at Cambridge, proposed that an Institute of Polar Research should be founded in Cambridge to encourage polar exploration and research, and act as a centre where polar explorers could meet, exchange views, and plan future research projects. His ambition was realised. In November, 1934, the Institute was officially opened by Mr Baldwin, the Prime Minister and Chancellor of the University.

The relics are part of history. The diaries of Scott and Wilson record the day's work in firm, legible handwriting, a glimpse of a life completely cut off from the rest of the world. Equally revealing are the diaries of Lady Franklin, Sir John Franklin's second wife. We see the sleeping-bag of Titus Oates, with one leg cut where he was frostbitten, and a statue of Fridtzof Nansen, the Norwegian explorer and statesman, who in 1893 sailed for the Arctic with Johansen in the *Fram* and reached 86°14′N on foot. There are examples of the art and cultures of the Eskimos and Lapps: their domestic equipment and clothing; methods of hunting and travel – an Eskimo kayak, hunting equipment, a cross-section of the sledges and different types of transport used by expeditions. Watercolour sketches made by Wilson during Scott's two Antarctic Expeditions and a signed photograph of the Queen which Vivian Fuchs took with him on the South Pole Expedition are also on show.

The Institute is Frank Debenham's dream come true. He was a remarkable man. During his years at Cambridge, Debenham became something of a folk legend, a role that appealed to his Australian temperament. During term he would often hold court in an upstairs café in Regent Street that produced excellent coffee and crisp rolls. Occasionally Edward Welbourne, the Master of Emmanuel, would join the table and invariably act as Devil's Advocate in any discussion – being bloody-minded was second nature. The only one to take the bait was usually Gordon Manley, President of the Royal Meteorological Society and an expert on polar climatology.

Above: By the entrance to the Scott Polar Research Institute is a statue of a boy with arms outstretched, titled Aspiration. *The sculptor was Lady Kennet, the widow of Captain Robert Falcon Scott.*

One of Welbourne's snide remarks was that Debenham only joined Scott by the back-door. In a way there was a grain of truth about it. When Scott and Dr Wilson visited Sydney on their way south for the journey to the Pole, Debenham was a sociologist at Sydney University working on the results of the Shackleton Expedition. Scott, anxious to involve Australia in the project and at the same time strengthen the scientific side, invited Debenham to join the team. It was an astute move. No man could have brought more enthusiasm to their group. The recollection of those days never left Debenham, and the sense of challenge was kept fresh. He used to say that stay-at-homes could never visualise the hazards or the fact that Antarctica is a continent larger than Europe with an area of some 5,450,000 square miles, or sixty times the size of Britain. On that score the Fuchs Expedition was a source of irritation: he felt the coverage by the media over-dramatised the situation when questions were raised whether the journey back could be made within the safety time-scale. Sir Leslie Martin, the architect, asked over dinner if such fears were justified and how its situation compared with Scott's plight. Debenham pointed out that such a comparison was difficult because conditions were so different. He felt that Fuchs' expedition was featherbedded. It only had to take equipment and provisions for the journey to the Pole. There it found shelter at an American research station. At its disposal it had mechanical snowcats, tracked vehicles, radio links, even plane-surveillance. As regards the return journey, once the polar plateau and the formidable Beardsmore Glacier had been conquered, everything should have been plain sailing. His outline of the route was so detailed it felt like plotting a journey from Liverpool along the M6, coping with Spaghetti Junction, then the M1 and home.

The Scott Expedition had set off on the 2nd November, 1911 on a round journey of more than 1,700 miles without radio-links and largely without maps. Beyond the Beardsmore Glacier, supply caches had to be established en route. The men were on foot because the dog parties had been sent back. Then came the terrible disappointment: they reached the Pole on the 17th January, 1912 to find the Norwegian flag had been planted a month earlier. They retraced their steps in worsening weather. They had to reduce rations and suffered appallingly in blizzards that never lessened. There was the accident to Evans that led to his death through the injuries, the gangrene and frostbite that caused Oakes to leave his tent during a blizzard to certain death, and the weakness that sapped the strength of Scott, Wilson and Bowers when only eleven miles from the One Ton Camp. The storm that never abated for ten days led the three men to perish.

To Frank Debenham that saga was engraved in letters of gold. On many scores he felt that Fuchs' expedition fell short of what Scott's men achieved. More to his liking would have been the feat of three young men in 1985 who trekked with primitive equipment 883 miles to the South Pole in the footsteps of the Scott journey: Robert Swan, Roger Mear and Gareth Wood are cast in the same mould of men whose deeds are preserved in the Polar Institute.

CONNOISSEUR'S CHOICE

The Fitzwilliam Museum is impressive – everything about it is on a grand scale. The Corinthian frontage sets the tone. The gates of iron and bronze and the massive bronze doors reflect the influence of succeeding directors, beginning with Sidney Colvin in 1876 and continuing with names like M. R. James, Louis Clark, David Piper and Michael Jaffe, but none, so far, have left their mark so thoroughly as S. C. Cockerell, who between 1908 and 1937 revitalised the Museum and its collections. His own assessment was typical – "I found it a pig stye. I turned it into a palace."

Below: *The Fitzwilliam, which houses the University collections of art and antiquities, is one of the oldest public museums in the country, founded in 1816 by Richard, seventh Viscount Fitzwilliam of Merrion, and designed by George Basevi in 1834. The foundation was laid in 1837 and the Museum opened in 1848*

The Museum is named after Viscount Fitzwilliam, who bequeathed to the University his collection of paintings and £100,000 to build a fitting museum to house them. A competition for the design was won by George Basevi in 1834, the foundation being laid in 1837. The Museum opened in 1848. Work continued under the supervising eye of C. R. Cockerall, Basevi being killed in 1845 through falling from scaffolding on Ely Cathedral. Shortage of funds caused delays, but finally it was completed in 1875.

The Fitzwilliam contains one of the finest collections of art in this country, but the size and variety of its treasures cannot be appreciated by a visitor with limited time. Unless selective in viewing, blurred frustration becomes boredom through walking at random from gallery to gallery. To avoid such an anti-climax I have short-listed exhibits that command attention. The Armour Room has a superb collection of armour and weapons covering a period from the thirteenth to early nineteenth century, with some swords dating from 1250. Of the helmets, the Milanese cold-chiselled Parade Helmer is a perfect example of the work of those sixteenth century armourer-artist brothers, the Negroli of Milan. This richly-embossed specimen of parade armour is damascened with gold. The visor is a lion mask. Any visitor who is susceptible to the atmosphere of history will be interested by the exhibit in the centre of the room. It is the Hearse Cloth of Henry VII, which was used at Masses read on the anniversary of the King's Death.

Equally evocative are the likenesses of historical figures in the large collection of portrait miniatures, in particular the earliest miniature in the Fitzwilliam of Henry VIII by Lucas Horenbout of Ghent, who worked at the English Court between 1525–40. The decorated borders incorporate the initials of Henry and Katharine of Aragon. Just as important is the detailed miniature of Queen Elizabeth by Nicholas Hilliard.

The connoisseur of rare illuminated manuscripts is spoilt for choice. The range includes the Hours of Isabella of France, *c.* 1270; the Metz Pontifical of 1302–6; the Peterborough Psalter, *c.* 1220; the Grey-Fitzpayen Hours, *c.* 1300; several leaves from a Psalter, *c.* 1240, illuminated and signed by the author "*W de Brazil me feit*" ("W de Brazil made me"); an early fourteenth century leaf from a Florentine choir-book by Pacino di Bonaguida. But for specialist taste, there is the Fitzwilliam Virginal Book, the most important folio in the music manuscripts. It is the finest collection in existence of six-

teenth and seventeenth century keyboard music with some thirty outstanding composers from some 300 works, faithfully copied out by Francis Tregian the younger, who died in the Fleet Prison after being found guilty as a recusant in 1608.

The Egyptian Section has much to offer including the huge granite lid of the sarcophagus of Rameses III, *c.* 1200. The cartonnage of Nekhtefmut's from the mortuary temple of Rameses II at Thebes has an inscription giving Nekhtefmut's titles as "beloved divine father, opener of the two doors of heaven of the Temple of Amun at Karnak". When the excavators split open the back of the cartonnage and the mummy was removed and unwrapped, amulets, scarabs and a posy were found on the body, which can be seen in the Museum. On show also are fragments of an eighteenth Dynasty papyrus of the *Book of the Dead*. There are many items from Tel-el-Armarna, including the mouth and chin from a huge sandstone figure of Ikhnaton, who abolished the old gods and substituted the worship of the life-giving sun in an attempt to break the domination of a rigid priesthood. Also in the Museum is the cast of the limestone bust of Nefertiti, the aristocratic consort of this idealistic Pharaoh. The terracotta model of Handel by Roubiliac is marked by an unusual informality. He is shown in a loose gown and nightcap with one of his slippers fallen off, leaning on copies of his work and playing a lyre as a cherub takes down his music. There are two sheets of a manuscript of John Keats' most famous poem, *Ode to a Nightingale*, written fluently with few alterations in the garden of Charles Brown's house in Hampstead in May 1819. This draft is entitled "Ode to *the* Nightingale", a slight variation to the published version. Also there is a lock of the poet's hair cut on his deathbed in Rome. Among other literary manuscripts is Blake's *An Island in the Moon*, Tennyson's *A Voice Spake out of the Skies*, and Rupert Brooke's *Grantchester*.

On show is the only recorded portrait of Erasmus by Quentin Metsys in cast bell metal, an exquisite example of this important artist's work. Equally outstanding is the miniature gold enamelled sculpture of *The Annunciation*, said to have been made in Paris for the Burgundian court and with a date *c.* 1400. Totally different is the figure in terracotta of a smiling girl, one of the few remaining examples of korai left unbroken when the Persian armies sacked Athens in 480 B.C. and destroyed the temples on the Acropolis. One of the finest pieces is a remarkable Maiolica dish from Tuscany, *c.* 1510. The decoration is quite spectacular. The Greek and Roman Rooms have collections dating from the prehistoric period to Roman times. I single out a diminutive ivory figure of a woman, alleged to have come from the Temple of Artemis at Ephesus, *c.* 700–650 B.C. Meissen figures produce a fine series, likewise Chelsea figures that include many rarities. The entire collection includes examples of fourteenth to sixteenth century Italian pottery; Islamic pottery of the ninth to nineteenth century; Turkish pottery from Isnik of the sixteenth to seventeenth century; Chinese pottery and porcelain of the Warring States period, 481–221 B.C., to the end of the eighteenth century; Korean porcelain and stoneware of the Silla Dynasty, A.D. 57–918, to the eighteenth century; Japanese pottery and porcelain of the sixteenth to nineteenth century; a collection of Chinese bronzes extending from the Shang-Yin period of 1766–1122 B.C. to the T'ang Dynasty, A.D. 618–906; and Chinese jades of the Chou Dynasty, 1122–249 B.C., to the nineteenth century.

Of the paintings, the sheer volume of masterpieces is overwhelming. Among the contemporary paintings in the English School are several by Augustus John, among them being *Thomas Hardy*, *George Bernard Shaw* and *Sir William Nicholson*, whilst *David and Dorelia in Normandy* at Dielette, near Cherbourg, depicts John's second wife, and son by his first marriage. There is also William Nicholson's famous study of *Girl with a tattered glove*; the romanticism of W. R. Sickert in the Old Bedford Music Hall; the English impressionist, Wilson Steer; the *Self-Portrait* by Stanley Spencer; and *November Moon* painted by Paul Nash in a friend's garden on Boar's Hill, near Oxford, and said to have been inspired by J. G. Frazer's *The Golden Bough*. The Pre-Raphaelites are represented by D. G. Rossetti, J. E. Millais, Ford Madox Brown, Arthur Hughes and William Holman Hunt. The last-named portrait of his eldest son is an outstanding example of Pre-Raphaelite studies. William Blake, who revived the lost tradition of medieval mystics and drew empassioned designs from the pools of his mind, is well represented. The vigour of David Cox and John Sell Cotman can be seen, likewise the long horizontal compositions of Peter de Wint. John Constable has three choice pictures, *Salisbury, Parham's Mill* and *Hampstead Heath*. J. W. N. Turner's oil *The Trossachs* is exhibited. Thomas Gainsborough's sensitive awareness of landscape combined with portraiture is seen in *Heneage Lloyd and his Sisters*. Also there are George Romney's choice study of *The Portrait of a Young Man*, Henry Raeburn's portrait of *W. Glendouwyn*, and David Wilkie's study of the Edinburgh beggar, *John Cowper*. Sir Joshua Reynolds, the first President of the Royal Academy, has four fine paintings: *The Braddyll Family, Henry Vansittart, Mrs Angelo*, and the unfinished *Edmund Burke and the Marquess of Rockingham*.

Works that should be seen are William Hogarth's conversation piece, the *Musical Party*; Van Dyck's portrait of *Archbishop Laud*; Peter Lely's *Portrait of a Lady*; *The Road to Calvary* by Antonio and Diego Sanchez; the comparison of treatment of the *Village Fete* in the Flemish Room by Brueghel the younger and Jan Steen; Rembrandt's *Self-portrait*; Hobbema's *Wooded Landscape*; *Portrait of a Man* by Hals; and *The Virgin and Child with St Anne* and *the infant St John the Baptist* by Rubens. Italian paintings include *Tarquin and Lucretia* and *Cupid with a Man playing a Lute* by Titian; Tintoretto's *Adoration of the Shepherds*; *Ecce Homo* by Guido Reni; and a selection of Old Master drawings including some by Raphael, Titian and Michelangelo.

The French paintings and drawings will please lovers of the Impressionists: *Le Coup de Vent* by Renoir; the shimmering translucency of *Garden at Pontoise* by Camille Pissarro; a landscape *La Foret* by Paul Cezanne; *Rue St Vincent* by Seurat; *Au Café* by Degas and *Danseuse rajustant son maillot* in charcoal; and *Portrait of a Woman* by Henri Matisse. Treasures like these are but a drop in the ocean. Hours spent browsing in the Fitzwilliam can be an overwhelming experience.

THE COLLEGE SHARED BY TWO QUEENS OF ENGLAND

The setting of Queens' is itself declamatory. Here is a rare example of a medieval college plan, the only one of its kind in Cambridge. The original court of red brick is based on the plan of a fifteenth century country-house with certain monastic features added, the lay-out incorporating butteries, kitchens, chambers, Library, Hall, Master's Lodge and Chapel. Cloister Court is outstandingly beautiful, the walks being based on William of Wykeham's plan at New College, Oxford. There are many features of interest to note. At the beginning of this century an unexpected discovery altered the appearance of the President's Gallery. The plastered walls were found to hide sixteenth century timber work that when uncovered revealed a perfect example of Tudor domestic architecture. It is all there – oriels, latticed windows and brick cloister arcades.

The Hall, richly painted, has had its share of alterations. Although a sixteenth century structure , it saw tastes change during the eighteenth and nineteenth centuries with the advocates of classical architecture and Gothic themes taking turns to satisfy the trends, several of the Victorian touches showing the influence of William Morris. Among the portraits is one of Sir Thomas Smith, who bequeathed a rent-charge to found lectureships "the balance of £1 to be employed one or two daies in the yeare to amende the cheare of the Fellows and scholars". The portrait of Elizabeth Woodville is a reminder that the College was shared by two queens of England. The original foun- der, Andrew Docket, Rector of St Botolph's and Principal of St Bernard's Hostel, obtained a royal charter in 1446 to establish "the college of St Bernard in Cambridge". In 1448 Queen Margaret of Anjou gave permission for the college to be refounded a sister institution to her husband's College of King's "to laud and honneure of sexe feminine", a gesture that would be applauded by today's militant women. Her motives in refounding the college were expressed by Fuller . . . "beholding her husband's

Below: The President's Lodge of Queens' College is a superb example of early sixteenth century domestic architecture with Cambridge's only medieval cloister

bounty in building King's College, was restless in herself with holy emulation until she had produced something of the like nature, a strife wherein wives without breach of any duty may contend with their husbands which should exceed in pious performances.'' The mental picture of Margaret in such a benign role is at variance with Shakespeare's assessment as a masterful woman with a sadistic streak that encouraged the bitterness of civil war. Historical evidence confirms this image rather than the romanticised female described by Gray in his Installation Ode, where she is described as ''Anjou's heroine''. On the other hand, when the College was refounded as the Queen's College of Ste Margarete – Virgin and Martyr, the Queen's patron saint – and St Bernard of Citeaux, contemporary comments suggest a good-looking, robust girl with tastes similar to her father, King René of Anjou.

The plan had a setback when the Wars of the Roses cut down the Lancaster cause. Henry was deposed, but through the initiative of Dokett in 1465, Elizabeth Woodville, Queen of Edward IV, continued her predecessor's work, granted the College its statutes and became true foundress by right of succession. In many ways the continuity was appropriate, for Elizabeth Woodville had been lady-in-waiting to Margaret and a close friend. Elizabeth's husband had been killed fighting for the Red Roses at the second Battle of St Albans in 1461. As these two Queens of England shared in its foundation, Queens' is the College of the apostrophe, in contrast to Queen's College, Oxford that had but Philippa, the consort of Edward III, as its foundress.

Among the many distinguished names associated with Queens' is John Fisher, the first Lady Margaret Professor of Divinity and Bishop of Rochester. As patron he invited Erasmus to lecture on Greek at Cambridge from 1511 to 1514 and was appointed Lady Margaret Reader. The rooms of this somewhat tetchy man were in the turret in the south-west corner of the Principal Court where he completed the edition of St Jerome and the New Testament in the original Greek. The work was scholarly but his thoughts were anything but charitable judging by letters to friends like Sir Thomas More, Ammonius and Dean Colet. He complained about the quality of life in Cambridge: ''Here I live like a cockle shut up in his shell, stowing myself away in college, and perfectly mum over my books . . . I cannot go out of doors because of the plague . . . I am beset with thieves, and the wine is no better than vinegar . . . . I do not like the ale of this place at all . . . if you could manage to send me a cask of Greek wine, the very best that can be bought, you would be doing your friend a great kindness, but mind that it is not too sweet. . . . I am sending you back your cask, which I have kept by me longer than I otherwise should have done, that I might enjoy the perfume at least of Greek wine. . . . My expenses here are enormous; the profits not a brass farthing. Believe me as though I were on my oath, I have been here not quite five months, and yet have spent sixty nobles: while certain members of my class have presented me with just a single one, which they had much difficulty in persuading me to accept. I have decided not to leave a stone unturned this winter, and in fact to throw out my sheet anchor. If this succeeds I will build my nest here; if otherwise, I shall wing my flight – whither I know not.''

He continually grumbled about poverty, though he received £700 a year. The scathing comments about his rooms were exaggerated, like so many of the criticisms. A letter written in 1680 by Andrew Paschal, Rector of Chedsey and a Fellow of Queens', gives some idea of what they were like: ''The staires which rise up to his studie at Queens' College in Cambr. doe bring into two of the fairest chambers in the ancient building; in one of them wich lookes into the hall and chief court, the Vice-President kept in my time; in that adjoyning it was my fortune to be, when fellow. The chambers over are good lodgeing roomes; and to one of them is a square turret adjoyning, in the upper part of which is the study of Erasmus and over ot leads. To that part beongs the best prospect about the Colledge, viz. upon the river, into the corne fields, and country adjoyning. So yt it might well consist with the civility of the house to that great man (who was no fellow, and I think stayed not long there) to let him have that study. His sleeping roome might be either the President's, or to be neer to him the next. The roome for his servitor, that above it, and through it he might goe to that studie, which for the height and neatnesse and prospect might easily take his phancy.''

It is hardly surprising that during Erasmus' stay, he was not over-popular with the Cambridge dons, who resented the criticisms and distrusted his new learning, yet they were able to acknowledge the Cambridge theologians. "In the University of Cambridge, instead of sophistical arguments, their theologians debate in a sober sensible manner and depart wiser and better men." Compliments were not always forthcoming. The President, Dean Milner, remarked to Macaulay that they had "no relique of Erasmus at Queens' except a huge corkscrew; and I am afraid that there was nothing in his principles to keep him from making very assiduous use of it." The oriental scholar, Claudius Buchanan, added a pertinent postscript. Apparently during a visit to Queens' he occupied Erasmus's rooms, and recorded that the corkscrew was "about a third of a yard long". Cambridge claims Erasmus, but at heart he preferred Oxford, in spite of the fact that the other place did not accept the new learning.

The mid-sixteenth century theological disputes skirted Queen's, though one Master, William May, was removed in 1553, reappointed in 1559, elevated to the Archbishop of York the following year, but tragically died on the day of his enthronement. The tempestuous seventeenth century troubles hit the College hard. The Master, Edward Martin, was sent to London by Cromwell for assisting the Royal cause. Dowsing left a trail of destruction in the Chapel. Of the features to notice, the cloister below the President's Lodge makes a genuine medieval setting for the Queens' Drama Society's performances of Shakespeare in May Week. The timber Mathematical Bridge is a copy of the original constructed in 1749–50 without any nails, the parts being pegged together. Wishful thinking gave the credit to Sir Isaac Newton; the same applies to the sundial over the Chapel, which is now used as the Library Reading Room. It was erected in 1642. To declare that Newton was the donor ignores the fact that he was only born in that year.

I have made no mention of modern additions. The new building in 1959 by Sir Basil Spence aroused criticisms from purists who disliked contemporary architecture on the Backs. The building by Powell and Moya's Cripps Building were also controversial. In such matters forbearance can be a virtue.

Below: *The timber Mathematical Bridge is a copy of the original constructed in 1749–50, that had no nails, the parts being pegged together*

A DECLAMATORY LANDSCAPE

Within a few miles of Cambridge it is possible to enjoy a Fen landscape, a canvas that stretches across acres of rich alluvial soil, a flatness that stretches from horizon to horizon without interruption. It is a unique background that can only be fully appreciated from the river. To do that a motor-cruiser can be hired from Chesterton boathouses for the afternoon. The stretch from Baitsbite to Bottisham Lock momentarily leaves the acres of corn and the sugar-beet fields and drifts in shadowy backwaters flecked by ripples and shadows of the overhanging willows. The fish are mostly roach or dace, whilst shoals of minnows flash green and silver. It is peaceful, not nearly as restless as described in the twelfth century records of the Crowland monks. Man had yet to change the countryside: "The whole country was almost dead flat, with here and there an inconsiderable eminence standing up from it. These heights were often surrounded by water, and when the autumnal and spring rains swelled the meres and streams and covered the flats, they formed so many detached islets. When were there in the world such eels and eel-pouts as were taken in the Ouse and Cam, close under the walls of the abbey of Ely (3000 eels, by ancient compact, do the monks of Romsey pay every Lent to the monks of Peterborough, for leave to quarry stone in a quarry appertaining to Peterborough Abbey; but the house of Ely might have paid ten times 3000 eels and not have missed them, so plenty were they, and eke so good).

"The streams, too, abounded with pike, and the meres and stagnant waters with tench and carp. Nor is there less plenty of waterfowl, and for a single half-penny men can have enough for a full meal. Nor was there a lack of fish that came up the river to spawn. Of wild boars of the forest in the Fen the head only was served up. The wild buck was less abundant in the fenny country. It was also facile to snare the crane, the heron, the wild-duck, teal, and the eccentric and most savoury snipe; the swallow-kite, the swarth raven, the hoary vulture, the swift eagle, the greedy goshawk, and that grey beast, the wolf of the Wold."

Times indeed have changed. The best we can do is to leave the Cam and go down Burwell Lode where we can find a tract of original fen, as wild as in the days of St Guth-

Below: Wicken is the only stretch of fenland preserved more or less in a medieval character. It has an atmosphere that breeds legends

lac. This square mile of Fens is as Hereward the Wake knew them. It is a stretch of dead water, reeds and bulrushes with narrow causeways of land intersecting it and includes Wicken Sedge Fen, St Edmund's Fen and Adventurers' Fen. It is stocked with rare plants and herbs. Laboratory-reared specimens of swallowtail butterflies have been released and are successfully re-established. Bird life is abundant, including the heron and bittern. As many as 1,500 duck have been seen on the mere at one time. From the tower hide, with its platform twenty-five feet above the level of the fen, it is possible to view not only Adventurers' Fen and the new mere, but also a large part of the Sedge Fen. Among the waders can be seen the stone curlew, wood sandpiper, greenshank, ruff and green sandpiper. Both the little ringed plover and great crested grebe have nested here, while observers have identified the song of Savi's warbler. Parts of the fen can be explored by boat, though some of the locals use the leaping-pole of a thousand years ago. A visit has its dangers. A stranger is well advised to go only with a guide, or, if alone, to keep strictly to the marked paths, for what looks like fine grass is often bottomless.

It is an atmosphere that breeds legends. Monks who saw marsh-fires beckoning over the swamps at night and heard strange cries of birds on the marsh must have found it easy to believe the weird tales about St Guthlac, the revered saint of the fens. They describe how Guthlac built himself a cell in the most haunted part of the isle, where he earned a reputation for healing and exorcising powers. This miracle-working saint lived in the fens for fifteen years. When he died the monks of Fenland built a chapel over his tomb as a shrine for pilgrims. From this sprang the celebrated Abbey of Crowland.

Reach Lode takes us to the beginning of the Devil's Dyke, the massive linear earthwork, seven and a half miles in length, with almost six miles of it in a straight line parallel to Fleam Dyke, which lies over the Icknield Way. By now the lymphatic landscape should be making itself felt. The monotonous elegy captures a mood. The very negation, neither ugly nor beautiful, has its own power. Look long enough at the scene and you find that, like some plain woman of character, it works upon your interest and wins you against will and reason. Everything is neutral. Time does not matter. The name of the lonely inn we pass at Upware emphasises this outlook – it is called No Hurry . . . Five Miles from Anywhere. With the fens stretching all round, the name is appropriate. It feels like 500 miles from anywhere, a sensation, with the slow, rhythmic progress of the boat, that makes you realise what no hurry means. It is a calming experience.

A feature of this stretch of the Cam is the heron. At dusk I have disturbed more than twenty of these huge silent birds. Seen in flight the heron is extremely handsome in its breeding-dress. Gone is the sombre grey of winter. Instead, all the under-feathers have a beautiful creamy tinge, only the longest wing-tips keeping their usual darker tint. The throat plumes are long and a delicately creamy white. As the bird goes downstream, the back and upper wings are a delicate grey – nothing like the coarse shades of autumn and winter. The head plume is darker than usual, and falls far down the neck. Occasionally, as one rounds a bend in the river, a heron can be caught standing philosophically on one leg, or poking majestically among the reeds with its long, infallible beak. The glimpse lasts a split-second. Then silently the bird rises, and leaves the landscape lonelier.

At the Fish and Duck Inn, the Cam merges with the Old West river and becomes the Ouse. We have a choice of continuing to Ely, turning sharply into the twisting of the Old West, or returning to Cambridge. The odds are that the time will necessitate the return journey. If we are sensitive to atmosphere, we shall long remember the pattern of straight rivers and dykes extending from horizon to horizon, the unending flatness broken only by stunted willow and the occasional fenland spire. The scene defies analysis. It is a hinterland of lonely spaces where the sunset paints in mud, water and dark soil with rich, even meretricious colours.

PETERHOUSE

Peterhouse is the oldest College in Cambridge. In 1281 Hugh de Balsham, Bishop of Ely and a Cambridgeshire man, established a house for "studious scholars living according to the rules of the scholars of Oxford called Merton". In one sense the decision was contradictory. The Merton Statutes were specific in that no friar, monk or canon regular could be a student, yet here was Hugh de Balsham advocating a system of education outside the monastic rule. It may be that being a Benedictine monk, an Order not so rigid as the mendicant Orders, he was attempting to counter the influence of these monastic houses by attracting a group of lay ecclesiastics to live by the regular canons of the Hospital of St John. The Augustinian brethren did not approve the "no religious" clause and their ways parted. As a result Peterhouse adopted the policy of the Sorbonne at Paris and Merton College at Oxford of training men for the secular priesthood. Hugh de Balsham's scholars were confirmed by Royal Charter in the possession of their *Domus Sancti Petri, sive Aula scholarium Episcopi Eleinsis* on the 28th May, 1284.

Hugh de Balsham died two years later. He left 300 marks to the scholars, who bought "a certain area to the south of the Church and built thereon a handsome Hall", which today is part of the south side of the main Court. Not much remains of the original structure, thanks to the restoring zeal of Sir Giles Gilbert Scott in 1866–8, but what are left are the oldest fragments of collegiate architecture in Cambridge. The parish church of St Peter, rebuilt about 1350 and known later as Little St Mary's, served as the College Chapel until 1632. In the late fifteenth century a gallery was built linking the College to the church. Inevitably there have been many alterations and modifications. The Combination Room was built in 1868 on the site of the old 1460 Stone Parlour. The Inner Parlour of 1595 has glass from William Morris in the windows and designed by Ford Madox Brown and Burne-Jones. The early Tudor cast-iron fireplace has tiles by William Morris whilst the walls are Morris-stencilled. The Chapel, built under the mastership of Matthew Wren, Bishop of Ely and uncle of Sir Christopher, is half Perpendicular and half Classical. It was consecrated in 1632 and completed four years later. When Cosin succeeded Wren, the brick construction of the Chapel was ashlared. Churchmanship was in line with Archbishop Laud's practices and was attacked by Prynne, the Puritan pamphleteer, who wrote, "In Peter House Chappel there was a glorious new Altar set up, and mounted on steps, to which the Master, Fellows, Schollers bowed . . . and on the Altar a Pot, which they usually called the incense pot . . . and the common report both among the Schollers of that House and others, was, that none might approach to the Altar in Peterhouse but in Sandalls."

Feelings ran high. Matthew Wren's experiences tell their own story. One of the Caroline masters, he enjoyed quick preferment through the sees of Hereford, Norwich and Ely. He supported Laud against the Puritans, then became involved in Laud's impeachment, followed by eighteen years in the Tower. He consecrated Peterhouse Chapel. In the light of Prynne's condemnation of the High Church ritual, an entry in Dowsing's diary is the sequel: "We went to Peterhouse, 1643, Decemb. 21, with officers and souldiers and . . . we pulled down 2 mighty great Angells with wings and divers others Angells and the 4 Evangelists Peter, with his keeis, over the Chapell dore and about a hundred chirubims and Angells and divers superstitious Letters . . ." John Coson, who was mainly responsible for the 1662 Book of Common Prayer, also used incense and vestments in accordance with the lawful heritage of the reformed English

Peterhouse is the oldest College in Cambridge. The Chapel was built under the mastership of Wrens' uncle, Matthew Wren. Its position, in the centre of the main Court, was later imitated in Emmanuel

Church. He lost the Mastership of the College through sending the College plate to Charles.

Of all the Masters so far, the most remarkable was Andrew Perne. His religious beliefs were so accommodating that they changed with the accession of a new Sovereign. In Henry's reign, he preached the Roman doctrine of the adoration of paintings of Christ. In Edward VI's he took a stand against transubstantiation and was so Protestant that he burned quantities of books in the University Library because they were too Catholic. In Mary Tudor's reign, he accepted the Roman articles and became so Catholic that the bodies of two German Protestant scholars were disinterred and burnt on the Market Hill because of their former beliefs. When Elizabeth became Queen, Perne was a staunch Protestant and reinstated the memory of the two Germans who had been cremated and preached a sermon in Latin denouncing the Pope. A Latin verb *pernare* was coined, translated "to rat, to turn, to change often", whilst the letters A.P. on the College weathercock were said to mean "A Papist" or "A Protestant" according to the way the wind was blowing. To restore the balance, it should be recorded that Perne, five times Vice-Chancellor, was a generous benefactor. He left his extensive library to Peterhouse with endowment to erect a building for it. Two College Fellowships and six scholarships were also endowed, whilst his astute opportunism undoubtedly influenced University development in a period of change. Incidentally the water which flows in front of the College is part of a water supply system first mooted by Perne.

Among the eminent personalities linked with Peterhouse was Richard Crashaw, son of a well-known anti-papal preacher and Fellow of the College, who was expelled for declining to subscribe the Solemn League and Covenant, and who later joined the Roman Church. Henry Cavendish entered Peterhouse in 1749 and is commemorated in the Cavendish Laboratory for physical research, which was founded by the seventh Duke of Devonshire in 1874. Cavendish discovered the constitution of water and atmospheric air, and also experimented on electricity and the earth's density. Peterhouse can claim Lord Kelvin, who came to the College in 1841 and graduated as Second Wrangler and First Smith's Prizeman. He furthered the science of thermodynamics and electricity, evolving the theory of electric oscillations, the basis of wireless telegraphy. It was through Kelvin that Peterhouse was the first Cambridge College to have electric lighting.

The College was also the home for a short time of Thomas Gray, the poet, but from the outset he found the rowdy behaviour of his fellow students too overpowering for his retiring nature. His rooms were in the corner of the top floor of the Fellows' Building. He dreaded fire and as a precaution had a bar fixed outside the bedroom window so that a rope ladder could be attached in an emergency. A bunch of undergraduates decided it should be put to use. A College servant was instructed to shout "fire" in the middle of the night, whereupon Gray made an undignified escape in his nightshirt only to find it was a practical joke. Not appreciating this type of humour, Gray left Peterhouse and moved to Pembroke College. In 1757 he was offered the Poet Laureateship but declined. In 1768 he became Professor of Modern History and died at Pembroke College on the 3rd July, 1771, aged fifty-four. He was buried in Stoke Poges beside his mother. On her tomb he had inscribed this epitaph:

> Dorothy Gray, widow; the tender careful
> mother of many children; one of whom had
> the misfortune to survive her.

SELWYN COLLEGE

Selwyn College, an Anglican foundation dating from 1882, is the Cambridge counterpart of Keble College, Oxford. It was founded by public subscription in memory of George Augustus Selwyn, the first Bishop of New Zealand and the eighty-sixth Bishop of Lichfield. Its aims were clear and uncomplicated . . . to provide academic education for men of moderate means, "willing to live economically in a College wherein sober living and high culture of mind may be combined with Christian training based on the principles of the Church of England." It was also an attempt to counter an expected backlash of a statute passed some years earlier that abolished the requirement that all prospective Fellows of Colleges and Professors had to provide evidence of being practising members of the Church of England. The fear was that it might encourage an anti-religious trend in Cambridge life. Such anxiety was groundless. The intention of the Royal Charter was realised though some resented the ruling that members had to belong to the Church of England or to a church in communion with it. On technical grounds the official status of the College was questioned. Even the title of "Hostel" was ruled out, but a Public Hostel was acceptable. The Master was not eligible to become Vice-Chancellor, nor could he appoint Proctors. However in 1926 Selwyn became an "approved Foundation by University Statute. Thirty-two years later came recognition as a "Full College".

Originally it had been intended to build the College in Lensfield Road on a site where now stands the Roman Catholic Church of Our Lady and the English Martyrs. Instead six acres in Grange Road were bought from Corpus Christi College. The architect, Sir Arthur Blomfield, favoured red brick in a Tudor style. The Chapel was consecrated in 1895 by Archbishop Benson. The west front turrets have bells given by W. S. Gladstone and T. H. Orpen. Behind the dais in the Hall that was built in 1908–9 is some choice panelling dated 1708 and taken from the English Church of St Mary in Rotterdam.

Selwyn lacks the feeling of age that can only come from the centuries, but it possesses an austere dignity of its own. The links with the Church of England remain strong, whilst the statutes require that the Master be a clerk in Holy Orders.

HISTORICAL CLUES

An enjoyable characteristic of the churches of Cambridge and outlying villages is their unending variety. After allowing for affinities of detail, there is often marked individuality, whilst the historical aspect, at times spanning almost a thousand years, adds a further dimension. The aesthetic appeal and atmospheric setting become aids to visualising what the people were like who over the centuries have walked down the aisles. Personal clues at times robust in flavour, can be found in *God's Acre*, providing a wealth of satire, jest, cynicism, optimism, pessimism, inevitably tinged with sorrow, but often eased with a note of good humour. Many an inscription forms a personal record of the person whose grave it covers. A tomb is the house of the dead. In that sense it is an expression of grief and bereavement, but the tombstone can become an autobiographical fragment. In the eighteenth century memorials frequently referred to occupations. A rough list includes such trades and professions as the blacksmith, which is fairly common, apothecary, grazier, carpenter, midwife, toolmaker, schoolmaster, cutler, hatter, butcher and watchmaker. These are orthodox classifications; others, particularly rural occupations, lend themselves to more imaginative treatment. Gamekeepers are high on the list. Domestic detail is frequent. What better than this simple expression of married contentment by a husband and wife than this last epitaph:

Lived Comfortably in this Parish . . . and had thirteen children.

More cryptic is the wording on a child's tombstone dated 1767:

By spots he died tho' spotless was his life.

Another epitaph is bluntly explicit:

Here lyes MARY the Wife of JOHN FORD
We hope her soul is gone to the LORD;
But if for HELL she has chang'd this life,
She had better be there than be John Ford's wife.

A touch of cynicism marks another tombstone of the nineteenth century:

The world is wide
And full of crooked streets
Death is the market place
Where all men meet:
If life was merchandise
As men could buy
The rich would live
And the poor must die.

Quirky inscriptions reflect a wry sense of humour:

> Underneath Lieth the Body of Robert Connonly
> Called Bone Phillip who died July 27th, 1793
> Aged 63 years At whose request the following
> lines are here inserted.
> Here lie I at the Chancel door
> Here lie I because I'm poor
> The forther in the more you'll pay
> Here lie I as warm as they.

Of the blacksmith's epitaphs few are better than this example:

> My sledge and hammer lie reclined,
> My bellows, too have lost their wind;
> My fire's extinct, my forge decayed,
> And in the dust my vice is laid.
> My coal is spent, my iron's gone,
> My nails are drove, my work is done;
> My fire-dried corpse lies here at rest,
> And, smoke-like, soars up to be bless'd.

These simple expressions conjure up mental pictures of what these people were like, a reflection of an attitude of mind to the inevitable, but are only word-pictures. They do not provide visual evidence of physical appearances. It is here that sepulchral effigy is so important. Cambridge is fortunate in having so many churches that have carved images of knights and ladies, poets and divines, mothers and children, squires and merchants, whose marble eyes have watched the worshippers over the centuries. Studied in detail they reveal the latest styles of different periods, recording with accurate detail and flavour the costumes of the Middle Ages, and the Elizabethan and Jacobean periods. Realistic portrayal of features was pronounced during the seventeenth and eighteenth centuries, when a series of portrait sittings would be given during the subject's lifetime. An instance of this was when the first Lord Salisbury commissioned his tomb from the sculptor, Maximilian Colt, in 1609 and only approved the sculpting of his head after several models had been made. In the majority of cases the sculptor is anonymous.

Effigies provide evidence of current items of dress. The vocabulary is that of a forgotten age – the Middle Ages of chivalry that knew the meaning of orle and basinet, barbe and houppelarde, tilting helm, crespine, nebuly, ailette and jambart; then later the swags and strapwork of Elizabethan and Jacobean times with the additions of lozenged pillars and obelisks. Angelic cherub heads are countered by the inclusion of spades, hourglasses and skulls. There was also a garish tendency to colour the monuments, whilst massive compositions commemorate figures in wigs and court dress with their ladies in attendance in a swirl of draperies and fluted columns. It is interesting to attempt identification of the different periods. Late fourteenth century fashion is reflected in the knight in a steel basinet with a curtain of mail hanging from it to protect the neck, a jupon to the hips worn over a breastplate, and an elaborate sword belt. Women of that period usually wear a plain cap relieved by close frills; the skirt is full and pleated, the bodice tight and long with often a back-flung cloak. Sometimes the gowns of the Queen Anne period are richly embroidered, whilst hairstyles are correct in minute detail. In this reign the basinet is enriched with a broad circlet of jewelled reliefs with the orle. The realistic touch was most marked in the seventeenth and eighteenth centuries, but all that ended in the nineteenth century. Neo-classical style and dateless draperies took over from fashionable clothes. The portrait head no longer predominated, but rather an idealised, impersonal study devoid of individuality. The tradition had been broken. It began with effigies like that of Bishop Northwold at Ely, a simple figure emerging from a plain stone slab, and evolved into the grand sarcophagus with the effigy in all its earthly finery lying fully in the round; the next phase saw the recumbent figure giving way to the effigy kneeling at prayer, reclining in a half-sitting attitude, or standing erect. Some of the most pathetic effigies are those of young mothers who died in childbirth but shown in choice, lace-trimmed nightgowns holding the sleeping babies denied in life. One of the most realistic figures can be seen in Ely. It is that of Bishop Gunning of the seventeenth century shown in the act of rising from the sarcophagus. The loose robes flow from the half-recumbent figure and the features are contorted with anxiety as he looks to the aisle with his right hand outstretched as if seeking assistance. For nearly 400 years that gesture had been made. Only our imagination can reach out to him.

The churches I have chosen are all within easy reach of Cambridge. They are living monuments as well as places of worship and reveal a great deal about the villages they serve. Effigies and brasses record the important local families going back some 600 years or more, the churchyards giving the names and ages of generations of humbler folk. Contemporary observations infuse life into these people whose likenesses remain in marble and alabaster, sources such as the Paston Letters that give a detailed picture of country life in these rural settings, whilst a Dutch historian comments how the women who graced these country houses were often kittle creatures. He declared, "they are well dressed, fond of taking it easy, and commonly leave household matters and drudgery to their servants. They sit at their doors, in fine clothes, to see and be seen of the passers-by. They spend their time walking, riding, visiting their friends, making merry with them at childbirths, christenings, churchings, and funerals. This is why England is called the paradise of married women. They lie till nine or ten every morning, then, being roused forth of their dens, they are two or three hours in putting on their robes, which being done they go to dinner, where no delicacies are wanting. Then, their bodies satisfied and their heads prettily mizzled with wine, they walk abroad for a time, or else confer with their families, as women, you know, are talkative enough, and can chat like pies, all the world knoweth it. Thus some spend the day till supper time, and then the night as before."

Against such a background can be placed many of the feminine effigies. In life they were full-blooded creatures. The early fourteenth century church at Bottisham, probably the best in the county, has two tombs worth examining: Sir Roger Jenyns and his wife sitting holding hands and wearing casually adjusted dressing gowns; and the monument by Bacon showing Margaret Coningsbye kneeling in prayer beside her husband, both in black robes and ruffs – the curtains of a stone canopy are drawn back by cherubs to reveal their children, Leonard and Dorothea, sleeping with buches of flowers in their hands. The inscription dated 1638 speaks for itself:

> These the world's strangers were, not here to dwell,
> They tasted, liked it not, and bade farewell.

I pick out the medieval church in my own village of Trumpington, not because of sepulchral figures on tombs but for its most treasured possession, the brass portrait of Sir Roger de Trumpington, the second oldest brass portrait in England after the Surrey knight Sir John d'Abernon. The Trumpington knight went on the Crusade with the future Edward the First, and died in 1289. He is 6 feet 4 inches tall. His head rests on a helmet secured to his belt by a chain. A dog by his feet holds the tip of the sword in his mouth. The brass itself is on a fourteenth century canopied tomb decorated with the heads of men and women.

In Little Shelford church the clues are on the stalls. They carry the arms of the Frevilles. In the chancel the alabaster figure of Sir John has lain since the beginning of the fourteenth century with an inscription in Norman French. Close by, a brass shows Robert and Claricia with a greyhound and two dogs at their feet. They clasp their hands, whilst their son does likewise with his wife. The date is 1405.

A few miles away at Sawston is a village with Mary Tudor links. In the manor house John Huddlestone gave her refuge after Edward VI's reign ended. Among many memorials John is remembered as "once Chamberlayne unto Kinge Phylipe and Captaine of his Garde, and one of Queen Maryes most honorable Privie Counsel." Nineteenth century portraits on brass show Sarah in a trimmed cloak over a gown and hooded headdress, Richard in medieval style, and Edward in a long cloak at prayer. More attractive is the wall memorial of kneeling figures in black gowns and white ruffs – a link with the Jacobean period.

Fulbourne is a pleasant village with all the trappings like Linton of thatched cottages, an old manor house, a windmill and a medieval church with a high tomb on which lie the chalk figures of Edward Wood of 1633 and his wife. Below them are two sons and a daughter. Under a canopy rests the lifesize figure of William de Fulbourn, chaplain to Edward III in richly embroidered vestments. At the beginning of the fifteenth century Walter and John Cotton built the moated hall and church of Landwade. The village, somewhat off the beaten track, has a wealth of medieval fittings and monuments to this family. Sir John Cotton of 1593 is sculptured as a knight in armour and kneels in prayer under the canopy of a striking tomb. His wife has a scent case hanging on a long chain. Sir John of 1620, also clad in armour, lies on an alabaster tomb. Below him on a ledge is one of his three wives, her fingers held in a book. Sir John of 1689 rests under an arch: the alabaster figure is in armour; the hair is long and wavy.

Chippenham, which has associations with George I and Charles Stuart, has a monument in its church of Sir Thomas Revet kneeling opposite his two wives, with four children below. Nearby is a seventeenth century woman by a prayer-desk in wood painted to resemble marble.

Isleham has a spacious, cruciform church with a fine clerestory and roof of unusual design. There are several features of medieval interest, items like gold cups and flagons, an Elizabethan charter with the Queen's seal, and a copy of the charter given by King Alfred for the building of a chapel in A.D. 895. It also has the thirteenth century tomb of Sir Geoffrey Bernard who went to the Holy Land with Prince Edward on the Crusades. In an adjoining transept is the figure of another Crusader, said to be Sir Geoffrey's son. The last male of the line is shown in brass – Sir John of 1450, who was at Agincourt and had to obey the order to kill the French prisoners. He wears plate armour, whilst his wife had a long gown and horned headdress. The details in the two fifteenth century brasses are interesting: Sir Thomas Peyton is in armour with huge elbow guards; his wife, Margaret Bernard, is in a brocade-patterned gown. Another brass of 1574 shows Sir Richard Peyton, a Reader at Gray's Inn, and his wife with a crown on her petticoat signifying she was a lady-in-waiting to the Queen.

Kirtling has a magnificent slate tomb decorated with shields of the first Lord North, Chancellor to Henry VIII, whilst the second Lord, who was host to Elizabeth, is under a massive canopy with six pillars and crowned by painted figures. Lord North is striking in black armour and gold markings. His head rests on a helmet, a griffin by his feet. The third Lord, who was prominent in the Court of Charles II, has no effigy, just a floorstone in the chapel. He achieved fame of a different kind – he discovered the springs at Tunbridge Wells.

Borough Green church possesses several fifteenth century monumental effigies of the de Burghs, who had the manor in the fourteenth century. Arched recesses hold several figures. One is a knight and his lady. He lies on a base of pebbles, his legs crossed, his head on a tilting-helmet. He is Thomas de Burgh of 1345, and the lady is Catherine de Burgh of 1410. Her gown is embroidered and the hair is in a net. Her husband, Sir John, lies on an adjoining tomb in armour and gauntlets. A third tomb has an armoured knight who holds a heart in his hands. Another figure on a tomb in the aisle is Elizabeth de Burgh with an ornate jewelled band round her draped headdress.

Horseheath has a church rich with brass and monuments of the Audleys and Alingtons. Outstanding is the alabaster monument of Giles Alington with his wife and six children. He is in slashed breeches and armour, she in ruff and hooped skirt. At Long Stanton is another elaborate tomb, that of Sir Thomas Hatton and his wife surrounded by six sons and daughters. They show the styles of the Commonwealth. Sir Thomas has rich armour and long curling hair. His wife has a hound at her feet, a bead bracelet, headchief, and a handkerchief in hand. Madingley church stands in a quiet park fringed by a lake and an impressive house built by Justice Huike in Tudor times. Three of the ladies who presided at Madingley Hall are remembered: Anne Heycock is in a medallion; Jane Hinde, who married Sir John Cotton and died in 1692, lies in a lace-trimmed nightcap and gown; Jane Cotton of 1717 kneels on a cushion. There is also an unusual sculpture of a baby wrapped in a shawl guarded by angels.

The interior of Harlton church is an impressive example of Decorated-Perpendicular transition. The mid-seventeenth century Fryer monuments are handsome, one reaching nearly to the roof. Dr Thomas Fryer is seen, bearded and grey, wearing a skull cap, black gown and ruff. His wife wears a gold chain, ruff and hooped skirt, whilst their son, Sir Henry, is in red and gold armour. His wife, who died in the time of Charles

Below: Jane Hinde, who married Sir John Cotton of Madingley Hall, died in 1692, and lies in a lace-trimmed nightcap and gown

They had Iſue
IOHN. THOMAS. IANE & ANNE
THOMAS & ANNE dyed young
IOHN & IANE surviv'd Them.

Stuart, is in a fashionable black and white dress and holds a handkerchief. Haslingfield church, with its magnificent fifteenth century tower, has the tomb of Thomas Wendy, physician to Queen Elizabeth. He is sculpted in alabaster, and clad in armour, kneeling with his wife in a farthingale and hooped skirt. Below is their son in armour, with his wife in a trimmed cloak and wearing a bonnet on her curly hair.

Wimpole church stands literally in the squire's courtyard. It is fourteenth century in origin but was virtually rebuilt by Flitcroft in 1749. It holds a remarkable series of monuments in the Chichele chapel by Scheemakers, Banks, Bacon, Flaxman and Westmacott. The scene is dominated by the huge alabaster tomb of Sir Thomas Chichele of 1616. He lies in gilded armour, a dog with a bone at his feet, and six children round the tomb with a baby in a cradle. The Earl of Hardwick, who was Lord Chancellor and presided over the trials after the 1745 Rebellion, has a large monument with a plaque of himself and his wife, and a portrait of his son, Charles Yorke, who was also Lord Chancellor.

This small selection of autobiographical fragments from past centuries is a reminder of what our ancestors were like. The introduction of neo-classical styles and dateless draperies destroyed authentic detail, thus their historic value ceased. Maybe it was a good thing that the tradition ended. Had the practice continued, it would have been difficult to introduce dignified effigies in contemporary fashions. Many look odd in their lifetime. Later generations might have found them near-hilarious.

Below: *Wimpole Church has a remarkable series of monuments in the Chichele Chapel. The scene is dominated by the huge alabaster tomb of Sir Thomas Chichele of 1616. He lies in gilded armour, at his feet a dog with a bone, and round the tomb six children, with a baby in a cradle*

ST CATHARINE'S COLLEGE

St Catharine's takes its name and crest – a wheel – from the mythical St Catharine of Alexandria, a patroness of learning, whose sanctity was so robust that it caused the wheel, on which she was about to be martyred, to break into pieces. A more practical origin of the name might have been the mother of the College's patron, Henry VI, who was called Catharine. In the statutes the founder Dr Robert Woodlarke, a member of a wealthy family, third Provost of King's College and one-time Chancellor of the University, said, "I have founded and established a college or hall to the praise, glory and honour of our Lord Jesus Christ, of the most glorious Virgin Mary, His mother, and of the Holy Virgin Katerine, for the exaltation of the Christian faith, for the defence and furtherance of the Holy Church and growth of science and faculties of philosophy and sacred theology." In spite of the build-up, the "House of Learning" was very modest in 1473. It had a chapel, library, cloister and hall with a Master and three Fellows in residence, a society of priests who spent their time praying for the soul of their founder and studying theology and philosophy. Medicine and law were expressly forbidden as were all non-religious subjects, but by the sixteenth century the scope had broadened. The College became a teaching body.

None of the original buildings have survived. Most of the existing fabric is a blending of seventeenth century architecture. The overall effect is plain and honest. The three-sided Court is an excellent example of seventeenth century taste that had been influenced by the Italian Renaissance. The dark-coloured brick was greatly admired by John Ruskin. Originally the Renaissance gateway was the main entrance for in the fifteenth century the College fronted on what is now Queens' Lane.

Several well-known men are associated with St Catharine's, like James Shirley, the dramatist, who graduated at the College in 1618. Thomas Bancroft, the epigrammatist, entered in 1644 and was a contemporary of John Ray, father of natural history. Precocity appears to have been encouraged. William Wotton, born 1666, was one of the youngest of Cambridge undergraduates. By the time he was six, Hebrew, Greek and Latin had been mastered. He entered St Catharine's at nine. By twenty-one he was a Fellow of the Royal Society, then he disappeared into obscurity. The College's decision to widen the scope of subject-matter benefited John Addenbrooke, founder of Addenbrooke's Hospital. He graduated as M.D. in 1711. In his will dated 1719 he left money to build and maintain a small physical hospital. He also left his medicine chest to the College.

These are but a few of the men who enriched College history, but there were others unknown by name, like the nine students who held their place on the river in the College boat in spite of the disadvantage of having a limited selection. The Pembroke Club had only nine members.

One man who should be singled out is associated with the phrase *Hobson's Choice*. It is Thomas Hobson, a well-known Cambridge personality, who lived in the town between the reigns of Henry VIII and Charles I. He was a carrier with a stage-waggon that plied regularly on the Cambridge–Luton road, starting from the extensive premises of the George Inn that used to stand where now are the iron railings of the College. Individual transport requirements were met from stables in which, according to the *Spectator*, were stalled "forty good cattle". Any could be hired along with whip and boots. It was a prosperous business in spite of Hobson's habit of treating clients indifferently. There was no haggling about picking and choosing. The horses went out in strict rotation. If

Opposite: *The College takes its name and crest from the mythical St Catharine of Alexandria, a patroness of learning, though the practical origin of the name suggests the mother of the College's patron, Henry VI, whose name was Catharine*

141

you didn't fancy the mount, the alternative was obvious. *Hobson's Choice* was just that. He died aged eighty-six and John Milton, an undergraduate at Christ's, compiled this serio-comic epitaph:

Ode to the University Carrier

Here lies old Hobson, Death hath broke his girt,
And here alas, hath laid him in the dirt,
Or els the ways being foul, twenty to one,
He's here stuck in a slough, and overthrown.
'Twas such a shifter, that if truth were known,
Death was half glad when he got him down;
For he had any time this ten years full,
Dodg'd with him, betwixt Cambridge and the Bull.
And surely, Death could never have prevail'd
But lately finding him so long at home,
And thinking now his journey's end was come,
And that he had tane up his latest Inne,
In the kind office of a Chamberlin
Shew'd him, his room where he must lodge that night,
Pull'd off his Boots, and took away the light:
If any ask for him, it shall be sed,
Hobson has supt, and's newly gon to bed.

Below: *The three-sided Court is a reflection of seventeenth century taste influenced by the Italian Renaissance*

Hobson's Conduit commemorates Thomas Hobson, a well-known Cambridge personality, who lived between the reigns of Henry VIII and Charles I. He was a carrier with a stage-waggon that plied on the Cambridge–Luton road, starting from premises of the George Inn where now stands the iron railings of St Catharine's College. He hired out horses in strict rotation, hence the phrase Hobson's Choice. The Conduit was moved from Market Hill to the corner of Lensfield Road. It was built to conduct water to Cambridge from Nine Wells near Trumpington

PEMBROKE COLLEGE

Pembroke College has the unusual distinction of being founded by a French lady a year after the Battle of Crecy. She was Marie, daughter of Guy de Chatillon, Count of St Pol and widow of Amoryde de Valence, Earl of Pembroke in 1346. The fifty-year-old nobleman married the seventeen-year-old Marie, who was said to be maid, wife and widow in a single day. Her husband was killed on their wedding-day at a tournament held to celebrate the marriage. The story is discredited in other records that state the Earl of Pembroke died of apoplexy three years after the wedding whilst on a mission to the Court of France. Thomas Gray referred to the first version in his *Installation Ode* performed at the Senate House on the 1st July, 1769 to mark the installation of Augustus Henry Fitzroy, tenth Duke of Grafton, as Chancellor of the University. Gray refers to the foundress as

> . . . sad Chatillon on her bridal morn,
> Who wept her bleeding love.

Either way, the lady, Lady Mary de Valence, withdrew from the world and endowed a nunnery of Minoresses at Waterbeach, later moving to the Abbey of Denny, whose nuns were under the Order of St Clare. In time she bought another site outside the town gates to establish a college of a Master, twenty-four Fellows and six scholars, enjoining "those who were elected into her college to be constant in their visits to this religious house as their ghostly counsellors and instructors". Denny Abbey is now part of history. The only parts to survive are traces of the ninety-four feet long refectory by the old cloisters and fragments of the square-aisled nun's church, the only architectural relics in England of the Order of St Clare. It is possible that another wealthy widow, Lady de Clare, who founded Clare College, encouraged the French girl to found a college herself.

During the centuries many changes have been made to the fabric of Pembroke. Little of the original remains. Instead, a mixture of dull, ugly buildings have accumulated. From the outset the scale was miniature. A print published by Loggan shows the College buildings huddled round a quadrangle little more than half the size of the present Front Court. It is little different to the fourteenth century plan. Pembroke was the first College in the University to have its own Chapel instead of scholars using the nearby church of St Botolph. The special licence needed to build a chapel was granted by Pope Urban V during his Papal exile at Avignon. The Papal Register records the fact in an entry dated July 1366. The wording reads:

> To the Warden and College of Scholars of Valence Marie Hall,
> Cambridge:
>   License, on the petition of their Foundress, Mary de Sancto
> Paulo, Countess of Pembroke, to have a Chapel founded and built by
> the said Countess within their walls, wherein Masses and other
> Divine Offices may be celebrated by Priests of the said College,
> saving the rights of the Parish Church

The privileges in question referred to the exclusive right of the parish priest to celebrate marriage and receive the dues of Easter offerings and surplice fees.

Pembroke College Chapel was Sir Christopher Wren's first building. When his uncle, Matthew Wren, Bishop of Ely and Fellow of Pembroke, was released from the Tower of London in 1659 after eighteen years' imprisonment, he decided, as an act of thanksgiving, to build a new chapel for his College. He asked his nephew, Christopher, then a professor at Oxford, to design it

The new Chapel was important through being the first work of Sir Christopher Wren and the earliest purely classical building in Cambridge. Wren was working on the Sheldonian Theatre in Oxford, but Pembroke Chapel was completed first. An outside factor influenced the decision. In 1659 Matthew Wren, Bishop of Ely, was released from the Tower where he had been imprisoned for eighteen years by the Puritans for his religious beliefs. He vowed that when freed he would "return unto Him by some holy and pious employment that summe and more, by which of His gracious providence was unexpectedly conveyed in unto me during my 18 years of captivity." That thanksgiving was to be a new chapel.

His nephew, Christopher, then a science don at Oxford, was invited to be the architect and £5,000 was donated towards the cost. The result was a building of finely balanced proportions. The altar-piece, a Deposition copied after Barocci, once belonged to Sir Joshua Reynolds. The east window is a tribute to Sir George Gabriel Stokes, one-time Master of the College, and shows the Crucifixion with Matthew Wren and the Countess of Pembroke beside the Cross. Figures in the background include William Smart by the wharf at Ipswich; Robert Hitcham, a seventeenth century benefactor; Laurence Booth, the fifteenth century Archbishop of York; and Henry VI by Soham Church.

Every College has its list of eminent members, but none had such distinguished Masters between the mid-fifteenth century and the Commonwealth. The clerics included Thomas Rotherham, later Archbishop of York and Lord Chancellor of England, who built two wings of the first University Library; Edmund Grindal, afterwards Archbishop of Canterbury; John Whitgift, who became Master of Trinity and Archbishop of Canterbury; Matthew Hutton, subsequently Archbishop of York; Lancelot Andrewes, successively Bishop of Chichester, Ely and Winchester; John Young, later Bishop of Rochester; Thomas Dove, later Bishop of Peterborough; Richard Foxe, Bishop of Winchester and founder of Corpus Christi College, Oxford; and Nicholas Ridley, the martyr, who wrote this farewell to Cambridge and his College just before execution:

> Farewell, Pembroke Hall, of late my own College, my care, and my charge . . . mine own dear College. In thy orchard – (the walls, butts, and trees, if they could speak, would bear me witness) – I learnt without book almost all Paul's Epistles; yea, I ween all the Canonical Epistles also, save only the Apocalypse – of which study, although in time a great part did depart from me, yet the sweet smell thereof I trust I shall carry with me into Heaven; for the profit thereof I think I have felt in all my lifetime ever after. And, I ween, of late there was that did the like. The Lord grant that this zeal and love toward that part of God's Word, which is a key and true commentary to all the Holy Scripture, may ever abide in that College as long as the world shall endure.

In Ridley's time the College had only thirty undergraduates. The reference to butts confirms that archery practice was a popular College pastime.

Among the laymen, Edmund Spencer matriculated at about sixteen years of age at Pembroke Hall in May, 1569. Thomas Gray was another poet of first rank, but a solitary. Dr Johnson referred to him as "a dull man in every way", in contrast to the warm, humorous spirit of his letters. With the exception of a few translations, all his poetry was published from Cambridge. In 1773 Gray's rooms were occupied by the younger Pitt. His father, Lord Chatham, unable to take the fourteen-year-old boy to Cambridge because of threatening gout, sent this letter to the College listing some of his son's qualities:

> He is of tender Age and of a health not yet firm, enough to be
> indulged, to the full, in the strong desire he has, to acquire
> knowledge. An ingenuous mind and docility of temper will, I know,
> render him conformable to your Discipline in all points. Too young
> for the irregularities of a man, I trust, he will not, on the other hand,
> prove troublesome by the Puerile sallies of a Boy. Such as he is, I am
> happy to place him at Pembroke.

Pitt's course of studies were apart from the other students. Privately instructed by his tutor, Pretyman, he graduated M.A. in 1776 without any examination. He became Chancellor of Exchequer at twenty-two and Prime Minister at twenty-five, a post he retained until 1801. He is remembered in Cambridge by a block of buildings built at Pembroke in 1908 and by the Pitt Press on the opposite side of Trumpington Street.

Among other Pembroke men of distinction, I single out S. C. Roberts, who brought to the Master's Lodge the thoughtful humour of an academic with a down-to-earth outlook. On one visit to the Old Mill House he brought with him the American poet, Robert Frost, who said that of all the Cambridge Colleges he had visited, Pembroke was the one in which he would have been happiest. A Fellowship there would have been a dream come true, just as he had come to England to receive honorary degrees from both Oxford and Cambridge. He was conscious of the honour and pointed out with quiet satisfaction that the only other American to be similarly honoured was James Russell Lowell in 1873 and that had been in part recognition of diplomatic services, and Longfellow in 1868, "but he didn't get both of 'em at the same time". Not that Frost had any need for comparisons. He had received almost every American literary honour – the Pulitzer Prize for poetry four times: in 1924 for *New Hampshire*; in 1931 for *Collected Poems*; in 1937 for *A Further Range*; and in 1943 for *A Witness Tree*.

Frost's refreshing vitality belied his eighty-three years. In fact, he made Roberts seem the older man. Knowing his association with the University Press, he recalled that his first volume of poems was published in England for the simple reason it has been rejected in America, adding in a deep New England accent, that success had always come slow. He was then thirty-nine. In self-deprecating mood, he regretted he had never been a real anything. Not much of a farmer, not much of a poet, he reckoned his output had been about ten pages a year over a period of sixty years. He was conscious of the formative influences of friendships with Edward Thomas, Lascelles Abercrombie, Wilfred Gibson, and in particular, Rupert Brooke. Frost reminisced about life in general and the early days. It was all unaffected, conversational, spiced with ironic humour and seasoned with simple home truths. The informality made it hard to realise that here was not only a great American poet who had influenced the work of young American poets and critics, but who was also a great American institution. One thing puzzled him. As a poet he always despised fashion, yet he had become fashionable. He wrote poems and about poetry in the plainest terms, yet critics discussed his work in terms of the greatest complexity. He had never consciously played any literary tricks. Looking down at his big, black boots, he said that maybe recognition had come from craftsmanship and integrity – at least he hoped so. There would have been no doubt had he been a Fellow of Pembroke.

THE UNIVERSITY PRESS

In 1584 the University received a charter from Henry VIII "to assign and elect from time to time . . . three stationers and printers, or sellers of books, residing within the University . . . empowered to print all manner of books approved of by the Chancellor or his Vicegerent and three Doctors, and to sell and expose to sale in the University or elsewhere within the realm, as well as such books as other books . . ." This authorisation was the foundation of Cambridge printing, but prior to that the University had its licensed stationers dating from the thirteenth century. Tradition claims that Erasmus introduced printing into Cambridge, but John Siberch of Sieburg in Germany was the first Cambridge printer to set up his press in 1521. He printed Erasmus' own treatise *De Conscribendis Epistolis*. Siberch was in no doubt about his status. He proclaimed himself *primus utriusque linguae in Anglia impressor*, or the first printer in England to set Greek in movable types. He printed only ten books, then returned to Germany.

The Stationers' Company of London objected to the charter. It weakened its monopoly. When Thomas Thomas, Fellow of King's College, was elected University Printer and prepared to print a book, it took drastic action and seized his press, maintaining that such a book would infringe the stationers' rights. The University contested the charge. Eventually the letters patent of 1534 were affirmed valid by the Master of the Rolls. The office of University Printer has since continued unbroken. In 1698 the classical scholar, Richard Bentley, who had been given a power of attorney to re-equip the Press, decided that the University Press should be governed by a University syndicate. In the terms of its charter, the Press shares with the Queen's Printer and the Clarendon Press at Oxford the right to print the Authorised Version of the Bible and the Prayer Book of 1662.

The building in Trumpington Street is a deception. The visitor is inclined to believe that the Pitt Press is a late fifteenth century building of ecclesiastical significance, instead of early nineteenth century. It is an excellent example of Gothic revivalism in Cambridge by Edward Blore, the architect who built Abbotsford for Sir Walter Scott. The name seemingly indicates that it was either founded by or in memory of William Pitt the Younger. Its origin is more prosaic. A public subscription to erect statues of William Pitt in Westminster Abbey and Hanover Square was so generously supported that the balance was offered to the University for erecting a building for the University Press on a site close to Pembroke which was the statesman's College. In the 1960s the Press built extensive buildings near the railway station, which were expanded in the 1970s as the headquarters of all its activities, both printing and publishing, but still under University control.

In 1804 the University was offered the surplus from public subscriptions raised to cover the cost of a statue of William Pitt, Prime Minister from 1783–1805. The money was used for a new building for the University Press near Pembroke College where Pitt was a student. The Gothic style of the Pitt Press gives it the appearance of a church

THE GODOLPHIN ARABIAN

The Gog Magog Hills are a pleasant walk from Cambridge. These gentle chalk slopes of 220 feet survey a landscape that is itself declamatory. The flatness stretches from horizon to horizon: on a clear day you can see as far as Ely. There are various theories on how the names originated, one being that the Emperor Probus stationed gigantic Vandal auxiliaries in the area and the much shorter Celts gave them the names of giants – Gog and Magog. The summit of these miniature hills is an earthwork named Wandlebury that was a sacred Iron Age site. There is another feature of interest. A horse lies buried in the passage that once led to his stable – a slab bears the name of the Godolphin Arabian who, with the Byerley Turk and the Darley Arabian, are the founding sires of the thoroughbred from whom all modern thoroughbreds trace their descent in the direct male line.

There is no record of the Godolphin Arabian having raced, but it is difficult to separate fact from fiction. One version claims he was discovered in Paris drawing a water-cart and sent to join the resident stallion, Hobgoblin, at Lord Godolphin's country seat at Gogmagog. Facts are not so colourful as fiction. Experts maintain that the Godolphin Arabian came from the Jilfan blood of the Yemen and was one of the four Arab horses presented by the Bey of Tunis to the King of France. Three of the horses were released in the forests of Britanny to improve the native stock. The fourth was bought by Edward Coke, who died in 1733, leaving his bloodstock including the Arabian to Lord Godolphin.

Whichever version is accepted, it is an established fact that the Godolphin Arabian covered Roxana. The union was fruitful, producing two notable horses, Lath (1732) and Cade (1734). The Godolphin Arabian line was perpetuated and has survived into the twentieth century, represented by Man O'War, one of the greatest horses ever to race in America, and by Hurry On and Precipitation in this country.

The Godolphin, who stood only 14 hands 3, died at the age of twenty-nine. An endearing characteristic was his affection for a stable cat, and this appears in many paintings. Even the stud-book has a reference to it. . . . "Sat upon him until he was buried, then went away and never was seen again until found dead in the hayloft."

CORPUS CHRISTI COLLEGE

Corpus Christi College is unique in that it was founded in 1352 by two town guilds – the Guild of Corpus Christi attached to the church of St Benedict and the Guild of St Mary attached to the church of St Mary's-by-the-Market. At that time religious guilds were prominent in Cambridge, although records are sparse until the reign of Edward I, when we learn that the Guild of St Mary was involved in conveyances of land. Mary Bateson in *Introduction to Cambridge Guild Records*, published by the Cambridge Antiquarian Society in 1903, described the purpose of St Mary's Guild. It was "primarily the provision of prayers for the members. The 'congregation' of brethren, sometimes brethren and sisters, met at irregular intervals, to pass ordinances and to celebrate solemn mass for dead members. The penalty for absence was half a pound of wax, consumed no doubt in the provision of guild lights before the altar of Our Lady."

In 1352 this Guild was permitted by Royal Charter, on the grounds of poverty, to merge with the Guild of Corpus Christi for the purpose of founding a college. The first buildings were close to the churchyard of St Bene't – in fact, until the nineteenth century it was known as Bene't College. The church served as the College Chapel. In 1500 a gallery was built linking church and College, like the one between Peterhouse and Little St Mary's.

From a visitor's point of view there are two features of outstanding interest. The Old Court is the most perfect and finest surviving example of an early medieval college court, the prototype of English collegiate architecture. It was built with great speed. Josselin says it was "entirely finished, chiefly in the days of Thomas Eltisle, the first master, but partly in the days of Richard Treton, the second master." In other words, the work was completed twenty-five years after the Charter had been granted. It consisted of a hall range, now the kitchens; the Masters' Lodge, later converted into sets of rooms for undergraduates; and chambers on the other three sides. The 600-year-old walls are of clunch, but plastered as so often is the case with clunch to give protection from the weather. The buttresses and garrets are later, *c.* 1500. A horizontal strip of uncoursed clunch rubble indicates the fourteenth century masonry. The original entrance to the College was through an archway opening into the churchyard and Free School Lane.

The second important feature is the Library with its magnificent collection of books and manuscripts presented by Archbishop Parker, one of the most eminent of Corpus men. In 1533 he was licensed to preach by Cranmer. Two years later he became Dean of Stoke-by-Clare and chaplain to Anne Boleyn. In 1552 he became Dean of Lincoln, gave support to Lady Jane Grey's cause, was deprived of preferment by Queen Mary and sought refuge from persecution in Frankfurt-on-Main. When Elizabeth became Queen, Parker accepted the Archbishopric of Canterbury, was consecrated by four Bishops in Lambeth Palace, and became identified with the Anglican group. Even in death Parker attracted controversy. He was buried in a private chapel at Lambeth and Dr Walter Haddon had an appropriate monument erected over the tomb. In 1648 his body was torn from the grave and buried under a dunghill. After the Restoration, Sir William Dugdale asked Archbishop Sancroft to recover the body and rebury it in Lambeth.

Many of the books and manuscripts in Matthew Parker's library became accessible through the Dissolution of the Monasteries. Such was his enthusiasm for collecting that one of his agents purchased over 6,700 volumes with items coming from the libraries of Winchester, Peterborough, Exeter, Lincoln, Bury St Edmunds, Bath, Christ Church and St Augustine's, Canterbury. As a collection, Corpus Christi Library inherited some of the rarest books, including *De Antiquitate Ecclesiae et Privilegiis Ecclesiae Cantuariensis cum Archiepiscopis ejusdem 70* which is alleged to be the first book privately printed in England; Jerome's Latin Version of the Four Gospels sent by Pope Gregory to St Augustine at Canterbury; Matthew Paris's own copy of his History; a fifteenth century copy of Piers Plowman's *Visions*; a copy of John of Salisbury's *Polycraticus*, which originally belonged to Thomas à Beckett; the earliest manuscripts of the *Anglo-Saxon Chronicle*, the vellum sheets having small holes made in Saxon times by ticks in the sheepskin; a folio manuscript of the *Iliad* and *Odyssey* saved from St Augustine's monastery at Canterbury; Thomas Bilney's Bible; two printed books by Caxton and one by Siberch, the first Cambridge printer; the First Draft of the forty-two Articles of Religion with Archbishop Parker's Psalter and Bestiary; Chaucer's *Troilus and Cressida*, *c*. 1450; Bede's Life of St Cuthbert, alleged to have been given by King Athelstan to the See of Durham; Alfred's translation of Gregory's Pastorale; and an Irish ballad, the earliest known example of Irish printing.

Below: The Old Court of Corpus Christi College, where John Fletcher, the playwright, had rooms about the time that Marlowe died

These and other treasures can only remain in Corpus Library if certain conditions are observed. Parker's deed of gift required that every year the Masters of Gonville and Caius College and Trinity Hall should carry out a check. Should six folios, eight quartos, or twelve smaller manuscripts be missing and not returned at the end of six months, the entire collection is handed over to Gonville and Caius College within one month. In the event of Caius experiencing the same trouble, the collection would be forfeited to

The fourteenth century Court said to be haunted by the ghost of Dr Butts, Master from 1626 to 1632, who hanged himself just before he was about to leave to preach the University sermon. He is said to have been seen looking out of the window by the sun-dial

Trinity Hall. A similar situation and the library reverts to Corpus. So far after nearly 500 years no such punitive action has been necessary.

Of other famous men claimed by Corpus, two are commemorated on a stone panel in the Old Court. The first is Christopher Marlowe. In the College list of members and the University Grace-book, his name is spelt Marlin. He was in residence between 1581 and 1587. *Tamburlaine* was written during that period here and published three years later to introduce a new development of blank verse. This son of a Canterbury shoe-maker was one of the first of the Canterbury scholars to benefit from the two endowments made by Archbishop Parker. The second name commemorated is John Fletcher, the playwright who entered the College about the time that Marlowe died. There is no reference to the belief that Fletcher shared the composition of Shakespeare's *Henry VIII*.

Other distinguished names in the Corpus annals include John Robinson, pastor of the Pilgrim Fathers; Robert Browne, the founder of Congregationalism; Sir Nicholas Bacon, Keeper of the Great Seal, whose statue can be seen in a niche at the entrance to the Chapel built by Wilkins; Thomas Tenison, Archbishop of Canterbury who, when Rector of St Martin's-in-the-Fields, preached the funeral sermon on Nell Gwynne; Thomas Cavendish, the circumnavigator. The Hall has several fine portraits . . . William Colman by Romney; Sir John Cust, Speaker of the House of Commons by Reynolds; Dean Spencer; and Sir Nicholas Bacon. One that failed to pass Dowsing's test was a former Master. The record states that Dowsing defaced "a Mayd praying to the Sonn and Virgin Mary" – the mistaken sex was probably caused by the full academic dress.

From fame to occult phenomena. The Old Court has its own ghost that haunts the corner where the Old Lodge was made into student's rooms. One version identifies the spirit with Dr Butts, Master from 1626–32 and Vice-Chancellor during the Plague of 1630. Such was his horror of the pestilence that in a letter to Lord Keeper Conventry, High Steward of Cambridge, he describes the frightful scenes in the town . . . it ends "Myself am alone a destitute and forsaken man, not a Scholler with me in College, not a Scholler seen by me without. God all sufficient (I trust) is with me, to whose most holy protection I humbly commend your Lordship with all belonging unto you." The strain finally broke him. On Easter Day, 1632, he was expected to preach before the University as Vice-Chancellor, but was found dead in his room, hanging by his garters. The second version concerns the lover of the daughter of John Spenser, Master from 1667–93. Disturbed during a clandestine meeting, the fellow hid in a cupboard and died of suffocation. The *Occult Review* for March 1905 describes the sequel: "In the Easter term of 1904, an undergraduate, who had rooms opposite those said to be haunted, happened to come in at three o'clock in the afternoon, and as soon as he had sat down to do some work, found himself seized with a curious feeling of uneasiness, which made it impossible for him to concentrate his mind. He got up and, looking out of the window, noticed the head and shoulders of a man leaning out of a window of the upper set of rooms opposite. The features, he was rather surprised to find, he could not recognise: they were those of a stranger with long hair, who remained perfectly motionless, and seemed to glare down upon him. For three minutes he stood at the window and watched, and then, thinking he might see better from his bedroom, he ran there, but by the time he had arrived, the man opposite had completely disappeared. The young man was now thoroughly excited and went across the court to the upper set of rooms opposite. However, he found the door locked, and when he called no answer was given. In the evening, after careful enquiry, he discovered that the owner of the rooms had been out the whole afternoon, and that it was quite impossible that anyone could have been in the rooms from the time of his departure at two o'clock to the arrival of his bedmaker at half-past six."

The spirit appeared on several other occasions, so efforts were made to exorcise: "The occupant of the rooms made up his mind to try to exorcise it, and got C – a friend of another College, who was interested in spiritualism, to come to his rooms for the purpose, with four other men. At the outset they all knelt down, said the Lord's Prayer, and called upon the Three Persons of the Trinity to command the spirit to appear. It was then seen, but by only two of the six men. Another said he felt a peculiarly cold and chilling air, but the rest saw nothing. The two who saw the ghost – the man interested in spiritualism and the occupant of the rooms – described it as appearing in the 'form of a mist of about a yard wide, which slowly developed into the form of a man who seemed to be shrouded in white, and had a gash in his neck'; that it then moved slowly about the room. The two men got up, and, holding the crucifix in front of them, approached the apparition, but seemed to be forced back by some invisible agency. They cried out, 'It drives me back', and then both completely broke down, becoming quite unnerved. A few days later they tried again to exorcise the spirit, with exactly the same result: the same men saw it, and no one else. They were again driven back, although this time they approached holding hands. The others allege that they appeared to grow stiff, and that they gripped one another convulsively. The meeting was again broken up without anything definite having been effected." The options are still open!

To end on a factual note, Corpus not only has the finest collection of silver plate in Cambridge, but the famous Wassail Horn, the earliest piece of plate belonging to a Cambridge College. The horn was given *c.* 1347 to the Guild of Corpus Christi by John Goldcorne, alderman of the Guild . . . . "a great horn, with feet silver gilt and the head of an emperor at the end, silver gilt; having also a silver cover, at the top of which are four acorns, silver gilt". It was used at feasts of the Guild before the College was founded, and is still used at College feasts, although it calls for skilful handling by guests, "the two silver feet having to rest upon the arm above the elbows, and a good lift of the right hand".

It is hard to remember that the original foundation of the College consisted of a Master and two Fellows whose only responsibility was the education of secular priests who would celebrate masses for the departed members of the guilds. Unfortunately this obligatory service was too early in point of time to comfort the ghost of the Old Court.

The magnificent collection of books and manuscripts in Corpus Library were presented by Archbishop Parker, one of the most distinguished of Corpus men, who accepted the Archbishopric when Elizabeth I became Queen

Corpus Christi Chapel was built in line with the gatehouse; its façade follows the tradition of the Royal Chapels of the Perpendicular style, with castellated ranges on both sides

THE STRUGGLE FOR ACADEMIC RECOGNITION

The struggle to gain full equality for women in education took time and was often acrimonious. The Victorian belief that women were only secondary adjuncts to the life of men died hard. The argument was that the education of women should only be concerned with developing qualities suitable for a wife. As divorce was not possible before 1857, the only alternative was life at home as an old maid or a genteel governess. Jane Austin described how she was obliged "to retire from all the pleasures of life, of rational intercourse, equal society, peace and hope, to penance and mortification for ever – to take up duties which seemed, under the more favourable circumstances, to require something more than human perfection of mind and body, to be discharged with tolerable comfort."

One of the pioneers for full educational equality was Emily Davies, who ignored the argument that it would result in improper behaviour, and raised sufficient money to establish the germ of a women's college in Hitchin for six students. Progress was slow. Official concessions were granted with reluctance. In 1868 Cambridge University instituted a local examination for women over eighteen who wanted to qualify for governesses and schoolteachers. The preparatory courses were arranged by the Association for the Promotion of Higher Education for Women, under the guidance of Henry Sedgwick, a Fellow of Trinity College.

In 1870 the Senate consented to issue informal certificates to students from Hitchin College and in the same year agreed that when £7,000 was raised, this College should have its own building, but not in Cambridge. In 1871 Sidgwick persuaded Ann Jemima Clough, sister of the poet, Arthur Hugh Clough, to take charge of a house in Regent Street, Cambridge. Eventually the new institution moved to Merton Hall in the grounds of St John's College, before acquiring its own site where Newnham Hall, now Newnham College, was opened in 1875. Building continued until 1910 to the designs of Basil Champneys, resulting in an exceptionally attractive William and Mary style. In 1873 Hitchin College had moved to a site near Girton village where Sir Alfred Waterhouse designed somewhat forbidding red-brick buildings softened by extensive grounds.

Unfortunately for the common cause of women's education, the relationship between Girton and Newnham was at times frosty. Davies did not always agree with Clough, accusing the Newnhamites of being too ready to compromise on matters of educational principle. In 1881 the University allowed women to take examinations but they were still not entitled to take degrees. London University had paved the way by giving degrees to women in 1878, whilst in 1890 Philippa Fawcett had upset the assumption that mathematics was too intellectual a test for the opposite sex by taking the highest marks in the mathematical Tripos. The University remained adamant. A ballot was taken in 1897 at which all Cambridge M.A.s were entitled to vote. The issue raised tremendous interest. Special trains were laid on for London voters. The scenes in Cambridge were close to riotous, but the outcome was overwhelmingly not in favour of admitting women for degrees. A lull of twenty years followed, then, in 1919, Oxford granted women students full membership of the University, but a Royal Commission investigating the affairs of Cambridge recommended that Cambridge should remain predominantly a men's university.

This prejudice died a natural death. In 1926 women were admitted as members of University Faculties and allowed to hold University teaching posts and compete for University prizes, then in 1947 women were admitted to full membership of the University by allowing them to take degrees. No protest was made. It was fitting that the first women Cambridge graduate was Queen Elizabeth, the Queen Mother, who, in 1948, received the honorary degree of Doctor of Law.

THE CAVENDISH LABORATORIES

The international reputation of the Cavendish Laboratories is due to the brilliance of its scientists, men whose discoveries and experiments have enriched the world, though some, wrongly applied, could destroy civilisation as we know it. Here it was that in 1897 J. J. Thomson established the existence of electrons; that Sir James Chadwick identified the neutron; that Sir John Cockcroft and E. T. S. Walton achieved the artificial disintegration of nuclei. These are but three of the scientific breakthroughs. In 1973 New Cavendish Laboratories were opened on the Madingley Road at a cost of £2.25, but somehow they lack the tradition and atmosphere of the old laboratory that stood on the site of the Botanic Garden in Free School Lane. No doubt by comparison the old laboratory was primitive with frequent improvisations that led to the "wax and string" image; nevertheless many of the early results were remarkable.

In 1869 a syndicate recognised the need for teaching Experimental Physics at Cambridge and recommended the appointment of a Professor and a Demonstrator, with premises of a lecture room, laboratory, classrooms and apparatus. Two years later James Clerk - Maxwell was appointed to the Chair. His portrait hangs in the hall of the Austin Wing of the laboratory, whilst at the Museum entrance is a marble bust of him by Boehm. It is inscribed dp/dt, the differential coefficient being Maxwell's favourite pun on his initials. In the second law of thermodynamics $dp/dt = JCM$.

The Maxwell apparatus that can be seen in the Cavendish gives some indication of the range of the early experiments. This includes the real image stereoscope; the colour top and prismatic colour box designed by Maxwell for his work on the quantative analysis of colour vision and colour blindness; apparatus for measuring the viscosity of gases; dynamical tops showing the motion of a rigid body rotating about its centre of gravity; the spinning coil to detect any inertia effect of the electric current; the pseudo-sphere and deformable cap which he made in 1854; a model illustrating a theory of the Rings of Saturn. In 1856 Maxwell won the Adams Prize in the University for his famous essay "On the Stability of Motion of Saturn's Rings". His Zoetrope or Wheel of Life is interesting. When he was eight years old he had shown interest in a mechanical device called the "Magic Disc" or Thaumatrope. A series of pictures were painted on a disc containing radial slits. Looking through the slits at a mirror and spinning the disc created the effect of motion. The flat disc made way for a drum which could be rotated on its axis. That dispensed with the need for the mirror. Maxwell added further modification by substituting concave lenses for slits and adding an ingenious series of slides for the Zoetrope.

After Maxwell's death in 1879, Lord Rayleigh was appointed Professor. Maxwell's workshop was enlarged to provide for the increased demands of teaching and research. Rayleigh's research concentrated on the increase in precision that was being demanded in electrical units. He reduced the level of uncertainty from about 3 per cent almost to the present high standards of accuracy and reproducibility. Rayleigh resigned in 1884 and was succeeded by the youthful Joseph John Thomson, who turned from mathematics to experimental work on electrical discharges in gases. From then on this tremendously productive research dominated the laboratory that became the centre of the first large research school in this country and achieved international fame from the galaxy of distinguished physicists presided over by "J.J."

In 1911 C. T. R. Wilson began the construction of an instrument, the Cloud Chamber, which had more influence on the development of modern physics than any other single piece of apparatus. Lord Rutherford became Cavendish Professor in 1919. An interesting reminder of his earliest scientific work is the detector for electric waves

Below: Sir George Thomson, physicist and Master of Corpus Christi College, showing a proof sent to him of the likeness of his father, Sir J. J. Thomson, physicist and Master of Trinity College, and a significant influence in world history through his discovery of the electron. This particular picture was reproduced on a Swedish postage stamp

which he built when he first entered the laboratory as a research student. It enabled signals to be detected at what was then a record distance of about one-and-a-half miles. On his return as Professor, Rutherford immediately resumed researches on radioactivity which had been interrupted. His first great achievement in Cambridge was to observe the disingegration of nitrogen nuclei by α-particles. F. W. Ashton's work on isotopes started when assisting Thomson with the research on positive rays. When Rutherford died, Sir Lawrence Bragg became Professor in 1938. One of the X-ray spectrometers with which early determinations of crystal structure were made by W. H. Bragg and W. L. Bragg, father and son, in 1912, is preserved in the Cavendish together with some of the first versions of the powder camera for X-ray crystallography. These are but some of the reminders of early experiments that are preserved in the Cavendish.

The 1895 change in the regulations of the University that allowed graduates of other universities to work on research projects in the Cavendish Laboratories enabled Ernest Rutherford from New Zealand to come to Cambridge. It also produced an agreeable postscript. It is not often that a leading Russian-born atomic scientist is welcomed to this country with genuine affection, but such was the experience of Peter Kapitza, the brains behind Russia's first A-bomb and satellites. At the end of the 1914–1918 war,

The Maxwell apparatus in the Cavendish gives some indication of the range of early experiments carried out by this Cavendish Professor of Physics (1831–79), in particular the improvements in devising an ingenious series of slides for this Zoetrope. It was a continuation of the interest shown by Maxwell at the age of eight years in a mechanical device called the "Magic Disc" or Thaumatrope, in which a series of pictures were painted on a disc containing radial slits. On looking through the slits at a mirror and spinning the disc, the effect of motion could be obtained

161

Kapitza was sent by the Russian authorities to visit various laboratories on the Continent with authority to buy or note any apparatus which might be of value to the Soviet Union. One such visit was to the Cavendish Laboratory where he met Professor Rutherford, who agreed to accept him as a research student. He made such spectacular progress that he was elected a Fellow of Trinity College five years later and eventually a Fellow of the Royal Society. Kapitza's work produced a magnetic field of far greater intensity than earlier ones. He constructed novel apparatus that could produce liquid helium and liquid hydrogen at temperatures near absolute zero. This, plus many more experiments, were recognised by the Royal Society's appointment of a personal Professorship and a grant from the Ludwig Mond Bequest for the building of the Mond Laboratory designed in particular for Kapitza's special work.

From 1926 onwards Kapitza made several visits to Russia, leaving his wife and family in Cambridge, but always getting a written assurance from the Russian authorities that he would be allowed to return on a specified date. In 1934 he again visited Russia to attend a conference to honour the Soviet scientist Mendeléeff, only this time he was ordered to stay and work in Russia, where he continued his researches, in 1944 being awarded the Order of Lenin and in 1955 the Stalin Prize. But it was evident from letters that he resented his enforced status.

Thirty-two years later Kapitza returned to Cambridge, where he received a warm welcome from the Cavendish scientists and the handful who had previously worked with him. He described how he and his wife had tried to create an English style of life. A magnificent villa had been specially built near Moscow, surrounded by a rose garden, a very English lawn and a tennis court. It was an attempt to capture something of the atmosphere of Newnham Cottage, Lord Rutherford's pleasant house with a large garden. In his study was a huge polar bear skin on the floor, again repeating a Cambridge touch, whilst next door had been built a specially equipped laboratory. One luxury was a car and chauffeur, but at heart he preferred the old bike that he used to pedal along the Backs.

One thing he was not able to copy was Rutherford's "Talking Foursome", a group that used to play a form of golf on the Gog Magog course. There were eight members of this select company: Francis Aston, Chairman of the International Committee on Atoms and Nobel Prize for Chemistry; Charles Darwin, Master of Christ's College; Charles Ellis, Wheatstone Professor of Physics; Ralph Fowler, Plummer Professor of Applied Mathematics; Frederick Mann, Reader in Organic Chemistry; Francis Roughton, John Humphrey Professor of Colloid Science; Richard Southwell, Rector of Imperial College of Science; and Geoffrey Taylor, Yarrow Research Professor of the Royal Society. As Kapitza remarked, rarely had such a battery of brainpower been applied to mastering the art of golf. The fact that they failed was some compensation for, on the two occasions that he played, the results were catastrophic, possibly accentuated by the fact that he adopted a stance on the tee some forty-five degrees to the right of the required direction. As a consequence he visited parts of the course the others never knew existed. The tactics adopted by this academic eightsome anticipated Stephen Potter's gamesmanship.

19TH AND 20TH CENTURY COLLEGES

Cambridge has several theological colleges whose students, though not members of the University, can sit the theological Tripos. Westminster College, founded in 1844, trains Presbyterian ministers. Ridley Hall and Westcott House are its Anglican counterparts. Wesley House looks after the Methodists, whilst St Edmund's House, founded in 1896, trains Roman Catholic priests and became a graduate college of the University in 1965. Homerton College is a teacher training college and an approved society of the University and accepts men and women for the education Tripos. Hughes Hall was founded in 1949 to train women graduates as teachers, being founded a University Institute. New Hall is an undergraduate college for women and was founded in 1954. It is housed on the Huntingdon Road in striking buildings with a dome of neo-Byzantine flavour that has become a landmark. Lucy Cavendish College, for women whose studies have been interrupted, was given University recognition in 1965. Robinson College was the first undergraduate Cambridge College to be founded for both men and women. The building was opened in 1980. The Chapel has stained glass by John Piper.

Below: Darwin College in Silver Street consists of George Darwin's family home, Newnham Grange, and the adjoining house, The Hermitage, joined together in 1964. A feature is the octagonal dining-hall on stilts

In 1964 Fitzwilliam House moved to new buildings on the Huntingdon Road, close to New Hall. An outstanding feature of the hall are the huge clerestory windows that rise gracefully to a well-proportioned roof lantern. In 1965 the University founded its own College for graduates in Barton Road, but when the cost was met by the Wolfson Foundation, the name was changed from University College to Wolfson College. Darwin College in Silver Street consists of George Darwin's family home, Newnham Grange, and the adjoining house, The Hermitage, joined together in 1964 in harmonious fashion. A feature is its octagonal dining-hall on stilts. In 1965, with the help of American benefactors, Clare College founded an independent graduate College, Clare Hall, providing modern facilities for academic family units. Churchill College, founded in 1960, was meant to be a national monument to Sir Winston Churchill. Architecturally the building is different and looks out of character in Cambridge with a chain of open courtyards. The Chapel was built in 1967 after heated controversy. Extremists argued that such a building was not in keeping with a strictly science-orientated college. The Library contains the archive of the Churchill family papers, and a tapestry by Jean Lurcat presented by General de Gaulle. In the grounds are sculptures by Henry Moore and Barbara Hepworth.

GRANTCHESTER

Grantchester is rightly named the Poets' Village for it inspired Chaucer, Byron, Wordsworth, Tennyson and Rupert Brooke. The phantom mill is just that, for it was burned down in 1928, but its memory has immortalised both mill and miller. Rupert Brooke wrote:

> Dan Chaucer hears his river still
> Chatter beneath a phantom mill.

Tennyson, remembering the romance of the Miller's Daughter, left these words:

> I loved the brimming wave that swam
> Through quiet meadows round the mill
> The sleepy pool above the dam
> The pool beneath it never still.

Wordsworth added these lines:

> Beside the pleasant Mill of Trompington
> I laughed with Chaucer in the hawthorne shade;
> Heard him, while birds were warbling, tell his tales
> Of amorous passion.

Then there is Chaucer's *Reeve's Tale* of the deceitful Miller of Trumpington:

> At Trompyngtoun, nat fer fro Cantebrigge,
> Ther goth a brook, and over that a brigge,
> Upon the whiche brook there stant a melle:
> And this is verray sothe that I you telle.
> A meller was there dwellyng many a day,
> As eny pecock he was prowd and gay;
> Pipen he coude, and fissh, and nettys beete,
> And turne cuppes, wrastle wel, and scheete.
> Ay by his belt he bar a long panade,
> And of a swerd ful trenchaunt was the blade.
> A joly popper bar he in his pouche;
> There no man for perel durst him touche.

It is sad that Cambridge, whilst preserving her ancient buildings, should be indifferent to others, essentially utilitarian but historically important. Having ceased usefully to serve the purpose for which they were made, they collapse through neglect and are scrapped, a fate that all too often befalls the windmill. My home in Trumpington had a well-known windmill in its grounds. It stopped working in 1887, and was then sold to the Master of Christ's College who, failing to let it, pulled it down – an act of vandalism regretted by the villagers, one of whom recalled how on wild nights they were sometimes called to unship the fan-sail because it was going too fast for the machinery to act. The mill would then have to be turned into the wind by the use of the hand winch. This attitude of the Master of Christ's is unfortunately common. All too often the fate of a windmill is disrepair, dereliction, demolition. Only a street-name records its existence, and in a few years it becomes difficult to visualise it in such a setting. Grantchester is an exception. The mill is no more, but everything else is still there – Byron's Pool, the water-meadows, the Old Vicarage and the orchard, apple blossom and the medieval church with its small Saxon window, Norman doorway and fourteenth century

Apple blossom in the Orchard at Grantchester, immortalised by Rupert Brooke

165

chancel. Records show that the church was used for "sanctuary". A murderer or thief could take sanctuary. As long as he remained in the church or churchyard, no one could touch him, but nobody could supply him with food. Once he left consecrated ground, he could be arrested. The outcome was usually that the Coroner arrived and gave the fugitive the choice of "surrendering to the king's peace", i.e., giving himself up to be tried in the court, or "abjuring the realm", i.e., going into banishment overseas. The latter was invariably preferable. The Coroner then assigned the port of departure, giving a brief period in which to reach it. Should he be found in England after that, the individual's life was forfeit.

History goes a long way back in Grantchester. Traces of Romano-British earthworks have been found near the village school, whilst bones of the mammoth and woolly rhinoceros have also been unearthed, but the visitor prefers the Brooke associations, happily still not over-commercialised. The church is no longer stopped at ten to three but by the mill-pond the poet's lines take on significance:

> . . . in that garden, black and white,
> Creep whispers through the grass all night;
> And spectral dance, before the dawn,
> A hundred Vicars down the lawn;
> Curates, long dust, will come and go
> On lisson, clerical, printless toe;
> And oft between the boughs is seen
> The sly shade of a Rural Dean . . .

Below: *This row of cottages in Grantchester is as well-known as Byron's Pool and the Old Vicarage*

Unfortunately the Old Vicarage does not lend itself to such spectral visions, but the memories linger.

UNIVERSITY LIBRARY

The central tower of the University Library, 156 feet high, is a familiar landmark. Designed by Sir Giles Gilbert Scott, completed in 1934, and opened by George V, it enjoys rights originating in the Press Licensing Acts of Charles II by which all publications should be licensed and registered at Stationers' Hall and three of each delivered to the Master of the Stationers Company for the use of the Royal Library and the Universities of Oxford and Cambridge.

Apart from this unceasing flow of new books, there are individual treasures like Chaucer's *Annelida and Arcyte*, printed about 1476 by Caxton; Bede's *Historia Ecclesiastica*, written about A.D. 730; the *Book of Cerne* of the ninth century; the first book printed in English, the *Recuyell of the Histories of Troy*; a manuscript of the Gospels given to the University in 1581; Chaucer's translation of *Boethius*, presented by John Croucher in the fifteenth century. To these can be added an unusual relic, a fragment of the shroud of Edward the Confessor (1042–66). Apparently when workmen were removing the scaffolding in 1685 after the coronation of James II in Westminster Abbey, the coffin of Edward was damaged. A cross and fragments of the shroud were taken out of the tomb. The cross and chain were taken to the King, who gave it to his Queen, Mary of Modena, who in turn passed it on to Prince James (the Old Pretender). The last reference to the cross was when Pope Benedict XIII received it from Charles Edward on the 17th June, 1729. A fragment of the shroud came into the possession of Symon Patrick, Prebendary of Westminster. Twenty years later he became Bishop of Ely and wrote a "Diary" of how the tomb was broken. This can be seen in the University Library, together with a piece of the shroud pinned to it.

Below: The familiar landmark of the central tower of the University Library that was designed by Sir Giles Gilbert Scott, completed in 1934, and opened by George V

A MILD PUB CRAWL

A mild pub crawl can be quite pleasant provided you know beforehand the sort of pub you want. Terminology is important. I use the terms inn, pub, tavern, and public house to describe places where alcoholic drinks are sold and consumed on the premises. In that way somewhat legal distinctions can be avoided. For instance, originally the tavern or the inn were controlled by different licenses and laws drawn up by the Act of Edward VI. The inn was limited to the lodging of travellers and the inn-keeper was required to keep an open door for such a purpose by day and night. Occasional drinking by the casual caller was illegal. On the other hand, the vintner, who usually kept the tavern, was only allowed to serve casual food and drink, was forbidden to provide sleeping accommodation and had to shut the doors at stipulated hours.

Today, though the licences are still different, their respective functions have overlapped. It is permissible to sleep overnight at a tavern, whilst a casual drink can be had at any inn. The *Oxford Dictionary* makes a broader classification when it defines a public-house as "an inn or tavern providing food or lodging, especially alcoholic liquors to be consumed on the premises". Even here there is the possibility of a further distinction between a public-house, which is licensed to sell all kinds of drink, and a beer-house, which is not licensed for spirits.

It all seems very complicated. All we want is a drink. It is simpler to use the terms in interchangeable fashion and conform to the general usage of someone in search of liquid refreshment and maybe food in convivial surroundings. There is no shortage of choice in Cambridge, though nothing like there used to be. At the beginning of the last century there were no fewer than thirty-one inns in the area around Bridge Street and Magdalene Street, whilst in the seventeenth century there were several inns alongside St Catharine's College in Trumpington Street. They were thirsty days. The sixteenth century building that is now the Folk Museum was once the White Horse Inn. The old Bar Parlour is still identifiable, but of the others, little remains, like the seventeenth century Three Tuns, the haunt of Dick Turpin remembered only by legends. Names are recorded. Magdalene Street had the Cross Keys, Swan, Plough Arms and King's Head. The house occupied by Professor Glyn Daniels, the archaeologist, had four previous identities as an inn . . . Wild Man, Freemason's Tavern, Royal Oak and Flying Stag. Whewell's Court in Trinity Street was built on the site of the early seventeenth century Dolphin Inn. Spacious, with some forty rooms, it housed the Judges of Assize. It was here that Cranmer fell in love with the landlord's niece. The infatuation cost him his Fellowship at Jesus, but after her death a year later, he was reinstated, eventually becoming Archbishop of Canterbury under Henry VIII.

Cambridge has lost many historic posting and coaching inns. As recently as 1986 the Blue Boar Hotel in Trinity Street has ceased to exist. In 1812 it was the inn of the Union London stage coach. St Catharine's College absorbed the Bull Hotel in the same way that in 1637 it swallowed up the George Inn, once owned by Thomas Hobson, the carrier. All we know of the seventeenth century Rose Tavern is that Pepys used to stay there – the former yard and coach-houses are now Rose Crescent. Occasionally the names of the inns have special significance. Signboards take us back to the days when few people could read and fewer still could write. Shops adopted pictorial signs, readily understood and easy to remember. For instance, the Pompeii excavations revealed tradesmen's signs made of stone and terracotta, some even painted: a goat indicated a dairy; a cupid with a shoe in either hand meant a shoemaker's shop; a slave carrying a wine skin marked a wine merchant; a chisel and adze suggested the tools of a carpenter; a millstone and ears of corn announced a baker. The sign of the inn had a special significance for the early landlords. Each was forced by law to show one. A record of 1393 tells of a landlord who was penalised for ignoring this ruling. Stipulations were clear: the sign could be hung on a post in front of the inn; suspended from an iron bar fixed in the wall; fastened on the ale-stake projecting from the building; or carved on the building façade. Signs were not cheap. "A meere vanite" sign in 1577 cost £40; semi-triumphal arches spanning the road, often in black oak, cost over £1,000. Later regulations made it illegal for signs to project the width of the roadway during Charles II's reign.

To produce an original sign calls for lively imagination and inventive ingenuity. Many do have commemorative significance, but others are a farrago of legend and fact. Cambridge has its quota. It would be interesting to trace their origins. A dozen at random produces a mixed bag . . . Hopbine and Barley Ear; Bees in the Wall; Cow and Calf; The King Street Run; Pike and Eel; Cricketers' Arms; Robin Hood and Little John; Dobblers Arms; Fort St George; The Grasshopper; The Hat and Feathers; Durham Ox. Cambridge tastes and humours are in line with the landlords of the past, Dickensian, Jonsonian and Shakespearean at heart.

For the would-be pub-connoisseur in search of a drink, my choice is narrowed to five inns, each of historical and unusual interest and convivial in welcome:

> The Pickerel Inn in Magdalene Street. Dates from the sixteenth century.
> The Baron of Beef in Bridge Street. Plenty of history and atmosphere.
> Bath Hotel in Bene't Street. Seventeenth century building.
> Eagle in Bene't Street. Galleried with yard. Shown in Loggan's plan of 1688 as a Post House called the Eagle and Child.
> Little Rose in Trumpington Street. Coaching inn that attracts many well-known personalities.

Even this brief pub crawl will confirm that no other country can match the atmosphere of the genuine tavern and inn. In this respect Cambridge is fortunate.

The Pickerel Inn in Magdalene Street with records as far back as the sixteenth century. In World War II it was a favourite hostelry for American servicemen

*The galleried Eagle that
appears on Loggan's 1688
plan as a Post House
called the Eagle and Child*

WILLIAM WORDSWORTH (St John's College)

The Evangelist St John my patron was:
Three Gothic courts are his, and in the first
Was my abiding place, a nook obscure;
Right underneath, the college kitchens made
A humming sound, less tuneable than bees,
But hardly less industrious; with shrill notes
If sharp command and scolding intermixed.
Near me hung Trinity's loquacious clock,
Who never let the quarters, night or day,
Slip by him unproclaimed, and told the hours
Twice over with a male and female voice.
Her peeling organ was my neighbour too;
And from my pillow, looking forth by night
Of moon or favouring stars, I could behold
The ante chapel where the statue stood
Of Newton with his prism and silent face
The marble index of a mind for ever
Voyaging strange seas of thought alone

A COLLECTION OF RARE CHURCHES

Cambridge is fortunate to have a series of churches of great diversity and unusual interest with a wealth of medieval and even earlier detail, an embarrassment of riches that makes churches in other parts of the country seem stereotyped by comparison. I have selected seven that should be visited by a discerning visitor.

1. The Church of the Holy Sepulchre known as the Round Church is one of the four round churches of England said to have belonged originally to the Knights Templar. Nicholas Pevsner had reservations about a claim, and pointed out that the link could not be proved, but the immediate neighbourhood of the Hospital of St John, even if it did not go back further than the early thirteenth century, might have had something to do with choice of shape. The style of the Round Church went well with that date. It is Norman, only unfortunately the Victorians, encouraged by the Camden Society, so restored the fabric that it is virtually a nineteenth century building. It is inconceivable that Salvin, the architect, was allowed to build on this Norman structure a chancel in

The Round Church or the Church of the Holy Sepulchre is one of the few remaining Round Churches in this country: the others are at Northampton, Little Maplestead in Essex, and the Temple Church in London. The Cambridge church has the distinction of being the oldest, though pin-pointing the actual date is not easy; the early part of the twelfth century is probable. Originally the church consisted of the ambulatory aisle and the circular nave. The fifteenth century saw the chancel and north aisle reconstructed. In 1841 the Cambridge Camden Society restored the church with regrettable thoroughness

imitation Decorated style. He also destroyed the polygonal upper storey of the circular nave containing four bells. Imitation Norman windows, copied from the remaining old ones, replaced those inserted in the fifteenth century, whilst new stone vaults and high pitched roofs were constructed over the nave and ambulatory. In spite of brutal iconoclastic restoration, the church has many points of interest. Standing in the nave is an unusual experience.

2. St Edward's Church in St Edward's Passage is closely linked with the events and personalities of the Reformation. Three of the martyrs who were burnt alive for their beliefs are remembered by a tablet in the church . . . "To the Glory of God and to honour those from this Parish who in the years 1523 to 1525 met near by at the White Horse Inn and there sought out the principles of the English Reformation:

Thomas Bilney   1531
Robert Barnes   1540
Hugh Latimer   1555"

Henry VI granted the advowson of St Edward's to Trinity Hall when the church of St John Zachary had to be demolished to clear the area of King's College. It became a Peculiar which put it outside diocesan jurisdiction. Two small chapels were added on each side of the chancel for the students of Clare and Trinity Hall who before had worshipped in St John Zachary.

The lower part of the west tower is dated about 1200, the nave being about 1400. The pulpit, *c.* 1510, is the one from which Latimer preached. Note the fine linenfold panelling. The night-watchman's chair, *c.* 1480, came from a Dorset church. It is kept as a reminder that King Edward, the patron saint, was murdered at Corfe Castle in A.D. 978. The parish register records that a woman parishioner died on the 17th August, 1650, aged 112 and is buried in the churchyard. These lines are added:

> Elinor Gaskin said
> She lived four-score years a maid
> And twenty and two years a married wife
> And ten years a widow, and then she left this life.

. . . the words have a touching finality about them.

3. Quite different is Holy Trinity in Market Street. The first church was destroyed by fire in 1174. The lower parts of the tower may be thirteenth century. A gallery in the south transept was built during the incumbency of Charles Simeon in 1836. His monument by Hopper has an epitaph in Gothic forms. The church is traditionally linked with the Evangelistic Movement.

4. St Mary-the-Less or Little St Mary's is a gem of the Decorated period. Originally it was called St Peter-without-Trumpington Gate. It was appropriated by Peterhouse when the College was founded and took its name from the church which served as a chapel until 1632. It dates from the twelfth century, was consecrated in 1352, and is basically a simple structure with a chapel in the crypt. A memorial to Richard Washington bears his coat of arms with the Stars and Stripes and an Eagle crest. In 1639 Richard Crashaw, the poet, was incumbent.

5. St Bene't's Church is the oldest church in town or county. In spite of alterations in later centuries, it retains some Saxon architecture dated between A.D. 350 and A.D. 1050. It is thought that it might have been the parish church of an East Anglican settlement when the Mercians commanded the castle. It was certainly standing when William the Conqueror landed. The tower, built in three stages, each slightly lower than the one below, was erected in A.D. 1025. The tower arch in the interior incorporates two Anglo-Saxon carved lions. It was used as a chapel by Corpus Christi College until the sixteenth century.

Thomas Hobson, the Cambridge carrier, was buried in the chancel in 1632, whilst Fabian Stedman, born 1631, was clerk of this parish in 1650. He invented changeringing. The first organised peal of bells in England echoed from the tower. The church is unusual in that it is served by Anglican Franciscans sent from the mother church at Cerne Abbas in Dorset.

6. Churches dedicated to St Botolph, the patron saint of wayfarers and beggars, usually stand near the gates of cities. In Cambridge such a church was just inside the Trumpington Gate. Very little is known about the saint, but he is mentioned in the Anglo-Saxon Chronicle. Folcard, Abbot of Thorney, wrote about him shortly after the Conquest. His name occurs regularly in the pre-Reformation English Kalendars. Forty churches in England are named after him, ten being in Norfolk. According to Sir Walter Scott it was a Prior of St Botolph who tended the wounded Ivanhoe, and it was the

Prior's ambling jennet, Malkin, that bore the injured man to the Castle of Coningsburgh.

Trumpington Gate has gone, but the church is a reminder of the days when a Saxon church stood on the site, though no traces remain today. It was succeeded by a Norman building and two Norman capitals can still be seen in the bases of the nave piers as well as fragments in the outer walls of the tower. The present church dates from about 1320 with the tower added in 1400. The body of the church is essentially early fourteenth century. Against the outer south wall of the chancel is a tablet to Robert Crumbold, the master-mason. The belfry contains a complete and untouched medieval ring of four bells, just as they came about 1460 from the foundry of John Danyell, a famous London bell-founder, who also cast the lost bells of King's College. The identity of the founder is established by the fact that all four have the same lettering, small and capital Black letters. All four have a floriated stop, which was Danyell's, and all except the treble have his shield with the arms of France, modern and England. The treble and second have one of Danyell's crosses and the treble has his initials J.D.

7. St Mary Magdalene on the Newmarket Road was originally the chapel of the Leper Hospital at Stourbridge. The surroundings are depressing. The ground, once known as the Common Field of Cambridge, was doubtless chosen for isolating a disease that became rare in England after 1300. The hospital was endowed in 1211 by King John

The churchyard of St Bene't's, the oldest church in town or county. In spite of alterations over the centuries, it retains some Saxon architectural features dated between A.D. 350 and A.D. 1050

with money from Stourbridge Fair, described as "the largest and most famous fair in all England and held in the Close on the vigil and feast of the Holy Cross".

At first sight, the chapel looks uninspiring, but in architectural value it is one of the most complex examples of solid Norman work and amazingly unspoilt. It is some fifty feet long by twelve and a half feet wide, built of flint except at the chancel end which is ashlar-faced. The roof was replaced in the fifteenth century. In 1816 Thomas Kerrick bought the chapel, then a stable, for £160 and gave it to the University. Fifty years later Gilbert Scott carried out some alterations, and inserted the west window, though the circular windows below are original. This gaunt chapel for lepers is an architectural treasure.

A church dedicated to St Botolph, the patron saint of wayfarers and beggars, stood just inside the Trumpington Gate. The Gate is gone, but the church is a reminder of the days when a Saxon church occupied the site

A CORNER OF A FOREIGN FIELD . . .
FOR EVER AMERICA

In Domesday Book the little village of Madingley is mentioned as containing some 150 inhabitants. Nearly a thousand years later its size had hardly altered, unless we add to their numbers a still, silent assembly of brave men.

In World War II, 15 million American men and women saw active service; 360,810 died overseas. In the majority of cases they were buried near where they fell in temporary graves. When the war ended more than half were taken back to America from some 250 temporary cemeteries in accordance with the wishes of relatives. Those who were left were laid to rest in fourteen permanent memorial cemeteries in the fields of North Africa, Luxembourg, Italy, the Netherlands, at Manila, near Bataan, Corregidor, and at the village of Madingley within sight of the towers and spires of Cambridge on land given by the University to the United States.

It is a moving sight. In the clearing among the trees, the silence broken only by the cawing of rooks, is an army almost 4,000 strong. Many belonged to the Army Air Forces; some died in the Battle of the Atlantic, others in training areas of the United Kingdom, in the invasion of North Africa and Normandy. Their final parade is row upon row of white marble crosses. On the headstones a Star of David records those of the Jewish faith, a Latin Cross on all the others. Wherever possible the name of the man, with other information, is cut upon the headstone. When identification was denied, the inscription reads, "Here Rests in Honored Glory a Comrade in Arms Known But to God".

On a long Wall of Remembrance is engraved a roll of 5,125 missing in action. The inscription is simple, "Americans, whose names here appear, were part of the price that free men for the second time in this century have been forced to pay to defend human liberty and rights." The chapel, designed by Perry, Shaw and Hepburn, Kehoe and Dean, of Boston, Massachusetts, is a memorial in itself. The mosaic created by Francis Scott Bradford of New York City portrays seraphim, Latin Crosses, the Star of David, and quotations from the Twenty-third Psalm. The altar cloth bears the first two Greek letters in the name of Christ. The chapel is representative of the American people, with illustrated battle maps, large murals, amplified with explanations of the campaigns.

The Stars and Stripes flag flies over acres that are now American soil, moving in the wind as if fingers were plucking the folds. It is a reminder of the sacrifices that were made. The tribute paid by Pericles to the dead of ancient Athens is appropriate: "In foreign lands there dwells also an unwritten memorial to them, graven not on stone but in the hearts of men."

When World War II ended, the University of Cambridge gave land to the United States for a permanent memorial cemetry. Row upon row of white marble crosses mark the resting-place of almost 4,000 American servicemen. The name of each man is cut upon the headstone. When identification was not possible, the inscription reads, "Here Rests in Honored Glory a Comrade in Arms Known But to God". The Stars and Stripes flag flies over these acres that are now American soil

GARDENERS' DELIGHT

Cambridge offers richness of variety to gardeners and botanists alike. Praise from Wordsworth, Tennyson and Henry James would have been even more fulsome today for the range is now bewildering. There is something for every taste, be it flowers, shrubs or trees, a mixture of rarity and commonplace. An obvious starting-point is the University Botanic Garden, but once through the impressive wrought-iron gates, the problem then is what to look for. First impressions are influenced by the lofty trees that dominate the scene, a noble array of massive oaks, beeches, chestnuts, pines, limes and birches. Also prominent is the great black walnut; the Tree of Heaven that was introduced into this country in 1751 from China; the American smoke tree, so rich in colour in the autumn; the Caucasian wing-nut; the delicate flowers of the Judas tree – legend declares that Judas Iscariot hung himself from one of its branches; the *Prunus serrula* from China with bark that has the deep bloom of copper; the *Tetracentron sinese*, possibly the most unusual tree of all; the Scots pine in the Old Pinetum; and the monkey-puzzle tree, said to have been introduced into Europe by Archibald Menzies, who slipped into his pocket some of the seeds being eaten as dessert at a Chilean banquet.

Exploration becomes a series of visual delights . . . the display of peonies by the herbaceous border, flowers that are mentioned in the *Chinese Book of Songs* of 3300 B.C.; the selection of saxifrages in the Rock Garden; the chronological beds that show when various flowers and plants first appeared in England, the sequence beginning with woad, then names like the almond, gillyflowers, primroses, columbines, periwinkles, and violets. For those to whom sight is denied the Scented Garden for the blind offers compensation with *Pelargonium odoratissimum*, *Pelargonium fragrans* and *Chrysanthemum balsamita*; also thyme, rosemary, mint, tobacco and stock. The lake and water garden are restful with willows, royal ferns and water lilies, not forgetting the white forest of pampas grass. The Winter Garden adds a splash of colour during the dark months with yellow Japanese witch hazel and the red *Salix alba Chermesina*, plus the heathers. Impressive in a menacing mood is the overpowering giant hogweed jungle. The pasque flower of purple and gold near the Rock Garden has a haunting beauty. Contrasts in rapid succession can be found in the Palm House, Alpine House, Stove House and Temperate House. Weird tropical specimens and menacing carnivorous plants are in a world apart. *Nepenthes rafflesiana* is a plant named after the elusive Raffles of Singapore. It is the base of a tranquilliser and flaunts its speckled bag as a trap waiting to snare its prey. The Conservatory is like a Victorian time-capsule with its arum lilies, passion flowers, coleus, poinsettias, chrysanthemums and cinerarias.

Should this profusion of specimens become too much, there can be lighter interludes. When we tire of the flowers, we can always scrutinise the people who are looking at them. They come, if not from the ends of the earth, then from all the soils of England, and make a fascinating subject of study, though they are not in themselves as beautiful as the flowers. Take their accents. It needs Henry Higgins, Professor of Phonetics, to do justice to them. Some are professional gardeners from the country and their wives, free for the day from caring for the kind of garden which owners throw open to the public on Sundays in aid of some odd charity. They are not to be confused with the occasional prosperous professional who owns a nursery, wins a gold medal for exhibits, and is really a successful businessman in an extra-mural kind of way. No one can confuse either class with the amateurs: men from outlying suburbs taking a quick look round;

young wives who have taken up roses and head straight for the beds illustrating their history with ramblers, medieval damasks, hybrid tes and China roses; quietly-dressed ladies with old-fashioned hair styles who jot down the names of varieties. They cannot all be vicar's wives, but they look as if they might be.

Many have problems with identification, which brings up the question of Latin. Some find botanical names irritating, changeable, difficult to remember accurately and ignorantly formed, whilst the question of pronunciation is made more complicated by the use of the old and new methods of speaking Latin. Those who seek the true pronunciation resort to a reliable gardening dictionary, maybe consult a professional gardener, or even listen to *Gardeners' Question Time* on the radio. If all agree, which is

The grounds of the Colleges and the University Botanic Garden offers a richness of variety that appeals to gardeners and botanists alike. Many are rare, and all are a visual delight

extremely unlikely, it is possible to mouth the words confidentially, but the satisfaction can be short-lived. Those who grumble should recall the ornithologists' *Troglodytes troglodytes troglodytes* and be thankful for *Robinia hispida, Salix Alba, Erica carnea* and other such pleasant-sounding names.

But such thoughts are for the professional. Rank-and-file gardening is more on a footing with Isaac Walton's fishing. It breeds in its devotees a feeling of quiet contentment, mainly because it is constantly reminding the gardener of his power to obtain desired and beautiful results. A garden is like a private study, where we can defy the outside world. This is the aim of the true gardener. In contrast to the severe, monotonous arrangements which too often constitute the gardens around some of our finest houses, there are also displays, not only in the University Botanic Garden, but in the Colleges, where every yard brings a surprise and a fresh interest. Old walls have growing from crevices such plants as Cheddar pink, sedums and sempervivums, and an occasional calculated disorder of flower-beds, all forming an expression of horticultural taste. In Cambridge all these varying aesthetic senses of beauty can be satisfied.

Authority in the Botanic Garden is not all official. The atmosphere encourages the expert-for-the-day. Gardeners can be disconcerting people. Either they know infinitely more about the subject than you do or else they know infinitely less. You seldom encounter one with whom you can discuss a common topic on equal terms. The gardener who knows more is impossibly highbrow and makes you feel as small as a child trying to discuss medieval Latin literature with a scholar. Nevertheless visitors occasionally take advantage of the botanic expertise for advice on problems. A diseased leaf was brought in an envelope from a bush in a garden. The questioner asked how the ailment should be treated. Another enquiry was whether a mushroom found on Midsummer Common and indentified as death cap was edible. For most people the name itself would have been enough, whilst its picture showing a slimy scarlet cap covered with yellowish warts is hardly appetising. The questioner thought it could be eaten in small quantities with nothing worse than an intoxicating after-affect. The botanic expert was not convinced and advised against sampling it.

It seems that mushroomers, like flower huntswomen, muddle themselves with print and illustration. Showing commendable patience, the expert told the lady that fungi with gills sinuate and decurrent, adnate and adnexed, fall into simply recognisable groups, varying in culinary charms from those unexcelled in flavour, though rather indigestible, to those causing intense suffering, followed by death. Timid gourmets ought to know better than place their faith in such names as panther cap, which gives off an unpleasant sickly smell; crested lepiota with its anti-social behaviour; livid entoloma and red-staining inocybe who unblushingly look their evil parts; and the bluish-green verdigris agaric, that suggests the most violent gastronomic consequences. The fairies who danced among the fairy ring champignons must surely have been the bad ones from their Titania downwards. As the Cambridge specialist observed, it is wiser to approach this enigmatic plant with conservative caution.

A feature common to all gardeners is their optimism: it is always enterprising and never satisfied. They are for ever planting and for ever digging up. They always look forward to doing better than they have ever done before. "Next year . . ." they say, and even as the words are pronounced, their enthusiasm becomes infectious, and you allow yourself to be persuaded that the garden will indeed look different, quite different, next year. Sadly experience tells us that it never does, but how poor and disheartening a thing is experience compared with hope. It is better to be sanguine even at the cost of future disillusionment. The ranks never thin of those amateurs with their notebooks and pencils, peering closely at the displays and taking notes. There is no elbowing or shoving for a particular courtesy survives, a gardener's courtesy, in a world where courtesy is giving place to rougher things.

The University Botanic Garden rewards the discerning eye. There is always the danger of missing specials among the profusion of old favourites, but they are always there. What can be done amazes the amateur, like the appearance of the blue poppy; snapdragons like church spires; delphiniums that challenge cathedral towers; bougain-villeas transformed into flaming sunsets bearing no resemblance to the old magenta curtains we used to know; and lilies competing with Jack's beanstalk. It would be churlish to criticise, but at times the amazing results produced call for careful assess-ment. Everyone welcomes the advances made by experiments in hybridisation that has led to some remarkable effects, but some of the older school hesitate to approve the turbescence among familiar flowers and dislike the unnatural specimens that are some-times introduced. The experts are not to blame. They are only doing their job using all the resources at their disposal, but many of those who look cannot emulate them, nor would wish to do so. On the other hand, it is right to cater for every taste. There will always be plant-lovers rather than garden-lovers, likewise the endless conflict between the advocates of garden-formalism and so-called landscapism, but the majority are those who turn to flowers that hold for them memories of gardens with happy associa-tions. In the University Botanic Garden they will not be disappointed.

SAWSTON HALL

Sawston Hall is the only Elizabethan courtyard mansion in the county that is built of clunch. The original house was burnt by a Protestant mob when they learnt that Mary Tudor had found refuge in the Hall from the Duke of Northumberland who had been instructed to capture her. She escaped disguised, but by the time she reached the Gog Magog hills, the Hall was burning. Protestant persecution meant that treason felony was committed if Mass was heard. If the priest was caught, the charge was high treason. If guilty he would be half-hanged, disembowelled, and quartered. The only answer was a priest's hole where vessels, books and vestments could be kept in safety. Sawston Hall has a remarkable one designed by Nicholas Owen, a Jesuit dwarf. "The entrance is so cleverly arranged that it slants into the masonry of a circular tower, without showing the least perceptible sign, from the exterior, of a space capable of holding a baby, far less a man. A particular board in the landing is raised, and beneath it, in a corner of the cavity, is found a stone slab containing a circular aperture, some-thing after the manner of receptacles for coal. From this hole a tunnel slants downwards, at an angle, into the adjacent wall, where there is an apartment some twelve feet in depth, and wide anough to contain half a dozen people . . . The opening is so massive and firm that, unless pointed out, the particular floor-board could never be detected, and when secured from the inside could defy a battering ram."

Nicholas Owen was tortured to death in the Tower for refusing the reveal the where-abouts of the priests' holes he had made.

THE UNION SOCIETY

The premises of the Union Society behind the Round Church is the final resting-place of a debating society that began in a room at the back of the now demolished Red Lion in Petty Cury; moved to rooms behind the Hoop Hotel; then to a depressing site in Green Street that was once a Wesleyan Chapel, before transferring to a red-brick Gothic-styled building designed by Alfred Waterhouse.

The formal opening on the 30th October, 1866 was attended by 800 guests and members with the Earl of Powis, the Lord High Steward, presiding. An interesting speech by Richard Monckton Milnes, later Lord Houghton, recalled the Cambridge of Thackeray, Tennyson, Sunderland, and the rooms in the Red Lion. Milnes expressed a degree of uneasiness about the comparative luxury of the new premises: "The *genius loci* entirely fails me. This is not my Cambridge Union. My Cambridge Union was a low, ill-ventilated, ill-lit gallery at the back of the Red Lion Inn – cavernous, tavernous – something between a commercial-room and a district-branch-meeting-house (cheers and laughter). How can I compare it with this superb building, these commodious and decorated apartments, these perhaps over-luxurious applications of domestic architecture which you will have to enjoy? Yet those old and humble walls had, at the time I first entered them, just ceased to echo voices which England will not willingly let die. The strange irony of destiny, which so often strikes exactly those whose long life we should imagine most needed for the welfare of mankind, has already taken from us Macaulay, the great historical orator and oratorical historian (loud cheers); Praed, that perfect master of light and social verse; Charles Buller, whose young statesmanship you will see recorded in Westminster Abbey, but whose charm of character and talent belong to the domain of personal regard; and John Sterling, whose tumultuous spirit and lofty temper still live, and will long live, in the biographies of Hare and Carlyle. Two still walk among us, whom I should unwillingly pass by – Charles Austin, who has refused to extend to a political or judicial sphere those wondrous faculties of speech and that perspicuity of mind which has won for him all that professional fame can give, and Bulwer Lytton, whose varieties of success place him foremost in the literature of our day, and with whose name Lord Derby has now illustrated the House of Lords (cheers). My lot was cast with a somewhat later generation, and I must beg you to pardon the affection and prejudice with which I am inclined to believe that the members of that generation were, for the wealth of their promise, a promise in most cases perfectly fulfilled, a rare body of men such as this University has seldom contained . . . . But you will permit me to recall some names dear to myself, and, it may be, familiar to you all. There was Tennyson (loud cheers) – the Laureate, whose goodly bay-tree decorates our language and our land; and Arthur, the younger, Hallam, the subject of *In Memoriam* – poet and friend now passing linked hand-in-hand together down the slopes of fame . . . ."

The motion for that inaugural debate was "That this House views with regret the late substitution of a Conservative Government for a Liberal Government". Nine months later, Lord John Russell resigned and Lord Derby had taken office. An amendment *For regret* read *satisfaction* was moved. It all seems very familiar. That debating pattern is as strong as ever today. Speeches maintain a high standard and past Presidents continue to find themselves in high office once maturity mellows indignation.

Opposite: The Union Society behind the Round Church maintains a high standard of debating skills that many past Presidents have continued in high office

RADIO ASTRONOMICAL RESEARCH

The expansion of the Cambridge research programme in radio astronomy, which was started in 1946 at the Cavendish Laboratory, involved the use of an extensive area of land. When the four-aerial radio telescope was completed in 1953, it became obvious that further developments on that site were impracticable. Plans were made to set-up a new observatory on a site five miles south-west of Cambridge at Lord's Bridge, where the Mullard Radio Astronomy Observatory, still part of the Cavendish Laboratory, carries out the radio astronomical work at Cambridge. The scope of the work baffles the comprehension of the layman. A visit to the Observatory emphasises man's comparative minuteness in space and the astronomical unimportance of our abode. Ours is one of the smaller planets of a typical star. By cosmic standards our solar system is minute. The nearest star is so distant that light travelling from it at 186,000 miles a second takes four years to reach us, whilst our information is a few thousand millions years out of date. Moreover, there is no indication that we are seeing anything but a small part of the total universe. Still, to however awe-inspiring a degree the scale is expanded, poets, philosophers and theologians continue to believe with Alexander Pope that . . . .

> All are but parts of one stupendous whole,
> Whose body nature, and God the soul.

The man who directed this research was Sir Martin Ryle, whose achievements in science and pioneer work in radio astronomy were rewarded by the Establishment with all the honours in its gift. The list made impressive reading: Fellow of the Royal Society, 1952; first Chair of Radio Astronomy at Cambridge, 1959; Gold Medal of the Royal Astronomical Society, 1964; knighted, 1966. Then, when Sir Richard Woolley retired in 1972, Martin was made Astronomer Royal, the first time in the 300-year existence of this office that the honour had gone to someone not previously the Director of the Royal Greenwich Observatory. In 1974 Martin was awarded the Nobel Prize for Physics, jointly with Anthony Hewish.

At that point such acceptance seemed to turn sour. Disillusionment set in. Martin began to rethink his priorities. Fellow scientists urged him not to waste his skills, to stop acting like an eccentric. They misjudged their man. Martin never did anything without careful thought and reasoning, particularly when so much was at stake. He felt deeply that his scientific researches had been misdirected. Failing health had made necessary an operation for lung cancer. In 1984 he died. His wife, Rowena, has given me permission to quote from a letter he wrote to Professor Chagas of the Vatican Academy of Sciences and some notes in his handwriting found in personal papers. . . . "I am left at the end of my life with the feeling that it would have been better to have become a farmer in 1946. One can of course argue that somebody else would have done it anyway and so we must face the most fundamental of questions, should fundamental science be stopped."

Remarkable words from a man whose scientific researches had achieved so much. The reasons he put forward to explain his change of heart were specific. They were not just a personal cry of despair that morality and personal responsibility were being pushed aside. It was much deeper. Before outlining them it is helpful to recall his career, the scientific breakthroughs, and remember what sort of man he was. He came

Opposite: Sir Martin Ryle, whose achievements in science and pioneer work in radio astronomy were rewarded by the Establishment with all the honours in its gift

from an academic background. His father was a Physician to Guy's Hospital, then Regius Professor of Physic at Cambridge, later Professor of Social Medicine at Oxford. Martin went to Bradfield College after leaving Gladstone's Preparatory School in Sloane Square, graduated at Oxford in 1939 with a First in Physics, then went to the Cavendish Laboratory to work with J. A. Ratcliffe on radio aerial design.

At the outbreak of the war Martin went to the Air Ministry Research Establishment where he joined one of the world's finest teams of electronic scientists, concentrated on the radar systems in the RAF, and became a specialist in radio counter-measures against German radar. The need for this was highlighted on the 12th February, 1942 when the German warships, *Scharnhorst* and *Gneisnau*, passed through the English Channel from Brest to Kiel undetected on the English coastal radar defence system because of massive jamming by German transmitters on the French coast.

After the war Martin returned to the Cavendish Laboratory. It was about this time that I first came into contact with him through a mutual interest in design techniques. He met our experts who designed, manufactured and built B.R.M. racing engines, one of the most complicated of engineering exercises. Martin studied the drawing-office prints with considerable knowledge and occasionally went with us to watch the finished product roar into action. Sailing was another form of relaxing, giving another opportunity for designing skills. It took the form of a sixteen-foot catamaran that he designed, built, and exhibited at the International Boat Show. Sailing on the Solent in his eighteen-foot auxiliary sloop gave him immense pleasure.

At the Cavendish he began a scientific investigation that skirted physics and other sciences involving analysing radio waves emanating from astronomical objects outside the earth. His initial equipment was a receiving aerial covering a wide area much larger than the length of the waves. He used two large aerials several hundred yards apart, their combined outputs becoming a radio version of the Michelson interferometer. Simple and effective. Suggestions that he might install a huge parabolic reflector like the one at Jodrell Bank were rejected. Instead Martin developed a new method called aperture synthesis which used eight parabolic reflectors set along a five-kilometre stretch of old railway line that simulated exactly the performance of a reflector that would have been too large to be constructed. These results were recorded by signals from the reflectors in digital-form fed into a digital computer. The computer-drawn images produced fine details of radio galaxies, work that earned a joint award with Hewish of the Nobel Prize for Physics.

The research of Martin and his team included many significant discoveries. The publication of the third Cambridge Catalogue of Radio Sources undoubtedly aided the development of radio astronomy and the discovery of quasars. He put forward the theory that radio astronomy could decide between the evolving universe and the continuous creation theories of cosmology. Martin favoured the former and became involved in controversy with Fred Hoyle and his supporters, the argument finally tipping in favour of the Ryle school. Then there was the occasion when the Ryle group tracked the first Soviet Sputniks and Martin suggested that artificial satellites could be used as navigational aids.

When the awakening of a strong social conscience caused such a change of heart, it is pertinent to look for the reasons. His fears were many, voiced in his letter to Professor Chagas. He said that some forty per cent of professional engineers and probably more physicists in the United Kingdom were engaged in devising new ways of killing people, and, whilst there were plenty of posts available in these areas, it was practically impossible for a young graduate or Ph.D. to find a socially-useful job. The misuse of science for military purposes inevitably meant that physics graduates would be absorbed into the defence establishment. He raised doubts about the energy programme based on fast breeder nuclear reactors, basing such fears on the danger of accidents and the refusal seriously to consider alternative energy sources like wind and wave-power. He used to say that Orwell's vision of 1984 might not be so wide of the mark, particularly in the light of Government's liking for surveillance. Martin had seen enough at first-hand to draw us back from the edge of the nuclear holocaust. He believed time to be very short and that either through error or a first-strike decision, a nuclear holocaust was likely within years rather than decades. A sentence scribbled in his handwriting among his papers says it all. . . . "Our world is one – yet evolution has now reached the stage where as a species we may soon die . . . we as scientiest should be able to see this more clearly than most and must use our influence to change the too limited aspirations of governments."

No one would disagree, but the question is how. This good man and prophet in his own time summed-up the sickness . . . our cleverness has grown prodigiously, but not our wisdom.

SOME DAY I'LL GO BACK . . .

Some day I'll go back . . . words that express in a generic sense the longing by many men and women to recapture hours that have been and can never be again, a latent yearning to go back to the spaciousness of one's youth and reconstruct the emotions of an hour, to put the years back and be one's own judge through purblind eyes. It is easy to believe that

> The porter will smile at my waistcoat and my ways,
> when I'm not looking, as he used to in other days.

Everything has the sameness of eternity . . . yet the end is as the beginning. . . . Some day I'll go back.

The inference is unavoidable. You can never return, at least, not in the guise you imagine. Those who do murder their memories: and yet, such a visit has its compensations. The wonder created by the eye of youth may be lost. In its stead comes truer appreciation of what remains. A mature mind has many bypaths of reflection. Evaluations take on fresh meaning. It is impossible to live even for a short time among these stones of learning without absorbing something of the unique atmosphere of Cambridge. It cannot be otherwise. The tempo of life is leisured and purposeful. On all sides is beauty of vision and sound. Kaleidoscopic impressions crowd the memory . . . murmurous chimes of clocks striking the evening hour in semi-unison . . . the avenue of trees by Trinity with shadows across the lawns . . . the cadence of madrigals rising from punts by King's in the summer dusk . . . the tranquillity of a warm afternoon at Fenner's with flannels as chaste as the June breeze . . . carpets of crocuses by the Backs . . . the lazy river procession of punts and canoes along the Granta to Grantchester . . .

evening mist swirling across Coe Fen . . . snatches of May Week music against a background of lantern-lined courts . . . the Proctor with bullers and "Bible" . . . epigrammatic gems in the Union . . . the torrent of bicycles streaming down King's Parade . . . men going to lectures in Mill Lane. Is it any wonder that generations of men and women in their time have murmured at the recollections of such years. . . . "Some day I'll go back . . ."

And if they do . . . what do they find? The attempt to reconstruct and recapture the past fails. It is like being a ghost in streets, courts and stairways peopled by alien spirits. The atmosphere is convivial but remote. Everything is the same outwardly, but the wonderment is missing. The darkness encircling Trinity Great Court is unghosted. Eyes do change with the years. What we see is no less beautiful, but it lacks the unthinking possessiveness of adolescence. In the old days the pressure of the moment was all-absorbing. It was the quaffing of new experiences rather than vintage appreciation. That undergraduate who walks across the bridges, pauses to glance at the greening willows that touch the water, and is quickly swallowed up by the shadows of the cloister . . . he is the latest inheritor in point of time of this tradition. Without knowing it, he mirrors his generation. That is one of the lessons we learn by returning. We see ourselves as a minute but integral part of an evolutionary pattern. In each century the gownsman has reflected the mannerisms of his age. Dress, habits and diversions have varied but the continuity of design has persisted. We are the unconscious inheritors of the past. That young man who prides himself on being different even for King's is merely the shadow of what went before. Anyone who has turned the half-way mark of life can indulge in such reminiscences. Each generation comes to realise that the wish to go back cannot be granted in its fullness. The ivory tower of remembrance knows only what has been. Such thoughts do not apply to the first-time visitor. It is sheer delight to note their reactions and unspoilt appreciation of the treasures of Cambridge.

MARY LAMB

August 20th, 1815.

In my life I never spent so many pleasant hours together as I did at Cambridge. We were walking the whole time – out of one College into another. If you ask me which I like best I must make a children's traditionary unoffending reply to all curious enquirers – 'Both.' I like them all best. The little gloomy ones, because they were little gloomy ones. I felt as if I could live and die in them and never wish to speak again. And the fine grand Trinity College, oh how fine it was! And King's College Chapel, what a place! I heard the Cathedral service there, and having been no great churchgoer of late years, that and the painted windows and the general effect of the whole thing affected me wonderfully.

INDEX

Gibbons, Grinling, 61
Gibbs, James, 17, 31
Gladstone, W. S., 133
Godolphin Arabian, 150
Gog Magog Hills, 150
Gonville and Caius College, 37
Gonville, Edmund, 37
Gonville Hall, 14, 37
Grantchester, 164
Gray, Thomas, 132, 146
Gresham, Sir Thomas, 40
Grey Friars, 58
Grumbold, Robert, 80
Grumbold, Thomas, 50
Gunning, Peter, 48

H

Hardy, Thomas, 84
Harlton Church, 138
Harrington, Sir John, 89
Harvard College, 97
Harvard, John, 97
Harvey, William, 38
Hawkes, Jacquetta, 101
Hawthorne, Sir William, 84
Haydn, Franz Josef, 35
Heath, Edward, 29
Hedley, William, 89
Heffer's, 52
Henry VI, 17, 19
Henry VII, 29, 75, 122
Henry VIII, 13, 14, 54, 84, 89
Hepworth, Barbara, 50
Herbert, George, 65
Hereward the Wake, 129
Herrick, Robert, 44
Hobbs, Sir Jack, 51
Hobbs, Robert, 36
Hobson's Choice, 141
Holy Trinity Church, 173
Homerton College, 163
Hopkins, Sir Frederick Gowland, 101
Hopkins, Gerard Manley, 101
Horseheath Church, 138
Household, John, 37
Hoyle, Fred, 186
Hughes Hall, 163
Humphrey, John, 162

I

Interim Club, 52
Isleham Church, 137

J

Jaffe, Michael, 121
James I, 84, 88
James, Henry, 43

James, M. R., 24, 121
Jesus College, 53, 87
Jockey Club, 93
Jowett, Joseph, 29, 46, 53

K

Kapitza, Peter, 161
Kelvin, Lord, 132
Kennet, Lady, 119
Keynes, Lord, 24
King Edward's Tower, 58
King's Chapel, 17, 19
King's Chapel Windows, 20, 21, 22, 24
King's College, 15, 17
King's Hall, 14, 54
King's Parade, 26
Kingsley, Charles, 84
Kipling, Rudyard, 84
Kirtling Church, 137

L

Laing, W., 89
Lamb, Charles, 26, 96
Lamb, Mary, 26, 188
Laski, Harold, 26
Latimer, Hugh, 47, 48
Le Fleming, Hugh, 58
Leach, John, 26
Leavis, F. R., 52, 116
Legge, Thomas, 40
Lely, Sir Peter, 92
Lewis, C. S., 84
Little Gidding, 48
Little Rose Inn, 169
Little St Mary's Church, 130, 173
Little Shelford Church, 136
Lopokova, Lydia, 24
Lucy Cavendish College, 163
Luddington, J. B., 58

M

Madingley War Cemetery, 176
Madox Brown, Ford, 88, 130
Magdalene College, 13, 82
Maharajah of Rajpla, 28
Maktoum, Sheikh Mohammed, 93
Mallory Court, 84
Mallory, George, 84
Manley, Gordon, 119
Mann, Frederick, 162
Margaret of Anjou, 125
Mariolatry, 20
Marlowe, Christopher, 154
Marsh, Grace, 28
Marsh, Marcus, 28
Marsh, Richard, 27
Martin, Sir Leslie, 120

Marvell, Andrew, 70
Mary Tudor, 14, 132, 181
Matthew, Bernard, 51
Mear, Roger, 121
Mey, William, 55
Michaelhouse, 14, 54
Mildmay, Sir Thomas, 99
Milne, A. A., 65
Milton, John, 96
Montague, Lord, 90
Montefiore, Hugh, 29
Morris, William, 88, 125, 130

N

Nansen, Fridtzof, 119
Nevile's Court, 59
Nevile, Thomas, 55
New College, Oxford, 18
New Hall, 163
Newmarket, 93
Newnham Grange, 9, 12
Newton, Humphrey, 63
Newton, Sir Isaac, 14, 62, 127

O

Oates, Titus, 119
Odell, Noel, 84
Old Schools, 32
Old West River, 129
Orpen, T. H., 133
Ouse, 129
Owen, David, 29

P

Paris, University of, 13
Parker, Archbishop, 152
Parr, Catharine, 55
Peck's, 26
Pembroke College, 144
Pepysian Library, 82
Perne, Andrew, 132
Perse, Stephen, 40
Persimmon, 27
Peterhouse, 75, 130
Petty Cury, 12
Philip, Prince, 16, 36
Pickerel Inn, 169
Piper, David, 121
Pitt Club, 52
Pitt Press, 147
Pitt, William the Younger, 146
Potter, Stephen, 162
Priestley, J. B., 45
Priory of St Radegund, 87
Proctors, 35
Public Orator, 36